The
REALITIES
of
WORLD
COMMUNISM

University of California, Berkeley

University Extension Series

on

Public Issues

No. 1   *The Realities of World Communism*

The
REALITIES
of
WORLD COMMUNISM

Edited by

William Petersen

PRENTICE-HALL, INC.

ENGLEWOOD CLIFFS, N.J.

"At least one claim of Soviet propaganda is thoroughly justified: no one can understand contemporary history, let alone intervene effectively in it, without clarity as to the nature of the present-day Soviet society."

Peter Meyer

Preface

The purpose of this book is to raise the level of discourse on one of the most complex political phenomena of our time. Many Americans display a sublime, and sometimes willful, ignorance of Communist ways. Their attitudes swing from cautious optimism through apathy to naked fear, and back again. When Khrushchev plays the jolly peasant, they think a deal might be possible. When Khrushchev is bilious, they have bad dreams about fifty Hiroshimas scattered over the United States. One reason for these pendulum swings is simple lack of information.

The mass media do not help much. The fifteen-minute television newscast devotes more time to selling the sponsor's product than to serious discussion of international problems. Most newspapers describe Soviet-American negotiations on any issue in terms borrowed from a TV western: there are good guys and bad guys; tall, lean, clean, smoothly shaven, quiet-talking good guys, and short, fat, unbathed, bearded, or at least mustachioed, robbers. This level of reporting may make the audience feel better, but not for long.

Instead of dispassionate informed analysis, Americans have been getting predigested pablum from self-professed experts with no standing in the scholarly community. Two such appeared at the campus of the University of California in Berkeley within a period of two or three weeks. One had made a career of preaching sympathetic understanding of the difficulties that the Soviet people were trying to overcome, and a sympathetic appreciation of their real or fancied successes; he was pleased to report on the new thaw in the post-Stalin era. The other had been even more successful in attacking Communism and all its works in the most simplistic terms, and in seeking financial and political support from some of the less responsible elements on the Right edge of American politics.

Some of us at University Extension, Berkeley, were appalled that at this reservoir of higher learning, with a half dozen experts of international reputation on its faculty, the students and the community had been offered this alternative on this important subject. University Extension is the arm of the University that extends its resources into the community. *The Realities of World Communism* was originally conceived as a series of lectures by members of the faculty to be offered in several cities of Northern California. The men who spoke were highly qualified authorities in the field, and they spoke to large, enthusiastic audiences. Newspaper editorials commented favorably that the University had sent its best minds into the community to help raise the level of citizen understanding.

This volume seeks a larger audience than could attend the lecture series. Its purpose, however, is the same: to offer an objective and scholarly analysis of the theory and practice of Communism.

MORTON GORDON
Head, University Extension
University of California, Berkeley

Contents

PREFACE—*Morton Gordon*   7

INTRODUCTION—*William Petersen*   11

COMMUNIST IDEOLOGY AND SOVIET FOREIGN POLICY
  —*Bertram D. Wolfe*   19

SOVIET SOCIETY UNDER STALIN: THE PROTOTYPE OF
  TOTALITARIANISM—*William Petersen*   41

THE SOVIET ECONOMY IN THE POST-STALIN DECADE
  —*Gregory Grossman*   62

SOVIET SOCIETY SINCE STALIN: CHANGES AND CON-
  TINUITIES—*Paul E. Zinner*   86

THE EAST EUROPEAN SATELLITES: VARIATIONS ON A
  SOVIET THEME—*Paul Kecskemeti*   109

COMMUNIST CHINA—THE FIRST FOURTEEN YEARS
  —*Robert A. Scalapino*   123

TRADE UNIONISM AND THE COMMUNISTS: AMERICAN
  AND INTERNATIONAL EXPERIENCES—*John Hutchinson*   164

THE JACOBIN LEFT AND THE FUTURE OF THE COM-
  MUNISTS IN LATIN AMERICA—*Robert J. Alexander*   188

WORLD COMMUNISM: A READING LIST FOR NON-
  SPECIALISTS—*William Petersen and Paul E. Zinner*   202

Introduction

In the 1930's the tiny groups of anti-Stalinist radicals used to return again and again to a discussion of what they termed "the Russian question": what kind of society is the Soviet Union? From today's perspective, it may seem appropriate that these scholastic logic-choppers should have concerned themselves so obsessively with a quality as medievalist as a society's essential nature. And yet in this case, as also in some others, they were asking the right question even when they did not find a satisfactory answer.

In every viable society there is a strain toward consistency, and thus a tendency to persist in fundamental respects. Unless we can identify, however approximately, this underlying bent, we are likely to misinterpret particular facts; for social facts are significant in relation to their social setting. Especially with respect to a civilization as complex as the Soviet Union, in which every datum has its political coloration, the "scientific" positivism of the "objective" analysis is likely to reflect, to one degree or another, the doctrine of the Party that defined any particular data as worth collecting. If we are really to see for ourselves, we must begin by deciding independently what we want to look for, and this means defining for ourselves the conceptual model into which our facts will be fitted.

The point is important enough to be worth spelling out with one significant example. In the moves and counter moves of the cold war, on the face of it one side looks very much like the other. Each defines its position as defensive, and the stance of the other as aggressive. Even Hitler, one recalls, used to claim that he wanted peace, and that his seemingly aggressive moves were merely responses to the West's intended, but not yet realized, aggression. The Communists maintain that war is a natural feature of capitalism, while socialism is naturally at peace. The strength of this argument is not in its validity, which is nil, but in its degree of generality

11

—because of which many in the West, not otherwise Communist dupes, half-accept this thesis of Lenin's *Imperialism*. One way of specifying the "aggressor," it might seem, would be to look at a world map, to see which side has spread over the continents since 1945; but apparently this is too simple. Is it true that a Communist society is "peace-loving"; is this part of its nature? What kind of society is the Soviet Union?

Answers to "the Russian question" can be classified into four broad types:

(a) The official doctrine, of course, is that the Soviet Union is socialist. Oppositionist Communists and non-Communists of various types have paraphrased this formulation in many ways. For example, Leon Trotsky (until the day he was murdered by a Soviet agent) defined the Soviet Union as a "degenerated workers' state"— a "workers' state" because the means of production were publicly owned, but "degenerated" because this abolition of private property had not resulted, as it should have by socialist theory, in improving the quality of life. Perhaps the typical American is in this respect a Trotskyist: he is likely to half-accept the Soviet Union's self-definition, while also half-aware that the Communist state is a world that 19th-century socialists never dreamt of. Similarly, he typically places Communists at the extreme Left of the political continuum, thus next to socialists and only two steps removed from liberals, but as far as possible from fascists.

(b) Some have termed the Soviet Union "capitalist" or "state capitalist." The prime purpose of the country's economic planning, it is argued, like the principal effect of 19th-century capitalism, has been to accumulate a stock of capital goods. However, it is obviously somewhat inadequate to define a society by only one important characteristic, passing over the great differences between a planned and a market economy—not to say the still greater differences outside the economic sector. Those who insist on this formula have been principally ex-Communists, enough liberated from the dogma to see that Soviet society is not socialist yet still caught in the Marxian dichotomy: if not socialist, then it *must* be capitalist.

(c) Increasingly in recent years, the Soviet Union has been defined as simply a "large-scale industrial society" (Alex Inkeles and Raymond A. Bauer). It is a "developed" country, and thus distinguished from "underdeveloped" areas, but approaching more and more closely the way of life of such other urban-industrial nations as the United States. This Deutscher thesis, as we may call it—for it has been associated especially with the British analyst Isaac Deutscher—is a comforting one. Indisputably, most of the world is striving to become industrial and at least some of this richly aided effort is succeeding. If in this process the world is also becoming more and more like the democratic West, then we need only batten down the hatches and wait till the storm of Communist aggression has passed. By this view, history is really on our side, even though the Communists believe it works for them. In their case, this faith has operated as a stimulus to bring the future nearer; in ours the belief in victory has meant usually that we sit down and wait for it.

Note that in these three concepts of Soviet society, the principal criterion of the definition is the country's economy. To designate the Soviet Union as "capitalist," which would seem to deny official Soviet claims completely, is merely the other side of the same coin. Such a designation follows Marx's dictum that a society—any society —derives its principal attributes from its economy, and not from what he termed the "superstructure" of politics, social relations, and culture. Just as Marx said he turned Hegel on his head, so in order to understand this self-proclaimed Marxian society, Marx must be turned on his.

(d) The Soviet Union has been termed a "totalitarian state economy" (Rudolf Hilferding), a "Party State" (Ruth Fischer), an example of "bureaucratic collectivism" (Max Shachtman), or of "Oriental despotism" (Karl A. Wittfogel). The precise term we use is less important than that we escape from the prison of economic determinism. The simplest of several alternatives, a "totalitarian society," is adequate, provided that we understand that this is not a mere epithet.

A totalitarian society is one dominated by a single minority Party, which, in order to realize its particular vision of a perfect community, attempts to achieve total control over the major workings of all significant institutions. The several components of the definition are all essential. Rule by a single minority party over a country with important loci of competing power is not totalitarian; in Ghana, for instance, the rule of the party can be challenged by traditionalist chiefs and the urban middle classes; in Franco Spain, by the army, the church, and the monarchist clique. And even if a group holds complete political power, it is not totalitarian if it does not also penetrate the social institutions in order to move them toward its utopian goal; the military dictatorship of a Latin American country or of a province of pre-Communist China is not totalitarian. No society, indeed, is completely totalitarian (just as none is completely democratic or completely capitalist), but Stalinist Russia was a close approximation of the pure type.

Indeed, almost all would now agree that Russia up to 1953, the year of Stalin's death, was a totalitarian society; and to recall the sharp, often bitter, divergences of the 1930's and 1940's in the light of this virtual unanimity suggests that some progress may have been made. After the end of the war, the evidence on Soviet terror, on Soviet slave labor, on the arbitrary controls over every sector of Soviet life, mounted higher and higher, finally to be capped by none other than Khrushchev himself addressing a Congress of the Communist Party of the Soviet Union. Eventually the most dedicated fellow-traveler, self-trained in blindness though he was, could no longer fail to see: the Soviet Union was a totalitarian society. It should be noted, however, that some who now make this declaration emphasize not *totalitarian,* but *was.* The agreement that has been reached about the past is almost irrelevant, for the old disputes continue with respect to the Communist present and the Communist future.

The complexity of present-day Communism as it has evolved in various countries is great enough to induce different interpretations and sometimes sharply contrasting prognoses from even the best informed analysts, observing the same events in the same Western democratic perspective. Some of this disagreement is represented in the essays of this volume. There has been no attempt to construct a monistic line, hiding honest differences of opinion responsibly arrived at by scholars qualified to have them. But the imposition of these legitimate criteria—scholarship, responsibility, honesty—has appreciably reduced the range from that between the apologists for the Left and the irresponsibles of the Right.

The theme of this symposium is the interaction between continuity and change in world Communism. In the first essay, on Communist ideology by Bertram D. Wolfe, the emphasis is on the permanent element in this changing world. Wolfe not only admits but stresses the many revisions that Khrushchev has made in the Stalinist system, but in his words (here quoted from another article of his) they have been within-system changes, not changes in the Soviet system. However one answers it, this is the crucial question:

which of the many important alterations in Soviet life can be reasonably taken as the beginning of a fundamental metamorphosis, a change to a different type of society? One step in answering this question is to supply a benchmark from which to measure the post-Stalin evolution; and this is given in the second essay, on Soviet society under Stalin, by William Petersen. The next two papers, respectively by Gregory Grossman and Paul E. Zinner, analyze the economy and the society of the post-Stalin decade. To the degree that any one-sentence summary of their richly detailed analyses can be adequate, both see the many significant changes under Khrushchev to be definitely within the same social and political framework.

Variation in Communism, however, is not only from one Russian dictator to another but also from one country to another. In Stalin's day (or in Lenin's, for that matter), the Communist Parties of the world were united in toeing the Moscow line. Each time that Russian foreign policy dictated another reversal in the international Communist policy, every Party turned about, whether in Europe or in Asia, in an industrial or a peasant country. Some of the present East European satellites, in particular East Germany, show something like the same obsequious subservience to the Kremlin. But others, Gomulka's Poland for example, are controlled on a much looser leash; and for a period Tito's Yugoslavia escaped Soviet domination altogether. These variations on a Soviet theme are analyzed by Paul Kecskemeti, who also regards the continuity in Soviet patterns as more significant than the deviations from them.

Is this true also of Communist China, Russia's principal competitor within the Communist bloc? Ideally, it would have been useful to replicate the three papers on the Soviet Union rather than crowding all of the analysis on China into the one essay by Robert A. Scalapino. But accurate data on this enormous, complex, and rapidly changing society are scarce. It is possible to skim the surface and present a reasonably accurate impression, but a more detailed discussion would have involved mainly the rather technical (and, for laymen, pointless) question of challenging the reliability of competitive sources. With respect to China, we are like the Westerners in the 1920's who tried to understand what was going on in Russia —balancing ignorantly hostile reports against ignorantly enthusiastic ones, measuring present misery against the misery of the past and the extravagant hopes for the future, hoping to establish some basis for credibility. That is why the question of whether "Maoism" differs fundamentally from Leninism is so important: if those are correct who hold that the same Party is fashioning both societies to essentially the same mold, then everything we know about Russia can be applied—remembering that these are different cultures—to China. But among the handful of Westerners genuinely informed about both Communism and China, this is still an open question.

The analysis of world Communism is not complete if it stops with those countries that have become Communist and passes over the international Party's efforts to establish new power. In the United States and other Western countries, these efforts were mainly through a special type of Party adjunct, known as a Communist front. This is an organization created or captured by Communists, who almost always constitute only a minority within it, in order to serve the Party's purposes in one particular field. By thus setting up a kind of associate membership—fellow-travelers, who adhere to only a certain portion of its program and discipline—the Party can increase its range of power enormously, both directly and by corrupting competing institutions that have been successfully infiltrated. The several million Americans who became members of one or more of the several hundred Communist fronts that flourished during the 1930's and 1940's, it is important to remember, were mostly *not* Communists; indeed, some of the more credulous may have been unaware that they were cooperating with Communists. The list includes important dignitaries of the Democratic and Republican parties, trade-union and corporation leaders, lawyers and actors, avowed atheists and clergymen of several denominations, and so on through almost the whole American social structure. When a person on the Right names the names on such a list, he draws the conclusion that, apart from the tiny sects that he supports, everything in American politics is tainted. From the same list, once he is forced to admit its validity, a person on the Left typically draws the opposite conclusion: organizations whose membership included so many distinguished, intelligent, *sincere* people could not be part of a totalitarian conspiracy. Both overlook the most characteristic feature of the front, that it is set up to enable a small nucleus to manipulate the large amorphous mass.

John Hutchinson's paper on trade unions is a case study on the Communist infiltration of democratic institutions. By concentrating on the facts concerning this one example, he is able to cut through some of the emotions surrounding this highly charged area and reach conclusions that, even so, go far beyond the labor organizations he analyzes.

Such Communist fronts as still exist in the United States have little influence, and in fact the strength of all Communist organizations has waned throughout the Western world. Currently the battles of the world revolution are being fought mainly in the underdeveloped areas of Asia, Africa, and Latin America. While these nations differ in many respects, they share a number of characteristics favorable to revolutionary change, and thus possibly to eventual Communist control. Many were recently the colonies of Western nations, which they are inclined to see still as the imperialist enemy. Traditional leaders are losing their power, in part because they typically refuse to adapt to new demands. The new heads of the countries are very often part of a rising class of radical intellectuals, hostile to the West and attracted to one or another school of revolutionary doctrine. The problems these new elites face are overwhelming—to build a nation out of inimical elements speaking a score of different languages; to satisfy the demands for social welfare and, at the same time, for rapid industrialization; to raise a population largely illiterate and almost totally unskilled in urban-industrial arts to the level necessary to attempt such goals; to ride with turbulent changes and yet stay in power. Even to plan tasks of this dimension suggests totalitarian methods, and the examples of Russia and China reinforce the suggestion. On the face of it, thus, the Communists have important advantages among the so-called uncommitted nations. The principal characteristic of the underdeveloped world is social fluidity: nothing is fixed. And the Communists see social upheavals not as disasters, but as opportunities. A Western democrat is at a moral disadvantage working in a social setting where democracy would be manifestly inappropriate: if he does not admit this, he feels himself to be a hypocrite, and if he does, he generally lacks any other social philosophy to guide his day-to-day activities.

It would be easy, however, to overestimate the Communists' advantages. In the paper by Robert J. Alexander on Latin America, the basic conclusion is that the Communists cannot control their radical allies. Fidel Castro in Cuba, a typical Jacobin, is indispensable to the Communists, for they could not rule without him. They can neither dispose of him nor absorb him; he is their indigestion.

And the Latin American wave of support for Castro has a similar ambivalence with respect to international Communism; for the first time in decades, Communists have a competitor to their Left, even more romantic and less responsible than they, and thus better able to gain from simplistic but vehement denunciations of "the system." Whether Jacobin violence can lead to a stable state with Communists in power, however, is still a moot question.

WILLIAM PETERSEN

Berkeley, California

Communist Ideology
and Soviet Foreign Policy

Bertram D. Wolfe

It was only towards the middle of the twentieth century that the inhabitants of many European countries came, in general unpleasantly, to realize that their fate could be influenced directly by intricate and abstruse books of philosophy.

—*Czeslaw Milosz*

For four and a half decades, statesmen and experts have waited confidently for the Soviet Union to mellow. Repeatedly they have thought they were witnessing the longed for change of dynamism, of direction, or of heart, which would make Communist totalitarianism in power just "one state among many"—different of course (are not all states different?), but a member of the comprehensive genus of orderly, constituted governments, content to tolerate orderly neighbors and to act according to the not too generous rule of live and let live by which governments, reluctantly, indifferently, or a little contemptuously, suffer one another's presence on the same earth.

A review of the pronouncements made on this theme over these forty-five years makes for melancholy reading. From the notion that Lenin's regime would last but a few weeks or months (Lenin himself shared this view for a while) to the certitude that power and responsibility always sober their wielders; from Lenin's New Economic Policy to Stalin's "socialism in one country" and Khrushchev's "thaw"; from the celebration of Russia's entry into the League of Nations through the shock of the Molotov-Ribbentrop Pact to the unity of the Grand Alliance that was to build "one world"; from Stalin's "peaceful coexistence" to Khrushchev's "peaceful competition"; from the "collective leadership" following Lenin's death to that following Stalin's to the personal rule of Khrushchev and the anti-Stalinism of the most apt of Stalin's pupils—at every *zig*

19

we have proclaimed, "At last a change has come," and at every *zag* muttered reassuringly, "Surely this cannot last."

I chanced some time ago on the diary of a deceased noblewoman, one entry of which noted that Fridtjof Nansen had come to tea, bringing glad tidings: "Our troubles with Russia are over; Lenin is returning to capitalism." The entry was made in 1922, and the lady's informant was one of his generation's most knowledgeable Soviet experts.

Four decades after that entry, I read in a recent work of an American sociologist a rejection of the very conception that "totalitarianism is a radically new social form," which, while it exists as such, will continue to maintain "its combative posture vis-a-vis democratic societies." The writer continued:

> Even on a simpler intuitive basis one can question the basic assumption of this theory—namely that society becomes completely atomized and rule is anomic and direct. In a *crisis* situation, a state can fragment all social life and through terror, perhaps, mold a people to its will. But can a society live in permanent crisis? Can it hold such a rigid posture without either exploding into war or relaxing? The basis of all social life requires not only a minimum of personal security, but the reasonable expectation by parents that their children will be educated, develop careers, and so forth. To that extent, a tendency towards "normalization" is at work in any crisis state.[1]

Leaving aside the assumptions outside our theme (namely, that rule by secretaries, cells, and transmission belts is "direct" rule; that totalitarianism is "anomic," i.e., without either a structure or a value system, merely because these are enforced from above; and that totalitarianism is incompatible with educating children for "careers"), the passage cited touches on the heart of the questions that concern us.

How can a regime that arose as the result of a crisis (a crisis both in Russia and in European civilization) endure as a "crisis regime" for forty-five years? Is there an automatic eroding factor which will compel it, before too long, either to "explode into war or relax into 'normalization' "? Is there a mechanical "convergence" factor which decrees that all industrial societies must ultimately become pretty much alike in political institutions and cultural attitudes because they use the same technology? Is the "simple intuitive basis" of Western thought a proper tool for understanding a society so different from the one in which that intuition was formed? Is the very concept of "normalization," of which Mr. Bell speaks, applicable to the ideology and structure of a militant totalitarian regime?

Or, turning to the opposite end of the spectrum of ways of analyzing totalitarianism, is it possible to deduce the twists and turns of Soviet policy by simple translation of the Communist ideology into an "operational code"?

In my view neither of these extremes is tenable. Soviet conduct, as we see it, is a resultant of the interaction of three disparate and conflicting forces, namely: (1) the preconceptions and drives of the intensely held ideology of the movement whose leaders seized power in 1917; (2) the influence of the tradition and geographical situation of Russia on those who seized power; (3) the deviations and alterations forced upon the new rulers by recalcitrant reality. Of these three components, the first is the driving force without which the Bolsheviks would not have seized power or held and justified it, the second and third act upon the ideology as a resistant factor, a brake or drag.

Forty-five years, it goes without saying, have brought important and cumulative changes, changes which come from expanding power and lengthening experience in power, changes in the land over which Bolshevism rules, and changes in the outside world.

Yet, among all these changes, the central question obtrudes itself: are there not manifest fundamental features of ideology and institutional framework which have endured, have continued to be decisive for the shaping of foreign policy, and with which we are likely to have to continue to reckon for the foreseeable future? [2]

II

Let us begin with the easiest part of the problem: the influence on Bolshevik policy of the Russian imperial heritage.

Lenin seized power, not in a land "ripe for socialism," but in a land ripe for seizing power. "It was as easy," he wrote, "as lifting up a feather." His coup was supposed to touch off a European socialist revolution; but while this revolution "matured," there was an opportunity to take power in the great Russian empire. "The point of the uprising," he chided his hesitant associates, uncertain about Russia's "ripeness" for his blueprint, "is the seizure of power. Afterwards, we will see what we can do with it."

Many of the things Lenin and his successors had to do were those which any new tsar would have attempted after an interregnum, a ruinous war, and a shrinkage of empire, namely: to end the war as best they could, to reestablish order (their kind of order), to reestablish Russia's frontiers, and to subdue and reconquer seceding provinces and peoples;[3] to identify Russia's interests in the mind of their subjects with their rule and resume under new forms and for new purposes Russia's secular expansion.

Insofar as there appears to be similarity between the policy of the stronger tsars and that of Lenin, Stalin, and Khrushchev, this springs from the fact that, more often than not, the same territories constitute the objectives of reincorporation or conquest. Georgia, Poland, Finland, the Ukraine, Belo-Russia, the Baltic states, Bessarabia, the Balkans, the Dardanelles, Persia, the Turkic empires, Sinkiang, Mongolia, Manchuria, Korea—all these have appeared previously in the pages of Russian history.[4]

The same geographical situation gives the same neighbors. The Soviet empire is still the Eurasian heartland, subject to pressure from East or West or both at once, capable of exerting pressure on East and West—on one at a time under the tsars with their limited aims; on both at once under the Bolsheviks with their unlimited aims. As before, Russia is the great landpower, many of whose policies are conditioned by the traditional contests between landpower and seapower. As before, in periods of strength, this landpower still strives for control of its bordering seas.

If the dream of controlling the Pacific proved to be a wild chimera and if Alaska and California had to be abandoned, the Caspian proved to be easy. With a little luck—and the Dardanelles—the Black Sea would be easy, too.

The conquest of the Baltic provinces and Finland had started Russia's way around the Baltic. Stalin's desperate effort to seize and hold Hamburg during World War II, his annexations in East Prussia, his claim to hold and fortify the Danish island of Bornholm in the Baltic, would have startled us less had we borne this inherited appetite in mind. Certainly the drive to turn adjacent waters into Russian lakes explains more concerning Russia's "geopolitical" attitude toward her bordering seas than does the journalistic cliché of "hunger for a warm-water port." Not as exporter or importer, but as the great landpower blocked in its secular ambitions by surrounding seapowers, does Russia look on her bordering seas.

The landpower's military advantage in any conflict is its inner lines of communication, provided its transport and logistics are adequate. But the seapowers are more mobile and can strike at any of its many frontiers, or several at once, compelling Russia to keep large armies in reserve at all her borders. This disadvantage is now aggravated by airpower, radar, plane and missile bases all around the empire, and the missile-launching submarine.

Another preoccupation of the power sprawling across the open Eurasian plain has been the "rectification of frontiers" by acquiring the Pripet Marshes, the only defensible line to the west, and the Carpathians, the natural barrier to the southwest. Of course, this was too bad for Poland and Austria-Hungary (or present-day Czechoslovakia), since a more defensible line for Russia meant the lack of a natural barrier for them. To the historian there was no novelty in Stalin's partition of Poland with Hitler, fumblingly reconfirmed by the Grand Alliance. The novelty was the military ignorance—or blind faith in Hitler—which led Stalin to station his main armies in front of the Pripet River and swamps, where these served only to break up the retreat of the Soviet armies instead of the Wehrmacht's advance.

The "rectification" of the western and southwestern borders of Russia has long been a traditional objective. Thus Kutuzov between 1812 and 1815 urged his sovereign to take advantage of Russia's advance on Paris to seize the Carpathians and retain the shortest line to the west along the Oder to the Sea. He proposed that Alexander I should "compensate" the Prussian king (as Stalin was later to "compensate" Poland) by "giving" him lands to the west. But here a notable difference arises between an Alexander and a Stalin: Alexander I had too much consideration for his brother sovereign, the king of Prussia, and for the diplomatic practices of his day. His forbearance in the face of a tempting proposal arose out of the code of conduct of 19th-century sovereigns, "cousins" all, and the generally limited aims that characterized the European system from 1815, when Napoleon fell, to 1914, when the first total war began.

Despite a certain archaism unconsciously carried over from the days of Russia's isolation, the foreign policy of the tsars was the customary policy of a great national state. Vague ideological overtones were not unlike those associated with the foreign policy of other nations. The belief that the tsar's power and duty came from God is analogous to the divine right of kings. The idea of the

"Third Rome" had no greater effect—indeed, not so great—as the doctrine of the Holy Roman Empire over the centuries from Charlemagne to Napoleon. Like Russia, France concerned itself with the "protection of the Holy Places," and St. Petersburg's fluctuating interest in the Ottoman Slavs was less intense and unremitting than Austria-Hungary's painful absorption with the stirrings of the South Slavs. Panslavism and Slavophilism remained feverish fantasies of isolated intellectuals, suspect at court, analogous to Pan-Germanism in the German empire but not so influential.

Tsarist diplomacy resembled that of Stalin and Khrushchev in its freedom from the overt, organized pressure of public opinion and in the natural inclination of autocrats to engage in summitry and personal settlements—a tendency to which the West has unwholesomely acquiesced, as a result of two total wars and repeated negotiations with dictators. On the whole, however, Russia's diplomacy was conventional, employing professional diplomats, following the practices of the worldwide diplomatic tradition that has almost vanished from memory, now that conferences and negotiations are habitually put to the uses of a revolutionary power. The aims of foreign policy were limited, usually pursued circumspectly and in a certain sequence, expressed in the prevailing terms of national interest, balance of power, concert of Europe, spheres of influence, rectification of frontiers, protection against incursions, respect for engagements and alliances, and readiness to take into account the opinions and pressures of the other great powers (as in the various settlements with Turkey). Just as the Russian autocracy, though it claimed absolute power, did not dream of totalist power within its own realm, so it had no global aims in foreign policy, no all-embracing plan for the world, no overall unifying idea. Neither an ideocracy nor insurrectionary, its generals brought no plans for revolution in their baggage. It had no fifth-column as its servant, no world to bury and no world to win.

Though it preferred autocracy in its neighbors, it did not feel impelled to set up replicas of its own regime wherever its armies entered, nor did it feel "insecure" and "provoked" until all the world should consist of autocracies. Alexander I marched into Paris at the head of the most powerful armies in the world, then withdrew leaving no permanent traces of his occupation on a France that remained much as it was before. The same was true of the other countries he occupied en route. Had Stalin possessed such overriding military power and led his armies into Paris in 1945, the result would have been startlingly different: he would have brought with him a set of rules, an ideology covering the whole of life, a totalitarian structure, and single-party rule.

III

It should be clear then that the men who make policy in the Soviet Union think and act differently from the tsars, and that we neglect their ideology to our peril. "The peoples of Eastern Europe are still paying for the illusion of the West that the Soviet Union was a state like any other, pursuing its power interests without regard to ideology." [5] To which one must add: and not only the peoples of Eastern Europe!

Once this pattern is recognized, it might seem that all we need to do is study their ideology to discover their "operative code," and thus foresee their every move. But ideology is no set of Euclidean theorems. Even for Communists there is no automatically "correct translation," no one-to-one correspondence, between any segment of ideology and any particular act. Their doctrine combines a religion and eschatology of salvation; a vast accumulation (prior to 1848 to the present) of political commentary and judgments, most of them out of date if they were ever valid; an economics now irrelevant; a historical sociology and critique of economic and social institutions, much of which is still suggestive; a philosophy that is little more than verbal casuistry. Every assertion, moreover, in the voluminous, contradictory writings of Marx, Engels, and Lenin is held to be part of a single science, a canon of which any sentence may be treated as having absolute probative value. Hence the application of the doctrine to any given situation is subject to argument, and it is not always easy for the Communist leaders themselves to deduce from it the appropriate conclusion or action.[6]

If it is hard for them (*they* solve this problem by forbidding factional controversy and institutionalizing the infallible leader as the sole authorized interpreter at any given moment), how much harder is it for us! Nothing could be more deceptive than the inclination to answer from within ourselves the questions: "What would I believe if I accepted this proposition which they accept? How would I act in the situation facing them if I held their beliefs?" The illusion that we can easily "put ourselves in their place" contains a built-in trap of putting them in our place, and thinking that they approach matters as we do. "What matters," Sir Lewis Namier once wrote of political ideas, "is the underlying emotions, the music to which ideas are the mere libretto." [7] All we can master is the words; to their music we are tone-deaf.

Though the doctrine operates persistently and powerfully to shape their vision, passions, thoughts, actions, it does not operate in a vacuum. It must be applied, in fragments and contradictions, to a real world of which even the doctrinaire, and particularly the adepts of this doctrine, take account. The masters of the doctrine have inherited from Lenin—and continue to develop—a distinctive Bolshevik blend of dogmatism and empiricism.[8] When we do pay attention to their ideology and its emotional context, we tend to be so impressed by its dogmatic character that we forget that it is *dogma applied to reality*.

It is true that this application of the doctrine to concrete reality has its ambiguities. When the faithful study the world for "theoretical" purposes, dogma has priority over reality, which is obliged to "confirm the truth of our science," which, of course, thus filtered, it does. However, the doctrine itself, they claim, is derived in all its parts from the empirical study of society and the universe. And it is their boast that the "science" thus derived enables them to appraise reality, react to it appropriately, judge at every moment the exact extent to which "the concrete, objective situation" and "the real relations of power" permit them to advance on the path it has marked out for them.

Moreover, we do them wrong to imagine that they will abandon this path and choose rather to blow up the world when given no other choice than open retreat.[9] This Götterdämmerung frenzy was a constituent of Hitler's spirit but not of Lenin's. Lenin was as proud of knowing "when to retreat" and "how to retreat in good order" as he was of knowing when to advance and push to the limit. For him, offensive and defensive, retreat and advance, probing and holding actions, open frontal attacks and simulated withdrawals and outflanking maneuvers—all were precious elements of a strategy of a protracted conflict which is to last until final victory. For every battle, his favorite adage was taken from Napoleon: *On s'engage, et puis—on voit!* [10]

Within rather strict limits, contact with refractory reality has forced upon these men adaptations ("creative extensions") of their doctrine. "Facts are stubborn things," Lenin would say. Facts could not, of course, refute "science." But they could show him that particular tactics, a plan of a given moment, had to be abandoned, or a particular proposition reinterpreted. Lenin and his successors have always been at pains to show that their "creative extensions" do not constitute a "revision." This is not mere casuistry, for it corresponds to a genuine psychological and political need.

Though the Marx of the last years was different from the Marx of 1848, there was an enduring framework of dogma and continuity of spirit that helped disciples convert his teachings into an ism and an orthodoxy. More fearful of "revisionism" than the founders, the "orthodox" tried to turn every element into dogma. Yet, most dogmatic of Marxists though he was, Lenin had, consciously and unconsciously, to transform what he adopted, to give it a Russian cast, to put on it the stamp of his own temperament. Repeatedly he "creatively developed" the doctrine, so that the Leninism of the foundation period (1902-1914) was profoundly different from the Leninism of the First World War (1914-1916). In 1917 he made even more drastic changes, so sweeping that he had to fight all the old leaders of his Party, who could quote the early Lenin against the new Lenin. Still more startling was the next transformation: from the pronouncements of April to November 1917 (anarchistic, decentralist, spontaneous mass-actionist, syndicalist, equalitarian) to the Leninism of firmly established power. Each of these stages represents a significant break in strategy and tactics against the background of a still more important and fundamental continuity of dogma, spirit, and long-range aim. Though in its day each of these creative extensions caused not only opponents but often devout disciples to believe that Lenin was "abandoning Leninism," all these variform pronouncements, like those of Marx, are now held to represent a single sacred canon.

With these complexities in mind, let us enter the thicket of Communist doctrine, to see what trails we can find leading from dogma to policy.

IV

Marxism-Leninism is a "science," indeed a superscience of the laws of motion of both nature and society. It makes into sciences history, politics, sociology, social and individual psychology, and all the subtle realms of the spirit.

Its God is personified History, the Future His Word and His Kingdom. Its mythology, as Herbert Lüthy has observed, has an astonishing "conceptual realism," which puts on the stage of history as living, thinking, and acting personages such abstract concepts as Capitalism, Imperialism, Socialism, as in the morality plays of the Middle Ages, Jealousy, Slander, or Avarice were accustomed to appear. Those who can juggle with these puppets and possess this conceptual wisdom are masters of the plot, bearers of History's will, beneficiaries of History's guarantees, executors of History's judgments.

A predictive science, it works to fulfill and is destined to fulfill its own prophecies. As it includes its own verification, so it includes its own morality—what history intends being at once scientifically and morally right. Whoever and whatever hastens the coming of the future is thus doubly sanctioned; whoever or whatever gets in the way is both unscientific and immoral.

The final victory of history's millennial intentions will usher in a state of absolute grace in which history-as-conflict ceases and loses its imperatives of harsh struggle; man can at last become human and humane, love can replace hatred, and all be made whole. This future of absolute grace exempts every "correct," i.e., scientific and moral, action of the present from the possibility of wrongdoing.

Weltgeschichte ist Weltgericht, but in this court justice is not blind, for judge's bench, jury box, attorney's stands, courtroom public and executioner are provided by the Party. Only the accused is an outsider, known in advance to be guilty as charged, undeserving of mercy. Mastery of the law carries with it the ability to penetrate subjective disguises and recognize the "objective meaning" of the assertions, acts, illusions, and very existence of the accused. Doubt, question, deviation, uncertainty, opposition, indifference, or willful attempts to escape the judgment or to absent oneself from the spectacle, or any impulse of sympathy with the accused, all are impermissible. "If we do not allow freethinking in chemistry," as Comte once wrote, "why should we allow it in morals or politics?" Why indeed if morals and politics are science?

The chief significance which the infallibility of the ideology and its adepts has for foreign policy is the combination of strength *and* flexibility which comes from knowing that you have History on your side. This goes far to explain the unresponsiveness to argument, the stubbornness and repetitiveness of Communist negotiators, the lack of communication in dialogues that are only ostensible dialogues. How can there be genuine dialogue without some consensus? How can there be give-and-take between that which is self-evidently and totally right, and that which is self-evidently wrong, both scientifically and morally? [11]

<h1 style="text-align:center">V</h1>

Marxism-Leninism is a combative ideology. At the core of things, it finds conflict, antagonism, clash. Progress (development) comes only through struggle. In this development the most important moments are those when accumulated tension and clash go over into open struggle, the highest point of all being apocalyptic, chiliastic, and eschatological. Toward this all history moves. With it, history as "the history of class struggles" will come to an end.

Until then, in the unending war, there can be frequent pauses, indeed there must be pauses. The ideology gives its possessors the wisdom to know when pauses are necessary, the pride to "crawl in the mud on your belly" without a sense of humiliation, the skill to "keep a clear line for maneuvering," for "retreating when possible and necessary" lest you lose all you have gained, for "renewing the attack" when that becomes possible, for "using treaties as a means of gaining strength," bringing up "fresh forces," obtaining a "better rather than a worse peace as a respite for another war," a "breathing spell." [12]

Even the Apocalypse is divided into stages. That is the meaning of the discussions on the possibility of "victory at first in several countries, or one country taken separately," of "socialism in one country," and of the scholastic distinctions between stages in "the construction of socialism," "the extended construction of Communism," and the "attainment of complete Communism." [13]

Ebbs and "compromises" are "necessary" then, but necessary only in an evil and wretched sense, because the enemy is tough and strong, and man is refractory material for the great experiment. The long war is made up of many campaigns and armistices before "final victory"; the road to revolution is "not as straight and smooth as the Nevsky Prospekt."

But Lenin trained his disciples to hate compromise for compromise's sake. His Hell is full of "compromisers," "opportunists" who

do not seize opportunities to advance, conciliators, procrastinators—
"Verily, procrastination is like unto death." And the lowest circle
of Hell is reserved for those who would compromise in order to come
to real agreement, settle matters, or call off the struggle in favor of
permanent and enduring peace. They would not succeed, of course,
for History decrees otherwise, but they must be cut off as dead limbs
lest they spread rot.

Clearly, in our relations with the Soviet Union we are not dealing with a "crisis" regime that will settle down to "normalcy" as
soon as it has solved the crisis which brought it to power. Lenin
managed to seize power because of a crisis in another regime. His
purpose was not to resolve the crisis, but to use the new-won power
as a mighty base for waging the war to which he was committed—a
twofold war: on his own people, until he had remade them according to his blueprint (the New Soviet Man in the New Communist
Society); and a struggle for the world, until that too is reconstructed
to the same blueprint. That is the meaning of all the gentle little
homilies with which Nikita Sergeyevich assures us that "Your grand-
children will live under Communism" and "Do whatever you will,
we shall bury you." This is not a crisis regime seeking to end the
chaos that arose in Russia during the First World War (that crisis
has long been ended), but a state-of-siege regime seeking to conduct
its own total twofold war until it achieves that total victory promised
by its ideology.

In this war, though armistices and temporary agreements are
necessary, the essence of any agreement is that it is temporary, not
that it is an agreement. The struggle may have to be continued "by
other means" for a "shorter or longer period." But war itself is
only the continuance of the politics of peace, and peace the continuance of the politics of war, "by other means." This is the wisdom which Lenin distilled from Clausewitz.

To continue an undeclared war or to launch an open war, no
casus belli is needed, only fresh breath and favorable circumstances.
The war itself has been decreed by history and was declared by
Marx once and for all in 1848 when he wrote: "The Communists
scorn to conceal their aims . . . the forcible overthrow of all existing conditions . . . a world to win."

Between irreconcilable opponents, one of whom is condemned by
History to be destroyed, the other sustained by History and destined
to conquer, agreement—like dialogue—can only be ostensible. It cannot form the basis of an enduring peace, for it aims only at respite

and advantage, or the limiting of disadvantage, in a continuing and scientifically and morally correct struggle.

The implications of these views are manifold. At the least, they suggest that in every encounter we remind ourselves that "negotiate" and "agree" have different meanings for them than for us. To them lulls cannot conceivably or decently be preliminaries to all-out peace. Nor are separate issues really separate, except in the sense that they have been separated out for strategical or tactical convenience from the general context of struggle. Every negotiation, every issue, even every day's session they regard primarily as a move in that irreconcilable conflict. While we doubtless must, according to our aims, treat each negotiation and issue on its own terms, we will be lost if we forget what it means in their aims, and what "negotiation" and "settlement" mean to them.

Only if we bear this in mind will we be less likely to be caught off guard by broken treaties (how many our government has noted in the past decade!); by agreements which, on the day after adoption, prove to be disagreements on what was agreed; by the helplessness of "neutral" "enforcement" commissions; by the "irregular" or "volunteer" or "guerrilla" detachments, officially disowned but quite openly recruited and supplied, which continue the efforts to unsettle what has been "settled." Only then can we remind ourselves that "agreements" must be defined with more than "Byzantine" rigor, and be self-enforcing—which, generally speaking, means that they must contain arrangements for ourselves and our allies to have the forces at key places to defend our interests.

Finally, the awareness should enable us to avoid the trap which we have set for ourselves by the practice of conventional diplomacy: to call off actual combat when negotiations are on, "in order to create an atmosphere favorable to peace." Theirs has been the revolutionary practice: to step up hostilities when negotiations begin, prolong them if the battle is going favorably, seek to gain by combat the most favorable position for a possible *status quo,* and the best jumping-off place for the eventual renewal of the conflict.

VI

In all politics, Lenin taught his followers, there is one central question. This he expressed in lapidary form: *"Kto kogo?"*—"Who whom?" In Russian no verb is needed; here the first word is subject the second object. But besides the compact form, Lenin's works supply various verbs in different contexts: Who beats whom? Who takes advantage of whom? Who uses whom? As long as the question "Who whom?" has not been finally decided by the victory of Communism on a world scale, tension is the breath of life.

Even the atom bomb and intercontinental missile do not permit the conflict to be called off, although they require more care than ever in preventing it from going over into all-out war. Early in 1961, Khrushchev said:

> Liberation wars will continue to exist as long as imperialism exists. . . . These are revolutionary wars. Such wars are not only admissible but inevitable . . . The peoples can attain their freedom and independence only through struggle, including armed struggle. . . . We recognize such wars and will help the peoples striving for their independence. . . . Can such wars flare up in the future? They can. . . . But these are wars which are national uprisings. . . . What is the attitude of the Marxists toward such uprisings? . . . The Communists fully support such just wars and march in the front rank with peoples waging liberation struggles.[14]

As with Lenin and Stalin, there are two things that Khrushchev tries with all his might and skill to avoid: all-out war and all-out peace. Because time is "on their side," and because they set the highest value on power and their possession of a great power base from which to accelerate History and fulfill their mission, they will not voluntarily jeopardize its possession. Hence all-out war has always been avoided. Fission and fusion bombs and missiles have served only to further strengthen this determination. But they have not persuaded the Soviet leaders to tolerate all-out peace.

For a movement whose essence is struggle, the most dangerous periods are those of comparative relaxation, entailing as they do the perils of loss of vigilance, acceptance of peace as natural, passivity, complacency, letdown, the danger of being "influenced" by the too "friendly" and persuasively powerful enemy—in short, the menace of spiritual demobilization and ideological disarming. "Revolutionary Social Democracy," Lenin wrote in mid-1906, when the high tide of the previous year seemed to be receding, "must be the first to enter on the path of the most decisive and relentless struggle, and the last to have recourse 'to methods that are more roundabout.' "

"Methods that are more roundabout"—Lenin abounds in instructions for going roundabout toward the unabandoned goal when it is clear that, for the moment, one cannot break through. Far from "losing face," a Bolshevik is tested above all by his ability to retreat in good order, and show skill in methods of struggle that are more roundabout.

To carry on a war for the overthrow of the international bourgeoisie [Lenin admonished the Communist International], a war which is a hundred times more difficult, prolonged and complicated than the most stubborn of ordinary wars between states, and to refuse beforehand to maneuver, to utilize the conflict of interests (even though temporary) among one's enemies, to refuse to temporize and compromise with possible (even though transient, unstable, vacillating and conditional) allies—is not this ridiculous in the extreme? Is it not as though, in the difficult ascent of an unexplored and heretofore inaccessible mountain, we were to renounce beforehand the idea that at times we might have to go in zigzags, sometimes retracing our steps, sometimes abandoning the course already selected and trying out various others? [15]

It is these "retracing of steps" and "zigzags" that have been the undoing of so many of our analysts. They have extrapolated the zig, prolonging it in a straight line out toward the horizon. Caught in outer space by the zag, they have rushed back to the turning point, only to prolong the zag on a straight line toward the other horizon. Perhaps this explains, as Leonard Schapiro once observed, the noiseless and not unwelcome obsolescence of so much of our Sovietology.

An awareness that the ascent of the mountain is tougher than the climbers thought carries with it no reassurance that they have abandoned the ascent. Lenin's retreats and zigzags were meant to circumvent impassable ravines, not renounce the climb. Flexible tactics can be undertaken without misgiving precisely because Bolsheviks are inflexible (certain) about their goal, and have History's guarantee that they must reach it. The peculiar Bolshevik blend of dogmatism and empiricism, tactical flexibility and goal-seeking inflexibility, action-affirming myth and pragmatic ability to take account of the "real relations of power," are all part of and reinforced by, a peculiar blend of rationality with what can only be described as a paranoic vision of self and "enemy" and "reality" that is not subject to rational refutation. And all these "blends" are at the heart of their movement and ideology, having been there from the beginning and having been reinforced by their long war.

I cannot therefore take comfort, as Chester Bowles does in a recent article, that "the power of indigenous forces, the pressure of events, and the increasingly pragmatic response of Soviet leaders have been steadily eroding the ideological foundations of Communism," thus creating "a crisis of faith" or at least a "private doubt" in the leaders about the usefulness of the ideology as a guide to the long war, and to the maneuvers and zigzags of each particular stage.[16]

In the past forty-five years has history not encouraged them to believe that they are the future and we the decaying past? At the outset—unless it should be saved by world revolution—Lenin barely ventured to hope that his rule would "last longer than the Paris Commune." It is rounding out four and a half decades secure in its might, the second power on earth straining to be the first, the stronghold of a "socialist camp."

What reason does a man looking with Khrushchev's eyes have for abandoning the view that "capitalism-imperialism" is decadent when it is losing all its colonies, did not show the resolution to protect Hungary's freedom or complete the unification of Korea, failed to make the military moves to prepare its sort of peace during World War II, thereby letting maimed and bleeding Russia pick up all of Eastern Europe and half of Germany, win powerful allies or partners in Asia, expand the "camp of Communism" from one-sixth of the earth to one-fourth, with one-third of the earth's population? We may offer our explanations of all this. None of them would seem to him to refute his simple explanation of "decadence" and "progress."

VII

Khrushchev was born in the ambience of his ideology, like a fish in water, and educated in that ideology's tenets and techniques. This ideology-technique guided his upward path from *rabfak* graduate and local student secretary to a place as one of Stalin's most vociferous and active claque-leaders, to wheelhorse of the post-Stalin machine, to sole authorized interpreter of the doctrine. In a world where power is knowledge, his power to interpret the ideology has given him knowledge of all things from breeding sows and raising corn to directing poets and philosophers and space-probers. When he bangs his shoe in disapproval the world trembles.

The monopoly power of the machine he heads, and the institutional framework through which it operates, are given legitimacy (insofar as the word is applicable) by the ideology which is the wellspring of the Party's power, and its image of the world. The Party is the word made flesh: Khrushchev cannot permit its wellspring to be polluted; it is the source of his emotions, his sense of the meaning of life, his insight into it, his vision of himself, his power and worth. What would give him the claim to rule over a great and ancient people and have his voice heard with awe in the councils of the mighty, if not his mastery of the remarkable machine deriving its energy from this ideology?

VIII

The vagueness of the ideology should not blind us to the definiteness of its myth-affirmed will to action or the intensity of the passions it evokes. It nourishes not so much love of the future, which is vague, as hatred of the present, which is clear and visible. Until the millennium, the God of History is a god of wrath. Only after Judgment Day's dreadful work has been completed will there be room for love among the saved. "Class hatred," wrote Lenin, "is the prime mover of revolution." Since hatred for "the oppressor" predominates over hatred of oppression as such or love for the oppressed, the movement finds no obstacle to sweeping away all existing restraints on power and developing a tyranny of its own, more systematically, pedantically, profoundly, and all-embracingly ambitious in its oppression than history has hitherto known. Since *a priori* there can be no evil in this system, the paranoid mechanism of projection attributes all evils, and evil itself, to capitalism-imperialism. Domestic shortcomings can be but "vestiges" and "survivals" of the enemy that has not yet been totally rooted out, or the work of conscious or unconscious agents.

But the mechanism of projection is notoriously invulnerable to fact and argument. The doctrine teaches that the enemy must be conspired against, subverted, overthrown: therefore the enemy must surely be conspiring, subverting, striving to overthrow the system which spells his death. In that field the dogma is not shaded by ambiguities of self-doubt or self-understanding. When the enemy offers gifts, fear him; when he offers kindness, then is he most suspect.

If the principle of reality could have penetrated this paranoid barrier, the Grand Alliance of wartime would have done it. "Experience" should then have said: "After all, there is not a single enemy as we thought; the imperialists have not formed a united, hostile camp; they did not gang up to put an end to us, their mortal foe; instead, the best and mightiest offered alliance and friendship." When the Axis should be obviously beaten, it might seem as if Communism were at last without an enemy!

But the ideology was equal to this, potentially the gravest crisis in its history. Even before the tide turned, as General Deane, Churchill, Djilas, and others have testified in their reminiscences, the men in the Kremlin were determined to keep it what it was to them all along: a "strange alliance." They could hardly wait until the tide had in effect securely turned at Casablanca and Stalingrad, to begin the "cold war" within the United Nations before the hot war was over. Even in 1943 they began to subjugate where their armies had liberated, to create by their acts, or re-create, the enemy, whom even as "ally" they had so carefully kept out of their citadel. The Zhdanov campaigns completed the rearming of those who had yielded to the illusion that Communism was now without a mortal enemy. When the "two camps" were separated once more by a no-man's land, the infallible interpreters of the infallible doctrine felt comfortable again in their totalist power at home and their total aspirations abroad.

Khrushchev's main accomplishments in this have been two: domestically, to reestablish the clear lines of Party control of all transmission belts (including police, managers, officials, and army) which Stalin's "many hats" and manias had somewhat blurred; externally, to apply Lenin's and Stalin's teachings about "depriving the enemy of even the weakest allies," in a new world of neutralist infant nations.[17]

IX

Finally, there is one aspect of the Communist ideology which distinguishes Leninism from all other varieties of Marxism, and it is central to our problem: namely, Lenin's absorption not with the dream of socialism but with the mechanics and dynamics of organization and power. In a world where most intellectuals were in love with ideas and accustomed to the gap between dream and deed, Lenin's idea was organization. He was an organization man, *the* organization man of whatever movement he participated in. He was an enemy alike to the dawn-to-dusk discussions of the intelligentsia and to the "unreliable," "spontaneous" flareups and subsidings of the masses; he was all his life at work on a machine to control untidy, unreckonable, detestable "spontaneity." [18]

Organization, control, and centralism were the sacred tripod of power. "*Now* we have become an organized party," he early wrote, "and that means the creation of power, the transformation of the authority of ideas into the authority of power, the subordination of the lower party organs to the higher ones." When a delegate to the 1903 Congress spoke liturgically of the Central Commttee as "Spirit, one and omnipresent," Lenin shouted out from his seat, "Not spirit, but *fist!*" This prosaic, repetitive, monotonous orator and crabbed writer was in his own way a poet: a poet of organization, centralism, control, and power.

It was on these issues that Lenin split the Social Democratic Party at its "unification Congress." They are the unifying thread running through all he has said and written, down to the occasional scraps. The party he created was made in his image: a party of *apparatchiki*—men of the machine—concerned with seizing power, holding power, extending power over all the spontaneous, free, and uncontrollable aspects of life, power to crush what must be crushed, to confine, direct, and control the rest. "We must organize everything," Lenin said in 1918 after he had taken power, "we must take every-thing in our hands." To the authoritarian trend inherent in an infallible doctrine, he added the further dream of an *apparat*, a machine, with "transmission belts," penetrating and using all organizations to "organize everything, take everything into our hands," make wayward, refractory life totally malleable and totally submissive to direction and control. Out of this, totalitarianism was born. Totally organized power over everything is the real core of its ideology.

In place of constantly seeking to close our eyes to this, I am afraid we must learn to keep it in the center of our thinking for the foreseeable future. For of all the appetites of man, the appetite for power is the one most known to grow by what it feeds on, the least likely by its exercise to diminish, be sated, or "erode."

FOOTNOTES

[1] Daniel Bell, *The End of Ideology* (Rev. ed.; New York: Collier, 1961), pp. 324-325.

[2] The enduring elements of the *institutional framework* I have discussed in a paper entitled "The Durability of Despotism in the Soviet System," presented at Oxford in 1957 in a "Conference on Changes in Russia Since Stalin's Death," first printed in *The Russian Review,* May 1958, pp. 83-93, and July 1958, pp. 163-175, and subsequently reprinted a number of times: in Alex Inkeles and Kent Geiger, eds., *Soviet Society: A Book of Readings* (Boston: Houghton-Mifflin, 1961), pp. 648-659; Samuel Hendel, ed., *The Soviet Crucible* (Princeton: Van Nostrand, 1959), pp. 553-568; Alexander Dallin, ed., *Soviet Conduct in World Affairs* (New York: Columbia University Press, 1960), pp. 262-282; Wolfe, *Communist Totalitarianism* (Boston: Beacon, 1961), pp. 270-293.

The present paper will deal only with the enduring elements of the *ideology.*

[3] In 1934, Karl Radek wrote: "The attempt to represent the foreign policy of the Soviet Union as a continuation of Tsarist foreign policy is ridiculous. . . . Tsarism, or any other bourgeois regime in Russia, would necessarily resume the struggle for the conquest of Poland and the Baltic states. . . . The Soviet Union on the contrary . . . considers their achievement of independence as positive and progressive historical factors." Radek, "The Basis of Soviet Foreign Policy," *Foreign Affairs,* vol. 12, p. 194.

Alas, poor Radek . . .

[4] On these continuities, see: Ivo J. Lederer, ed., *Russian Foreign Policy* (New Haven: Yale University Press, 1962); Peter Scheibert, "Die sowjetrussische Aussenpolitik und ihre Traditionen," *Schriftenreihe des Forschungrates des Landes Hessen,* 9te Veröffentlichung, 1961, pp. 25-32; Michael Karpovich, "Russian Imperialism or Communist Aggression?," in Dallin, *op. cit.,* pp. 186-195.

[5] Richard Lowenthal, "The Logic of One-Party Rule," in Dallin, *op. cit.,* p. 67.

[6] See Donald MacRae, "The Appeal of Communist Ideology," in Inkeles and Geiger, *op. cit.*, pp. 104-113.

[7] Sir Lewis Namier, *Personalities and Powers* (New York: Macmillan, [1955]), p. 4.

[8] On this see Zbigniew K. Brzezinski, *Ideology and Power in Soviet Politics* (New York: Praeger, 1962).

[9] This was written several months before Khrushchev provided one more spectacular example by his retreat from Cuba in October 1962.

[10] First you get into battle, then see how far you can go.

[11] "They say," Khrushchev declared in Albania on the eve of the Foreign Ministers' Conference of 1959, "that 'with the USSR you must negotiate in the following fashion: concession for concession!' But that is a huckster's approach! . . . We do not have any concessions to make, because our proposals have not been made for bartering. . . . [Their] proposals do not contain a single element for negotiation. . . . They are not based on a desire to find a correction solution."

[12] All the quotations are from Lenin *Selected Works*, V. 7 (New York: International Publishers, n.d.), where he discusses the Brest-Litovsk Treaty. Similar views are found throughout his works. Analysts who become aware of the apocalyptic element in Communism are apt to overlook this realistic, calculating, pragmatic element. This is one of the main sources of our continual misunderstanding of Communist peace maneuvers, retreats and "agreements." Lenin taught his disciples: "If you are not able to adapt yourself, if you are not ready to crawl in the mud on your belly, you are not a revolutionist but a chatterbox." Neither Lenin nor Stalin was a chatterbox. Khrushchev, despite his unending chatter, analogous to a stage magician's line of patter, is not a chatterbox either.

[13] The first quoted formula is Lenin's, the second Stalin's, and the others have been used by Stalin and Khrushchev.

[14] Speech of January 6, 1961, "For New Victories of the World Communist Movement." It was originally delivered at a closed meeting in the Kremlin and released for publication abroad some ten days later. Khrushchev has returned to the same thought a number of times since. On July 15, 1963, while a partial test ban was being negotiated in Moscow by Lord Hailsham, Harriman, and Gromyko, *Pravda* carried an "Open

Letter from the Central Committee of the Soviet Communist Party to All Party Organizations of the Soviet Union," in which the same idea was once more reaffirmed. In the translation supplied by *Tass* to the *New York Times* (July 15, p. 12), it reads:

> Expressing the line of our Party, Comrade Nikita Khrushchev said: "There will be wars of liberation as long as imperialism exists, as long as colonialism exists. These are revolutionary wars; such wars are not only permissible but even unavoidable, since the colonialists do not grant independence to people voluntarily. Therefore it is only through struggle, including armed struggle, that the peoples can win their freedom and independence."

[15] Lenin, *Selected Works,* v. 10, pp. 111-112.

[16] Chester Bowles, "Is Communist Ideology Becoming Irrelevant?" *Foreign Affairs,* July, 1962.

[17] To be sure, Khrushchev is not finding this road as smooth as the Nevsky Prospekt either. The interregnum between Stalin and Khrushchev has left the "monolithic camp of socialism" somewhat fissured, while Lenin's injunction "to temporize and compromise with possible—even though transient, unstable, vacillating, and conditional—allies" is proving more complicated than the formula suggests. To analyze these difficulties, Khrushchev's attempts at meeting them, and the effect of these difficulties and devices upon the ideology itself would require a separate study.

[18] Lenin even created heresies of his own such as *khvostism* ("tailism")—"dragging at the tail of the spontaneous mass movement," and "slavish kowtowing before spontaneity." In 1920, Lenin told the 10th Congress of his Party: "Petit-bourgeois spontaneity is many times more terrible than all the Denikins, Kolchaks, and Yudeniches put together!"

Soviet Society Under Stalin:
The Prototype of Totalitarianism

William Petersen

By lifting their hands against Comrade Stalin, they [the defendants in the 1937 show-trial] lifted them against everything that is best in humanity, because Stalin is the hope, Stalin is the expectation, Stalin is the lighthouse of all progressive humanity. Stalin, our banner! Stalin, our will! Stalin, our victory!

—Nikita S. Khrushchev, 1937

In 19th-century England Marx distinguished the bourgeoisie (the owners of the means of production) from the proletariat (who owned nothing but their "labor power"); and this distinction still holds for the West, even though mere ownership of corporation stocks has become far less important than control of boards of directors. In a totalitarian state, the class structure is determined mainly by political, rather than economic, attributes. The Soviet Union of the Stalinist period had three broad social classes—the Party at the top, the slave laborers at the bottom, and the mass of free non-Party people in between. We shall begin at the top and move down through the social structure, restricting the analysis to the roughly thirty years (out of the forty-five since the 1917 revolution) that Stalin was either in ascendancy or in power.

The role of the dictator in a Communist dictatorship, though seemingly not a problematic matter, has often been misunderstood. In the first portion of the Stalinist era, from the death of Lenin (1924) to the 16th Party Congress (1930), Stalin took pains to deny the special importance of his personal role. His achievements were ascribed to a "collective leadership" of the Party, through which the inevitable forward march of History was being realized. The Party embodies perfect wisdom and is, unlike any mere individual, infallible. And it is true that Stalin won the fight for control because he was an *apparatchik*—a man of the Party apparatus. The heir apparent was Trotsky—the closest associate of Lenin, a brilliant orator and writer, who used his excellent mind to grapple with problems of national and international scope; and in these respects he was typical of the Party's intellectuals. Stalin, on the other hand, was appointed as early as 1919 to the Party's Organizational Bureau, established simply to put the policies adopted by the Central Committee into operation. From this seemingly routine post, he was able to organize the most effective personal machine, so that when he was made General Secretary in 1922, it was in recognition of *de facto* power he had already achieved. Trotsky, his first and principal rival, was not alone in his puzzlement over Stalin's success. Stalin was, in Trotsky's often repeated word, a "mediocrity," a man incapable of greatness. Yet by Trotsky's analysis (recently revived by Khrushchev), Stalin so deflected the country from its true Leninist course that Trotsky found it necessary to coin a term, "Stalinist," to describe the many aberrations.

For years this was a word used exclusively by critics of the regime, but from the middle 1930's on, the official Communists not only accepted the appellation "Stalinist" but rejoiced in it. The name and the picture of the *Vozhd*, "the Leader," were everywhere. He was the first and final authority on all subjects. The constitution of 1936, which behind a facade of democratic verbiage established his personal dictatorship, was officially proclaimed the "Stalin Constitution." Regions and cities were renamed in his honor, not only the well-known Stalingrad but Stalinabad, Staliniri, Stalino, Stalinogorsk, Stalinsk, and so on; and those unfortunate towns not so blessed made do with renaming one of their streets or squares.

All public occasions were marked by ritual obeisance to "the wise and beloved leader of the toilers of the universe, the great Stalin." Indeed, this ritual became so fixed that informed Western analysts were able to predict from its absence or diminution a change in the regime's power structure.[1] In Ancient Rome, once the republic became an empire, the dictator's subjects vied in finding ever more obsequious expression of their total subordination, finally making gods of their emperors. So also in the Soviet Union, Stalin rose from his post as General Secretary, to the all-wise leader of humanity, to the verge of becoming a deity. An Uzbek poet printed in *Pravda* attributed to him the creation of the world.[2] At the end of World War II, shortly after one fuehrer had committed suicide in the ruins of Berlin, the major poet of the German Communist Party, Johannes

Becher, wrote to another fuehrer an ode,[3] the flavor of which can be indicated only by a partial quotation:

> When in the reconstructed plant
> Machines again begin their roar,
> They sing a song, and we understand it all,
> A hymn of praise rung out—Stalin, we thank thee.

> When again the peasant walks his fields,
> Freed from the foe, and sows again,
> Often he stands and looks afar
> And offers a thanksgiving prayer: Stalin . . .

After Stalin's death, while Malenkov, Beria, and Khrushchev were struggling to succeed to first place, the Party organs denounced this "cult of personality" and demanded, once again, a "collective leadership." The parallels with the post-Lenin period, though striking, are not exact; the precise excesses of the Stalin cult need not be replicated in detail under his successor. But it is also true that Khrushchev's efforts to heap all the blame for all of the now admitted atrocities on the personal head of one man constitute, to put it no stronger, an exaggeration—as well as a strangely non-Marxian interpretation of social history. Khrushchev follows many analysts during Stalin's lifetime, both Communist and anti-Communist, in grossly overstating the personal role of his predecessor. For instance, the notion that, like Napoleon, he would found a personal dynasty was based on a false comparison. Napoleon depended on the army but his power was as a man of destiny; Stalin was always the General Secretary of the Party. While he had this post, his personality (or, as some have put it, his paranoia) was a political factor of some importance, just as in an absolute monarchy the foibles of the king can affect the whole state. But the monarchy is larger than any king; when one dies, his subjects cry, "Long live the king!" Stalin died, and the institution he reflected lives on.

The Communist Party of the Soviet Union, the social base from which the dictator operates, also represents only a tiny minority of the population.[4] At the beginning of 1917 there were fewer than 25,000 members, and by the end of the year, after the Bolsheviks had taken power, there were only about 116,000, or still only 0.08 percent of the population.[5] During the following years the number of Party members grew, but never to a very large fraction of the population, and not steadily. When Lenin died in 1924, the membership was about a third of a million, and over the next decade it increased to more than two million. Part of this growth represented Stalin's successful maneuver to "proletarianize" the Party, or, in effect, to flood out his opponents among the Old Bolsheviks with large numbers of the crudest, politically most inexperienced workers, who were most susceptible to demagogic appeals. After the murder of Kirov, the Leningrad Party secretary (1934), the Party instituted a great purge, which spread in widening circles and over the next four years depleted the membership by almost half. Beginning in 1938 there was a renewed membership drive, which was intensified during and immediately after the war, when the threatened regime sought to establish a better rapport with the populace. In the middle 1950's the roughly 7.2 million members made up something under 4 percent of the population, and since then there has been an increase to about 5 percent. The Party is not the same self-consciously elitist organization that Lenin created, but it is still an elite.

The social composition is difficult to estimate, for the sparse statistics are often deliberately misleading. Before 1917 the Party was indeed what it was supposed to be by Leninist theory, a hard-knit core of professional revolutionaries; but by the time Stalin rose to full power, the Party membership—at least on questions relating to social change in the Soviet Union—was about as revolutionary as the DAR. In theory it was a "party of workers and peasants," and the available statistics emphasized these components. New members were classified as "workers" on the basis of their social origin irrespective of their actual occupation, as though proletarian status were an inherited factor. Many higher administrative personnel in industry and agriculture were labeled deceptively. One must interpret such statistics carefully to see what they mean. According to one painstaking analysis,[6] in the middle 1950's the Party's membership was distributed among sectors of the labor force as follows:

Political and administrative hierarchies..................... 21%
Armed forces and police.................................. 14
Senior administrators in industry, mining, and transportation.. 18
Senior administrators of collective or state farms............   9
Educational, medical, scientific, and cultural professions...... 10
Junior foremen and rank-and-file workers in industry, mining,
  and transportation...................................... 18
Junior foremen and rank-and-file workers in agriculture...... 10

Thus even after the postwar recruitment, which had concentrated on bringing in a greater number of peasants, hardly more than a quarter of the total Party membership could reasonably be termed "workers and peasants."

A Communist Party member in the Stalin era lived well.[7] An enormous disparity between the incomes of the ruling class and of the masses, though it cannot be documented from national data, is indicated by what information we have. In the middle 1930's, in Moscow, the monthly incomes of top Party, state, and industrial officials were about forty times those of wage-workers. In judging the meaning of this contrast, two facts must be kept in mind. Workers in the nation's capital were a relatively favored group, far better off than peasants, not to say slave laborers. And, second, for the upper class the official money income was appreciably supplemented by all sorts of free items—homes complete with furnishings and servants, cars complete with chauffeur, vacations at spas or beaches, and so on through the full, well-publicized range of Soviet social welfare. Even basic consumer goods like food and clothing were distributed through rigidly segregated outlets: all of the better commodities were reserved for Party stores, to which only the upper classes had access.

If the upper class led a good life, it was also a dangerous one. The Soviet counterpart of our business cycle is a regular alternation between greater and lesser terror, "a constant balance between oppression and relaxation."[8] During the boom period superhuman goals are set and everyone tries to march toward utopia at double-quick time. When another failure becomes manifest, a scapegoat is found, perhaps the Party leaders who seem most to threaten the dictator. But the structure of the Party and its associated bureaucracy is such that the toppling of a member of the Politburo may often be accompanied by a general purge.

Factions in the Party have been forbidden since 1921, but this was never a prohibition that could effectively enforced. A Communist is a political animal, a man who needs an arena for political activity, and who is trained to make one for himself if the rules do not provide it. Even apart from their recurrent effort to change the Party's policy, members are pushed into factions by the very nature of their institution. A man close to the top of the hierarchy generally tries to move up the last rung by building a personal machine in the Party, the army and state police, the industrial bureaucracy, even the Comintern. From the other side, a man lower down and ambitious to advance himself through the channels that the Party affords must have a patron who can open doors for him. This informal cooperation between patron and client the Russians term *shefstvo*—from *chef*, French for "boss." [9] The protection a patron is able to give his client, however, is often ambiguous. An astute chess player never attacks the queen immediately, or even a knight; he tries to take an exposed pawn. The first attack on a member of the Politburo is typically against a much less powerful figure who is known, or suspected, to be his adherent. The patron defends his own if he can, if only because he knows that he is the real target. If he falls, he drags down with him as many of his entire faction as can be identified.

Like Lenin before him, Stalin cleared the way by a succession of purges, of which the culmination was the so-called *Yezhovshchina* of 1936-38. Nicolai Yezhov, the head of the state police during those years, deserves a place, alongside Genghiz Khan and Himmler, in the annals of monstrous inhumanity. In three show-trials fifty-four defendants (including almost all of the surviving prerevolutionary Party leaders except Stalin and his few associates) were accused of heinous, improbable, and—whenever the charges could be tested by evidence outside the Soviet Union—demonstrably false crimes, to which they confessed in open court. They were executed, together with tens, or it may be hundreds, of thousands who were afforded no public accusation. According to no less a witness than Khrushchev, speaking at the 20th Party Congress in 1956, when he was trying to establish himself by attacking the now safely deceased Stalin:

> Many thousands of honest and innocent Communists have died as a result of this monstrous falsification of such "cases," as a result of the fact that all kinds of slanderous "confessions" were accepted, and as a result of the practice of forcing accusations against oneself and others. . . .
>
> The vicious practice was condoned of having the NKVD prepare lists of persons whose cases were under the jurisdiction of the Military Collegium and whose sentences were prepared in advance. Yezhov would send these lists to Stalin personally for his approval of the proposed punishment. In 1937-38, 383 such lists containing the names of many thousands of Party, Soviet, Komsomol, Army and economic workers were sent to Stalin. He approved these lists.[10]

Even for Russia, the terror was on a new scale. Of the 139 members elected to the Central Committee by the 17th Party Congress (1934), 98 were later shot. While in past elections to the Central Committee, some two-thirds to four-fifths of those elected had been incumbents, at the 18th Party Congress (1939), after this mammoth bloodletting, of the 71 members elected 65 were new to the Central Committee.

The human impact of the purge can be better appreciated from the details that we know about the Party in Smolensk. That town suffered from an adept practitioner of purge tactics, one Rabinovich, who became highly skilled in pouncing on his comrades and colleagues with fantastic charges—in one case, for example, that a member of the cell was an impostor who had taken the place of a good Communist, now dead. He was able to fling such wildly inaccurate accusations and depend for their substantiation on the fear-drenched atmosphere of the Party, in which no one dared deny even patent nonsense. Eventually Rabinovich, like Yezhov himself, fell victim to the purge. We learn from the Smolensk archive, also, that the purge had its beneficiaries as well as its victims; as some sociologists would put it, the purge was functional. Men or women with no more than an elementary education, and in one case with a public record of excessive drinking, became officials of the district court and leaders of the militia.[11] Also at the national level, many of those who survived, or who replaced the purged, were grossly inadequate for their new posts. Stalin perceived these deficiencies, especially if they were past doctrinal deviations, as advantageous to him, for persons so encumbered were particularly dependent on the Stalin faction and susceptible to its pressure. For example, Vyshinsky had remained a Menshevik for three years after the Bolsheviks took power, and this association with the Devil was certainly one reason why as state prosecutor he was so assiduous in digging up similar heresies, whether real or fancied, in the defendants' pasts. With this indelible flaw on his record, he was a wholly malleable tool in Stalin's hands.

II

In the abstract, as we noted, Marx divided capitalist society into bourgeoisie and proletariat, but whenever he wrote an account of a specific country—France, or the United States, or India—he found it necessary to specify six or seven classes. Similarly, the intermediate political class of free non-Party people, which we have defined preliminarily by the negative fact that they are neither at the top nor at the bottom, varies greatly within itself. In a more detailed analysis this middle group can be usefully broken down into three subclasses—the technical elite, the industrial workers, and the peasantry.

The Russian word *intelligentsia* is not properly translated by "intellectual"; it means rather "a social stratum comprised of persons whose vocation involves mental work," including "scholars, engineers, writers, teachers, physicians, agronomists, state and Party functionaries, directors of industrial enterprises, of machine tractor stations, of collective and state farms, military officers and generals, persons employed by the state cultural and educational institutions, artists." [12] If we wish to distinguish this "stratum" from the Party itself (which by this definition is included in it), we must use another designation, such as technical elite, or James Burnham's "managers." There is, of course, a great interpenetration between the Party and the associated bureaucracies. In the first years of the Soviet regime, trusted Party members were "colonized" (to use Communist jargon) in all important institutions, in order to ensure their revolutionary integrity. Later large numbers of the technical elite joined the Party, which in certain periods (for instance, 1938-41) particularly sought them as new members.

In the early years of the Soviet regime, many Western analysts believed that the "managers" or "technocrats" would gradually assume dominant power, and this hypothesis has been revived since Khrushchev's accession to Party leadership. Perhaps the strongest argument in favor of this view is the Marxian dogma that those who control the economy must also come to be the political leaders, but in several senses this begs the question. There are at least three reasons for supposing that administrative personnel will retain much the position in Soviet society that they presently have—highly favored in income and prestige but decidedly subordinate to the Party in power.

a) In the Soviet Union as in the United States, "managers" are more an analytical classification than a nascent social class. There is no evidence that higher technicians, industrial and agricultural administrators, writers and intellectuals, and the other professional and administrative categories actually see themselves as a single social unit with common interests. Burnham's "managerial revolution" is hardly likely to be staged if its main actors are not even dimly aware of the roles he wrote for them.

b) Even if the "managers" became conscious of their membership in a new administrative class, they would not necessarily oppose the rule of the Party. Technical education at the university level always includes an especially heavy indoctrination in Marxism-Leninism, and while most engineering students dislike this extra work (just as engineering students in the United States generally see liberal-arts subjects as a waste of their precious time), the inculcation of one system of values, reinforced by the exclusion of all alternatives, affects their views. Once he acquires professional status, moreover, the "manager" works closely with the Party, with a typical division of labor congenial to both sides. Engineers and administrators are trained in narrow technical skills; they know *how* to do particular things. If, atypically, they begin to consider *why* things should or should not be done, they are more likely to join the Party than to oppose it.

c) In any case, the Party takes good care that whatever power is implicit in formal economic controls shall not be realized. Every Party unit in the Soviet Union has what is known as its *nomenkla-tura,* or the list of administrative positions under its jurisdictional control.[13] This system is not publicized; the very word seldom appears in the Soviet press. It is known, however, that applicants for higher positions in industry (in the broadest sense), not only directorships but also lesser posts, must be passed by the Party, which also maintains a regular check on their continued loyalty. There have been repeated purges of the technical elite. The First Five-Year Plan was opened with the Shakhty trial (1928), in which a group of non-Communist engineers and administrators were accused of treason and sabotage. Yezhov's purge of the Party extended to the officer corps of the Soviet army: in 1937, Marshal Tukhachevsky, eight generals, and an estimated 15,000 officers were ousted. According to Khrushchev's later report:

> During these years [1937-41] repressions were instituted against certain parts of military cadres beginning literally at the company and battalion commander level and extending to the higher military centers. . . . [Some] managed to survive, despite severe tortures to which they were subjected in the prisons. . . . However, many such commanders perished in camps and the Army saw them no more.[14]

And in the post-Stalin period the Party has established firmer authority not only in the state police (the Beria purge of 1953), but also in the army, in agriculture, and in industry.

Of all the elements of the intelligentsia, scientists and artists may find the Party's rule most difficult to accept. The one searches for scientific truth, the other tries to create artistic values; but the Party has a monopoly on both truth and values. Indeed, one often reads that this opposition is so complete that not even a partial resolution is feasible. Thus, if Galina Ulanova, the country's prima ballerina, is a truly great dancer, or if A. Y. Khinchin's studies on the theory of probability are excellent, then the Soviet Union is not a totalitarian society. Or, in reverse terms: since science can flourish only in a free society, and since modern wars are won by science, therefore democracy must overcome any totalitarian opponent. This special version of the doctrine that History fights with us is as false as any other variant.

The relation between the Party and science is complex. Sometimes the concentration of personnel, money, and effort on a single task has resulted in remarkable advances; sometimes the doctrine of "Party science" has effected a retrogression not only from present levels in the West but, in the worst cases, from pre-1917 Russian levels. There is no wholly satisfactory generalization to explain this contrast.[15] (a) In some cases, what the state can use to enhance its prestige or military might is fostered; but a whole generation of distinguished geneticists was killed off and supplanted by Lysenko's men, and this in spite of the fact that Russian agriculture certainly needs whatever assistance science can give it. An even more telling example, perhaps, is sociology, which hardly can be said to exist in the Soviet Union even though certain sectors of this discipline could be very useful in social planning. (b) Another generalization might be that the most abstruse sciences are relatively free. For example, mathematicians have had to make a ritual bow in the general direction of dialectical materialism, but then in some cases have been able to make real contributions. Yet the theory of relativity, expunged from Nazi Germany as "Jewish physics," was denounced in the Soviet Union as "metaphysical" and "idealist," which are terms of equal opprobrium. (c) Perhaps the only valid generalization is that the Party supports or denigrates scientific studies depending on how *it* sees them, and that since this view is both prejudiced and ignorant, it is often arbitrary. However arbitrarily, it is the Party that controls. Scientific work is coordinated through the USSR Academy of Sciences, a state organization, and the Party maintains units in every institute and research laboratory to keep a watch on their activities.[16]

The conflict between the Party and artists is potentially much stronger. For about two hundred years, a segment of the artistic world has proclaimed the doctrine of absolute social irresponsibility, *l'art pour l'art* and for nothing else, and this is a much greater affront to Communist sensibilities than the ideology of Western science. Moreover, a scientist who, in spite of metaphysical deviations, is permitted relative freedom may produce in his laboratory something of use to the state, but no Communist would ever believe this of an artist given freedom to create. In 1932, the Party established a single Union of Soviet Artists, both completely subordinate to itself and enjoying a total control over all facilities for creative painting—exhibition halls, commissions for specific works, even artists' supplies. Parallel organizations were set up to control writers, architects, musicians, and other creative artists. The doctrine these organizations were supposed to enforce, Socialist Realism, remained elusive even to those officially responsible for its formulation.[17] On one occasion Stalin told a group of writers that it meant that they should "write the truth"—certainly a dangerous interpretation. According to Zhdanov, Soviet art must be "national in form and socialist in content," a formulation that meant little more than that workers in the arts had to obey the Party. Every country, it is true, has its calendar painting, its national anthems, its monumental state architecture; but in the Soviet Union, under the doctrine of Socialist Realism, *all* art was restricted to this level.

III

Below the intelligentsia are the workers, officially the dominant class of this "working-class society." The Soviet Union collects more economic data of all kinds than any other society; and it is no accident, as Marxists would say, that in this mass of statistics the Stalinist era gave analysts no index of real wages. Lacking such data, we must make do with more or less inadequate substitutes. For example, in 1939 and 1940 the American Embassy ascertained the prices, in Moscow retail stores, of a typical basket of consumer goods, and calculated that average prices had risen by more than twenty-two times since 1913. Over the same period the money wages of workers had risen by less than fourteen times, so that their real wages had fallen by more than a third from before the revolution. The decline after 1928, which marks the beginning of the five-year plans, can be calculated with greater precision. If we designate the real wages in that year as 100 and use a cost-of-living index based on 1928 weights, then the real wages after taxes and compulsory bond purchases were 57 in 1937, 40 in 1948, and still only 63 in 1952.[18] In short, it is likely that the material welfare even of industrial workers declined from just before the revolution to the end of the NEP, and it is absolutely certain that such a decline was suffered during the Stalinist era *per se*, from the beginning of the planned era to Stalin's death. Such figures do not take into account the simultaneous decline in quality, which is generally much more difficult to measure. But in urban housing, for instance, whose quality can be gauged with available data, even Soviet apologists admit a serious deterioration during the 1930's.

Perhaps the clearest indication both of the relative status of workers and of the Party's intent is the country's tax structure. In the United States the major portion of the government's income comes from the progressive income tax, which for the highest incomes is 90 percent of the total, and American liberals have always opposed the sales tax because it imposes the heaviest relative burden on those least able to bear it. In the Soviet Union, most consumer goods, including even staple foods and cheap clothing had (and still have) a sales tax of about 50 percent, and almost half of the government's income was from this source. The highest rate of tax on personal incomes, on the other hand, was only 13 percent. "It is time it was understood," Stalin declared, "that Marxism is an enemy of equalization." [19]

The worker under tsarist autocracy was a relatively free man compared to his counterpart under Stalin. Indeed, one of the prerequisites of the planned economy was the total subjection of the trade-union movement, which up to the 16th Party Congress (1930) had retained a modest autonomy. From that date, industrial workers were subjected to one onerous restriction after another. From 1932 on, every Soviet subject had to carry an internal passport—a revival of one of the most hated of tsarist institutions. Travel abroad was prohibited for all except the favored few, and travel within the country was either highly restricted or imposed, depending on the needs of the planned economy. In addition, each industrial worker had a "work book," in which were entered all infractions of discipline, absences from work, and other "work offenses." The specific punishments imposed varied from industry to industry and from one period to another, but any would be described in the West as draconic. One day's absence from work or being twenty minutes late was ground for dismissal, which meant the loss of one's ration card and, probably, of one's dwelling space. Later, being more than twenty minutes late at work was made a criminal offense, punishable by six months of forced labor, preferably at the same site with a 25 percent reduction of wages. Increasingly, wages were paid by piecework, at rates set by specially trained and favored "Stakhanovites," named after a husky young coal miner, who allegedly overfulfilled his quota by sixteen times. Stakhanov was made a full member of the Party without passing through the usual candidacy; he received the Order of Lenin and the Red Labor Banner. He was the prototype of the happy workers that visiting friends of the Soviet Union were taken to meet. Since the ideology favored the working class, a few workers, particularly if they were also of working-class stock, earned a pleasant livelihood as such show-pieces.

Throughout the Stalin era the peasantry was both the largest economic stratum and, in the whole free sector, the one most alienated from the regime. The main social consequence of the Bolshevik revolution, after the abortive attempts to establish a socialist economy had failed and the Party had retreated to the mixed economy of the New Economic Policy, had been—paradoxically— the distribution of land among the peasantry. This was not in accord with the long-range Communist program, but a matter of temporary expediency: it was necessary to neutralize the peasantry while the Party took power. That many peasants had acquired their land only in 1917-18 did not mean that they regarded it lightly; if anything the peasant's proverbial attachment to his plot was stronger in Russia than elsewhere. Efforts to coax peasants to abandon their holdings and join the state-sponsored collective farms failed completely; by mid-1928 only 1.7 percent of the peasant households and 2.3 percent of the crop area had been collectivized. The major program of the First Five-Year Plan (1928-34), thus, was to collectivize agriculture, to convert the peasantry into a landless proletariat, peons of the state, and to use their expropriated property as the capital for the subsequent industrialization.

This program was carried out, first of all, by reinforcing the jealousies and hatreds in the village, recreating the moods of the civil war, engaging the poor peasants against the so-called *kulaks*. Kulaks were "wealthy" peasants (their average per capita income in 1926 was $88 per year!), defined by legal criteria that were changed repeatedly as collectivization proceeded. Eventually all who tried to fight the Party program were defined as kulaks or, if this was too preposterous, as kulak-followers. But while the "middle" and "poor" peasants were often willing to benefit from the expropriation of neighbors slightly better off, they did not willingly give up their own property to the state. Anna Louise Strong, the devoted American Communist, traveled in the Russian countryside in these years, and her glowing account tells us, sometimes between the lines, how the "voluntary" votes for collectives were obtained—by traveling courts administering barrelhead justice, by threats of terror, and, when the threats did not suffice, by terror.[20] The Party made pariahs of the kulaks, a whole social stratum expropriated of its means of subsistence, disfranchised, deprived of ration cards and of the right to purchase in cooperative stores; their children were expelled from school, their sick were excluded from medical treatment. In some cases villages were brought to submission by depriving them of water; other villages or whole areas were surrounded by troops and starved into submission.

Within three years Russian agriculture was collectivized, but in the process it was ruined. More than half of the livestock had been killed off, either to assuage hunger or as a last gesture of desperate sabotage. Virtually all of the most efficient peasantry had been either killed or sent off to forced-labor camps, and their places as leaders were taken by 25,000 city youths, anxious only for the Party career they could establish by successfully corralling the peasant mass. The first catastrophic consequence of the enforced collectivization was the famine of 1932-33, when several million persons died of hunger, especially in the Ukraine, which once had been Europe's wheatbasket.[21] The famine of the 1840's, we know, still is a potent factor in Irish politics, and there is every indication that the effects of Stalinist terror in the Russian countryside will persist as long. Communist boasts about the achievements of the planned economy are sometimes well based, but as every Party conference makes clear, the regime still does not know either how to mitigate the peasants' antipathy or how to drive them to more efficient production. In the

United States, as in most industrial countries, the agricultural problem is what to do with surpluses; in the Soviet Union it is still how to feed the cities.

IV

A few weeks after they had taken power, the Communists established the Cheka, or Extraordinary Commission for Combatting Counterrevolution, Sabotage, and Speculation. Its name reflected its intended purpose, limited even in the middle of a civil war; it was an "extraordinary" body for specific aims. Over the years the designation of the state police was changed repeatedly, from Cheka to GPU to OGPU to NKVD to MVD (to take the process only to Stalin's death), reflecting a continual reorganization and enlargement of its functions. As the NKVD or MVD, standing for People's Commissariat (or later, Ministry) of Internal Affairs, it became an outlandish combination of routine civil administration and terror apparatus. Its functions ranged from tasks like the registration of births and marriages or fire-fighting to the resettlement of whole ethnic minorities and the administration of slave-labor camps. To understand this system one must keep this contrast in mind—the barbaric cruelty administered routinely by the Department of the Interior.

By now we have hundreds of detailed accounts of Soviet slave labor. One of the most interesting still is a volume written by a team of Soviet writers headed by the renowned Maxim Gorky, translated into several languages, and distributed by Communist outlets throughout the world. At this time, at the height of the euphoria occasioned by the beginning of the planned economy, Soviet propagandists were capable of celebrating forced labor as a positive achievement of the Stalin regime, as a system that simultaneously rehabilitated criminals and built the economy. The project so eulogized was the White Sea-Baltic Canal, which shortened the distance from Leningrad to the Arctic ports by some 2,500 miles. In one sense, to build a canal is a job that must be supervised by trained engineers. But the 70,000 slave laborers who did the work had to be controlled, and this was a task at which the state police (or "Chekists," as they were then called) were adept. "Experience has almost made the Chekists engineers, and has taught the engineers the Chekists' style of work." [22] When the canal was finished, the "reforged" "criminals" "volunteered" to work on another project, and were shipped off with their two types of directors.

Another especially interesting account is by Margarete Buber-Neumann, the daughter of Martin Buber, the world-famous Jewish philosopher, and the wife of Heinz Neumann, a German Communist who had fled to Moscow after the Nazis came to power. Both Neumanns were arrested during the Yezhovshchina and put in camps, where he died. After the Molotov-Ribbentrop Friendship Pact was signed, his wife and a number of other former German Communists were turned over to the Gestapo, and Margarete Neumann spent several years more in a German camp. Miraculously she survived also this, and her book is a detailed comparison of the undersides of the two totalitarian states.[23]

From such accounts—by former inmates, by GPU officials who had defected, by Western analysts of the half-hidden information in official records—we know where the camps were, and we know how the inmates were treated. The one point on which there is substantial disagreement among Western scholars is also one of the most important—how many slave laborers were there?

Up until 1928 the figures were relatively negligible; at the beginning of that year there were only 30,000 men detained in the camps. In the next two or three years, with the forcible collectivization of agriculture and the beginning of the planned economy, the number jumped to perhaps 4 million. How high did the camp population ultimately rise? Estimates by informed persons (for example, Walter Krivitsky) have ranged as high as 20 million, but this is almost certainly too large a figure. Immediately after the war, Dallin and Nicolaevsky estimated the total as between 7 and 12 million,[24] and for the same period Wolin has recently estimated it at 12 to 15 million.[25] Other Western scholars suggest that the figure may have been closer to half this. The differences are due in part, of course, to the inherent difficulties in interpreting the incomplete and defective data; and these difficulties cannot be wholly overcome.

It may be, however, that a portion of the range in estimates reflects the considerable variation in the total camp population from one period to another. To borrow the terminology of the economist, slave labor was a commodity with a rapid turnover, so that it is important to distinguish between stock and flow. Most camps were situated in the most inhospitable areas of the Soviet empire, where temperatures might fall to 50 or 60 degrees below zero. Clothing and shelter were inadequate, and the no more adequate food was rationed out according to what portion of the daily work norm had been completed. The first time a man was unable to work at the pace his guards set, his weakness was aggravated by semistarvation. Under such conditions, the average life expectancy of camp inmates was probably no more than three or four years, perhaps five or six at the outside. The number of slaves, whatever it was at any time, could hardly have been maintained by the routine terror of normal Stalinism. It must have depended on the extraordinary spurts that recurred every several years. We can distinguish three periods of major recruitment: 1929-32, when the principal source of slaves was the disaffected peasantry; 1936-38, when Yezhov, starting in the Party and its periphery, was eventually able to uncover traitors in every sector of the society; and 1941-45, when substantial percentages of conquered nations (Poles, Estonians, Latvians, Lithuanians), of Soviet ethnic minorities (Volga Germans, Chechen, Ingush, Tatars, Karachay, and others), of prisoners of war (German, Japanese, and others), and of former Russian prisoners, who were presumed to have been contaminated, were used to renew the camp population. At the height of these drives the total was at a maximum, and during the intervening periods of relaxed terror at a minimum. Depending on where in this cycle estimates happened to fall, they could be quite precise and yet vary by a factor, say, of one to three.

The importance of the camp system in Stalinist society, in any case, cannot be measured by even the most accurate inventory of inmates. The smell of fear and death emanating from this hell permeated every corner of the free society. This was indeed "a new civilization," in the words that Sidney and Beatrice Webb used in the title of their mammoth apologia, but its novelty derived in large part from an institution they took care never to observe. Slavery has been a commonplace of history, but not slavery in an industrializing economy, not socialized slavery. We know that significant sectors of the Soviet economy—mining, heavy construction, logging, fishing (including the production of caviar)—partly depended on slave labor directly. We can only surmise to what degree this ultimate threat against the population enabled the Stalinist faction, a minority group within a minority Party, to impose its bloody will on the whole people.

V

If we try to sum up the most characteristic feature of Stalinist society, each of us will use the index that strikes him as most important. Western critics have pointed to the total lack of a private life, the absolute conformity to the precise Party norms that intrude into every corner of society, the drab grayness of artistic life, the low level of consumer goods for the masses and the dramatic contrast with the affluence of the upper classes. While all these features are both characteristic and abhorrent to a Western democrat, in my opinion the way to measure the effect of Communism on the Russian population is to count the people who were killed. To talk of the loss of privacy is like—to use one of Stalin's favorite folk expressions—lamenting the loss of hair of one who has been beheaded.

Strangely, we can estimate this figure with reasonable accuracy. The most telling datum is the sex ratio revealed by the 1939 census, when there were some 7.2 million males short of the normal balance. Note that this was before the war (in the 1959 census, after that slaughter, the shortage of males was almost 21 million), but it marked the end of a quarter-century of domestic terror: World War I, the seizure of power and the elimination of all political opposition, the forced collectivization of agriculture, the hyperrapid industrialization with all the attendant problems of labor discipline, the forced russification of Soviet minorities, the imposed settlement of immemorial nomadic peoples on state-controlled farms, the development of terror from a means of achieving such social goals to an end in itself, a Soviet way of life, a new civilization. Not all types of extraordinary mortality, of course, are included in this lacuna of 7.2 million males. Famine, for example, does not generally result in a grossly unbalanced sex ratio, and the Soviet regime has brought about two devastating famines, one in 1921-22 and one in 1933-34, in each of which millions died of hunger or accompanying diseases. Must we double the 7.2 million to arrive at a total of those killed? This would probably be a conservative figure. "During the years 1915-23 the Russian people underwent the most cataclysmic changes since the Mongol invasion of the early 13th century." [26] And in the Stalinist heyday this Leninist prelude must have seemed a mere curtain-raiser to the drama yet to come.

FOOTNOTES

[1] Perhaps the most remarkable instance of this art of "kremlinology" is an article by the late Franz Borkenau. He noted that a resolution of the Central Committee of the Socialist Unity Party of Germany (that is, the Communist Party of East Germany), passed on January 4, 1953, contained only a single quotation from Stalin, and that a mere half-sentence dating from 1910. There was no specific derogation of the Leader, but the remarkable absence of the routine adulation could be explained by only three hypotheses: a suicide pact among the authors of the resolution—improbable; an impending complete shift of power in the Russian Party, no hint of which had reached the West—hardly likely; Stalin's imminent death. Borkenau predicted this last in print, and indeed it took place seven weeks later. Borkenau, "Was Malenkov behind the Anti-Semitic Plot?" *Commentary*, May 1953.

[2] A portion of the poem is translated from *Pravda* of August 28, 1936, in Victor Serge, *Russia Twenty Years After* (New York: Pioneer Publishers, 1937), p. 131.

[3] See Ruth Fischer, *Stalin and German Communism* (Cambridge: Harvard University Press, 1948), p. 662, translated from the first postwar issue of an official Party journal, *Internationale Literatur, Deutsche Blätter,* June-July 1945.

[4] See the compilation of membership data in Merle Fainsod, *How Russia Is Ruled* (Cambridge: Harvard University Press, 1957), pp. 212 ff.

[5] The estimated population in 1917 was 145 million. See Frank Lorimer, *The Population of the Soviet Union* (League of Nations; Princeton: Princeton University Press, 1946), p. 30.

[6] T. H. Rigby, "Social Orientation of Recruitment and Distribution of Membership in the Communist Party of the Soviet Union," *American Slavic and East European Review,* October 1957.

[7] A compilation of data on incomes in this period is Peter Meyer, "The Soviet Union, A New Class Society," printed originally in *Politics,* March-April 1944, and reprinted in

Julien Steinberg, *Verdict of Three Decades* (New York: Duell, Sloan, and Pearce, 1950), pp. 475-509. It is also one source of the famous analysis of "Soviet Myth and Reality" in Arthur Koestler, *The Yogi and the Commissar* (New York: Macmillan, 1945). See also W. W. Kulski, "Classes in the 'Classless' Society," *Problems of Communism,* January-February 1955.

[8] Zbigniew K. Brzezinski, *The Permanent Purge* (Cambridge: Harvard University Press, 1956), p. 168.

[9] Franz Borkenau, "Getting at the Facts Behind the Soviet Facade," *Commentary,* April 1954.

[10] Nikita S. Khrushchev, "The Crimes of the Stalin Era: Special Report to the 20th Congress of the Communist Party of the Soviet Union, Closed Session, February 24-25, 1945," *New Leader,* section 2, July 16, 1956, p. 32. This edition of the speech is valuable for the annotations by Boris I. Nicolaevsky.

[11] Merle Fainsod, *Smolensk under Soviet Rule* (Cambridge: Harvard University Press, 1958), pp. 191-192.

[12] *Bolshaya Sovetskaya Entsiklopedia* (2d ed.; Moscow, 1953), Vol. 18, p. 270.

[13] Jerry F. Hough has written a doctoral dissertation on this subject at Harvard. Perhaps the best analysis of this institution that is generally available is in Fainsod's *Smolensk under Soviet Rule.*

[14] Khrushchev, "The Crimes," *op. cit.,* pp. 39-40. This purge of the army was one important reason that the Nazi armies, when war started in 1941, cut through the Soviet defenses like a hot knife through butter.

[15] For one interesting effort, see Walter Hirsch, "The Autonomy of Science in Totalitarian Societies," *Social Forces,* October 1961.

[16] See Alexander Vucinich, *The Soviet Academy of Sciences* (Stanford, Calif.: Stanford University Press, 1956).

[17] *Cf.* Vladimir Slepian, "The Young vs. the Old," *Problems of Communism,* May-June 1962.

[18] Janet G. Chapman, "Real Wages in the Soviet Union, 1928-1952," *Review of Economics and Statistics,* May 1954. For a more detailed analysis reaching the same general conclusion, see Abram Bergson, *The Structure of Soviet Wages: A Study in Socialist Economics* (Cambridge: Harvard University Press, 1946).

[19] Speech of January 26, 1934; reprinted in *Problems of Leninism* (Moscow: Foreign Languages Publishing House, 1953), p. 635.

[20] Anna Louise Strong, *The Soviets Conquer Wheat: The Drama of Collective Farming* (New York: Holt, 1931).

[21] *Cf.* Ewald Ammende, *Human Life in Russia* (London: Allen & Unwin, 1936); William Henry Chamberlin, *Russia's Iron Age* (Boston: Little, Brown, 1934).

[22] Maxim Gorky *et al.*, *Belomor: An Account of the Construction of the New Canal between the White Sea and the Baltic Sea* (New York: Smith and Haas, 1935), p. 326.

[23] Margarete Buber-Neumann, *Under Two Dictators* (London: Gollancz, 1949).

[24] David J. Dallin and Boris I. Nicolaevsky, *Forced Labor in Soviet Russia* (New Haven: Yale University Press, 1947), pp. 86-87.

[25] Simon Wolin, "Concentration Camps," in Michael T. Florinsky, ed., *Encyclopedia of Russia and the Soviet Union* (New York: McGraw-Hill, 1961), pp. 112-113.

[26] Lorimer, *op. cit.*, p. 42.

The Soviet Economy in
the Post-Stalin Decade

Gregory Grossman

As one seeks to reconstruct a picture of the Soviet economy in those late winter days of 1953 when the dictator lay dying, the epithets "grim," "oppressive," and "bleak" haunt the mind. True, the repair of the enormous wartime physical damage had been nearly completed. Industrial production had been rising rapidly since the end of the war, and even the output of manufactured consumer goods was already considerably above the 1940 level.[1] The consumer's lot had also improved markedly from the extremely low levels of the early postwar years.

But grim, oppressive, and bleak the economic picture still was. Although the war had been won, the economy continued mobilized on a quasimilitary footing to speed reconstruction, to conduct the cold war, to master atomic weaponry and rocketry, and to support the war in Korea. (The burden of the Korean War on the Soviet economy should not be minimized. Among other things, it led to a perceptible decline in the production of civilian machinery.) The notorious labor control laws of 1940 were still on the books, though apparently no longer fully enforced, while a separate and equally severe set of laws and regulations controlled, or at least were intended to control, the mobility and activities of collective-farm peasants. The "cult of personality," that is, Stalin's unbridled and capricious despotism, was felt by everyone and in everything. Millions of persons—the exact number is still unavailable—were leading a semihuman existence in forced-labor camps, many of them only recently impressed during Stalin and Beria's last major wave of arrests. For those outside the camps, and even for the populations of the satellite states, the terror and the political and cultural controls were at a new peak of intensity.

The real wages of the urban population were already substantially above their relatively low level in 1940, just before the German attack, although still considerably below their level before the five-year plans began; but peasants' real incomes were still lower than in 1940, and very much lower than in 1928.[2] Urban housing was a particularly dismal element in this picture, with living space per person, though more ample than in 1940, still one-fifth below what it had been in 1926.[3]

It is difficult even to begin to catalogue the economic problems and headaches that Stalin bequeathed to his successors. To start with agriculture (for reasons not only alphabetical), the output of that sector per head of the total population was then barely at the 1928 level, while the net output of livestock products per capita was substantially below 1928.[4] Of course, even in 1928 the Russian diet was one of the poorest in Europe. The facts that in 1952 an urban population three times as large as that in the earlier year was fed, and some agricultural products were exported, are tributes to the effectiveness (if not efficiency) of the collective-farm system as an instrument of extracting produce from the village—a success bought by Stalin at the price of depressing both farm production and peasant morale. If we ask what in Soviet agriculture at Stalin's death caused this deplorable state of affairs, we find, to put it crudely, that nearly everything was wrong: planning, organization, management, the price system, taxation, the physical equipment and facilities, the composition of the labor force, the distribution system, and, above all, incentives.

The other sectors of the economy had their share of woes, too, despite—and at times because of—the rapid growth of industry and related branches. To mention a few: overcentralization and over-bureaucratization, especially in the form of hypertrophied industrial ministries; cumbersome and often inept planning, which paid virtually no attention to economic efficiency; technological conservatism at most levels; an elaborate incentive structure, in part ineffective and in part perversely effective; a bad price structure, though with the saving grace that it had relatively little to do with resource allocation; emphasis on quantity of output at the expense of quality; chronic shortages of industrial supplies and equipment; and so on. The list has become well known to students of the Soviet economy.

Stalin allayed the economic emergency implicit in these ills by repressing at least the more visible symptoms. ("With sufficient political power one can suppress the operation of economic laws for some time," is the way a Polish economist once put it to the writer.) But the symptoms, and the emergency, became more apparent and painful under his successors, especially since the dynamics of the situation—the pent-up consumers' needs, the unstable economic relations with the satellites, the demands of the cold war, the scientific and technological race with the West, the challenging emergence of the "third world"—now called for early remedial measures.

II

But before turning to the remedies that were adopted, let us glance at the Soviet economy's overall record of performance during the first post-Stalin decade. In sheer size, it has gone a long way indeed in these ten years. The gross national product, measured in rubles but with Western methods, probably nearly doubled between 1952 and 1962, implying an average annual rate of growth of somewhat under 7 percent.[5] This is of course a very creditable performance, though not entirely without parallel in the last decade among major industrial countries even in the non-Soviet world. The output of industry, the favored sector, probably grew on the average at about 9 percent over the ten years.[6] Both the national product and industrial production grew appreciably faster during the first five years of the post-Stalin decade than during its second half, a point to which we shall return.

Agricultural production seems to have expanded by about 60 percent over the same years, nearly all of the increase taking place by 1958.[7] The total population has simultaneously increased by 18.5 percent (about 1.7 percent per annum), so that agricultural output per capita has increased by some 35 percent. And speaking of population, we should also note that its urban component has grown very much faster—by about 45 percent, or some 4 percent per year—so that the whole absolute increment in the total Soviet population over the decade is accounted for by the increase in the urban population. In the course of 1960 the Soviet urban population passed the rural population in absolute size.[8]

Consumption per capita also increased very considerably. Precise and reliable data are lacking but, taking the country as a whole, a per capita increase of 50-60 percent for the decade, or 4-5 percent per year on the average, probably expresses the right order of magnitude. Most of this improvement occurred by 1958. Some of it of course reflects the rapid urbanization, urban per capita consumption being much higher than rural. The variety of goods made available to the consumer has also widened considerably, but the improvement in quality and sales service has apparently been less marked. Shopping is still a relatively time-consuming and arduous matter, and sometimes the goods are not on the shelves, particularly outside the major cities. A growing volume of imported commodities, typically from East European or Mediterranean or tropical countries, has also been made available to the Soviet consumer. By virtue of their nature, quality, and design, the imported goods have constituted, so to say, the frosting on the Soviet consumer's cake. As for urban housing, it has benefited from enhanced attention by the government, and the annual rate of construction was sharply stepped up beginning in 1958. Nonetheless, housing construction has usually been under the planned rates, while the urban population has grown more swiftly than anticipated. Consequently, the improvement in dwelling space per person has been only moderate in relation to the pressing need: probably not quite 25 percent over the decade (after allowing for the underrecording of dwelling space in earlier years).[9]

Great as the expansion of the Soviet economy has been, the relative allocation of its gross national product among the major end uses—personal consumption, communal (free) services, government administration, defense, and gross investment—has changed comparatively little (with the exception to be noted) between 1952 and 1962, though there was some appreciable fluctuation *within* the decade. Personal consumption represented around 45 percent of the national product in both these years (though around 50 percent during 1954-1958). The one major shift was the steady decline until mid-1961 in the share of the defense and the correspondingly rising share of gross investment. The latter averaged about 30 percent of the gross national product over the decade, but now seems to stand at appreciably above this ratio.[10] Similarly, the general distribution of funds for fixed capital investment—between industry, agriculture, housing, and other sectors, and between heavy and light industry—has remained quite stable. In other words, relatively small shifts apart, the emphasis in Soviet resource use has remained where it was under Stalin: on state power and rapid growth. The current seven-year plan (running through 1965) and the twenty-year program (1960-1980) do not change this emphasis in any significant way.

III

There is no mystery behind the rapid growth of the Soviet economy during the post-Stalin decade (or, for that matter, in earlier years). In explaining the performance, we must surely list first the single-minded determination of the regime to maximize economic growth, and its willingness to sacrifice very much, economically and in human terms, to this end. Secondly, and consistent with this, a relatively large share of total resources has been steadily devoted to growth. As we have already seen, from 1952 to 1962 the average gross investment rate has been approximately 30 percent and has been rising lately. This is of course a very high proportion; the corresponding U.S. figure has been around 18 percent, although other non-Communist countries (Japan, Norway, Finland) have approached or exceeded the Soviet rate, while many West European countries have maintained percentage rates in the 20's. In addition, the USSR has been allocating large sums to education and training,[11] research and development, scientific and technological intelligence and publication, and other growth-inducing activities.

Thirdly, the Soviet economy continued to benefit from the existence of a large pool of underemployed manpower in agriculture. While between 1952 and 1962 the population of working age increased only moderately—about 11 percent—because of the small cohorts reaching the working ages in the second half of this decade, employment in nonagricultural sectors of the economy increased by some 50-55 percent, or by 4-4.5 percent per year on the average. The agricultural labor force, after rising moderately for several years as well, has been declining since 1956, and at the end of 1962 was probably smaller than ten years before—even though, as we have seen, agricultural output has risen about 60 percent over this period. In an economy which still has substantial underemployment in large areas of its agriculture, it is of course the rate of growth of nonagricultural employment that primarily affects the speed of overall economic expansion.[12]

Fourthly, the Soviet Union was able throughout the past decade to benefit from what the economist calls "advantages of backwardness." The overall technological level of the Soviet economy in the early Fifties was quite low relative to the state of knowledge and practice in the advanced Western countries, and of course also relative to subsequent technical progress at home and abroad. In short, there were (and still are) many areas to be exploited by taking over Western technology. The seizing of many such opportunities was no doubt a major factor in the rapid growth, especially industrial growth, of the post-Stalin decade. But the opportunities in fact went beyond this. The decade was also a period of assimilation (*osvoenie*) of the enormous productive capital and human skill accumulated during the quarter century between the start of the five-year plans and Stalin's death. The feverish and often chaotic construction and training of the early Thirties, the collectivization crisis and its many repercussions, the terror, the great purges of the later Thirties, preparation for war and the war itself, the grimness of the postwar years and the Korean War, the inadequate and often warped incentives to producers and innovators throughout the period—these and many other factors prevented reasonably full use of what had been accumulated and acquired with so much toil and suffering. Yet these defects of the Stalin era also harbored promise for the Fifties; they were "productivity reserves" in Soviet parlance. An appreciable part of the growth after Stalin probably depends on the relative normalization of the political and economic climate and the consequent "shakedown" of the previously built-up productive capacities and skills.

Fifthly, there were several special, in part nonrecurring, favorable factors during the ten years. Examples: the 100 million acres put under the plow in the "virgin lands"; or the reduction of defense outlays in relation to the national product and of the armed forces in relation to the civilian labor force, which permitted the relative share of investment to rise substantially without throwing a corresponding burden on consumption; the release of a large proportion of the inmates of forced-labor camps and their return to normal civilian employment. Merely from a narrowly economic standpoint, the camps were very wasteful of both human and material resources, even by Soviet standards.

Naturally, not all developments during the decade were uniquely favorable to the tempo of Soviet economic growth. On the other side were such major factors as the extension of economic and military aid to underdeveloped countries; the sharp increase in defense outlay after mid-1961, apparently in part at the expense of investment; and, last but not least, the reduction of the standard work-week (outside agriculture) from 48 to 41 hours.[13]

Rapid growth must not be confused with dynamic efficiency; the latter is the relation of the rate of growth to the resources devoted to it, such as rate of expansion of the capital stock (or the proportion of investment in the national product), rate of increase of total employment or, as argued above, of nonagricultural employment, and the outlays on training, research, and development, etc.[14] The advantages of backwardness should also be kept in mind in this connection. While we cannot here go into detail, it would seem that the dynamic efficiency of the Soviet economy during the past decade has not been particularly high. In other words, the Soviet economy has been growing fast by devoting a very large proportion of its resources to this end and by rapidly shifting the relative structure of its labor force in favor of the nonagricultural sectors, rather than by converting each unit of such resources into overall economic growth with unusually high efficiency. This of course is not to minimize the accomplishment such as it was. Many underdeveloped countries find it particularly difficult to divert even relatively much smaller resources from current needs to economic growth.

IV

While our time-perspective is admittedly still short for reliable judgment, the post-Stalin decade seems to consist of two fairly well-defined subperiods. The dividing point is not the 20th Party Congress in February 1956, as it is in the realm of economic thought and in the political and cultural fields, but rather the second half of 1958. Our first subperiod therefore extends for somewhat over five years (or just five years if we prefer to date it from the launching of the "New Course" in the summer of 1953), while the second extends for some four and a half years to the time when these lines are being written at the end of 1962. Whether the important reforms introduced by the Central Committee Plenum in November 1962 constitute in some real sense the end of the second subperiod and the start of yet another phase, it is of course too soon to tell.

The first subperiod, 1953-58, can be most succinctly characterized as a vast, if not always very profound or radical, rescue operation that resulted in rapid expansion of the Soviet economy along a broad front. More specifically, this was the time for urgent and sometimes hasty redressing of the most serious imbalances inherited from Stalin, righting of some of the worst injustices and inequities, salvaging incentives, eliminating some of the grossest organizational inefficiencies, and directing resources to some areas where they were urgently needed. It began with the New Course—concessions to the consumer, the peasant, the forced-laborer, and the satellite economies—a set of hasty, even emergency measures designed not to rock the political boat.

The reforms in agriculture, which began in earnest in September 1953, set off a long series of remedial measures in this sector, the end of which is not yet in sight. At the very first, their emphasis was on the various elements of incentives: prices, taxes, and delivery obligations. At the same time, controls over the peasants were also tightened, following the frequent Soviet assumption that a larger carrot not only serves its own purpose but also makes the bigger stick more effective. But the two measures that received most of the publicity and attention, especially from Mr. Khrushchev himself, were the plowing up of the semi-arid and arid "virgin lands," begun in 1954, and the expansion of acreage under corn, started in 1955. Both were designed primarily to augment, radically and swiftly, the feed-grain base of livestock husbandry—the latter directly, the former largely by shifting bread-grain production to the new lands and thereby releasing some of the old areas for feed grains, including corn. The magnitude of the virgin-lands campaign is vividly indicated by the fact that the land newly brought under the plow there since 1954, about 100 million acres, is equivalent to almost one third the *total* cropland currently harvested in the United States.

These measures, and many others that cannot be discussed here for lack of space, contributed in varying degree to the quick and large increase in agricultural output—about 50 percent overall— during 1953-58. On the other hand, attempts to free local initiative by decentralizing planning and management in farming, especially by virtue of a decree published in May 1955, remained almost entirely on paper. The "campaign" methods, the constant pressure for larger deliveries to the state, the inadequate incentives on the farm (especially in animal husbandry), the ingrained habits of the high and petty bureaucracy and the daily intervention of Party officials, and all the other modes of operating carried over from the past, combined to thwart any extension of meaningful autonomy for the individual collective farms. Moreover, toward the end of the first subperiod the authorities began to tighten the squeeze on the collective-farmers' private plots. These are of considerable significance not only for the welfare of the farmers but also as a source of food supply: in 1958, together with some other, smaller forms of private cultivation, they accounted for one-third of the agricultural output of the USSR, although covering less than 4 percent of the total sown area.[15]

One of the most important structural reforms in post-Stalin Soviet agriculture took place toward the very end of the first subperiod, in mid-1958. We are referring of course to the abolition of machine and tractor stations (MTS), the sale of most of their equipment to collective farms, and the attendant thorough revamping of the farm price structure. The MTS had been not only virtually the sole source of the services of large-scale machinery for collective farms, but also played a most significant role in connection with procurements and political control in the countryside. They were also quite wasteful and inefficient. The reform of mid-1958 eliminated dual authority on the land, did away with much of the waste and inefficiency, and largely abolished the baneful multiple-price system. It happened that in the same year extraordinarily favorable weather conditions prevailed. Agricultural production rose sharply to a new plateau in that year.[16]

In the field of labor controls and welfare measures, the first five years after Stalin also saw a number of very significant reforms, mostly by way of reducing certain inequities and improving work incentives. Decrees were issued beginning almost immediately after the 20th Party Congress in February 1956, to reduce the length of the work-week, overall and for certain categories of workers, and to eliminate criminal provisions against tardiness, absenteeism, and unauthorized quitting. These and later decrees cut the standard work-week from 48 hours in 1953 to 41 hours in 1962, as already mentioned. Also in 1956, pension rates were augmented and minimum wages and salaries were raised (and later raised again), thus substantially improving the position of two underprivileged groups in Soviet society. The whole wage structure soon came under careful study; and many reforms were introduced to increase incentives and to adjust comparative earnings of different categories of workers. Numerous other labor and welfare measures have been introduced since 1956 affecting work rules, grievance procedures, tax reforms, and various social security provisions.[17] And, finally, we must mention again the release of many of the inmates of forced-labor camps and the transformation of some camps into so-called corrective-labor colonies, which are claimed to have a milder regimen.

The major reform with regard to industry and construction in the first subperiod was the abolition in mid-1957 of economic ministries and their replacement by a little over 100 regional economic authorities, the so-called sovnarkhozes, or economic councils. Apart from its political motives and implications, this measure was intended to abolish ministerial autarky ("departmentalism"), bring middle-level administrators closer to the enterprises, and rationalize the organization of production and supply on a regional basis. The enterprises themselves, however, gained few additional powers and little additional freedom of action in the process, and it is very doubtful that the term so frequently applied to this reform in the West (but never in the USSR)—"decentralization"—is at all apt. But as time was to show, the creation of the sovnarkhozes raised about as many problems as it solved, among the former particularly a new kind of autarky, "localism." [18]

A new breeze of economic realism, and even rationality, began to be felt in the Soviet Union at about this time. Stalin's death had already made possible some widening of the extremely narrow range of discourse among economists and considerably more candid public discussion of economic problems (e.g., the industrial conference of May 1955). In this realm, too, the 20th Party Congress (February 1956) gave a mighty push that in a few years swelled into an avalanche of frank, practical discussion and theoretical debate, occasionally accompanied by new departures in economic policy. This is not the place to describe the new, vibrant, sanitizing, and at times exhilarating spirit and reason that in 1957-1958 suddenly entered the stagnant, stale, highly scholastic air of Soviet economics. The whole question of economic calculation and rational choice began to be reexamined from the bottom up, the Soviet price structure came under close theoretic scrutiny, traditional policies and planning methods came to be questioned, mathematics was once again admitted into the economist's toolbox, and mathematical methods of planning and problem-solving suddenly became of the most intense interest. Dogma came under mounting attack, though Marxist doctrine still set definite limits to the search for rational answers.

From the spring of 1956 on, what used to be a trickle of statistical publications grew swiftly into a veritable flood (though still with significant gaps and not of uniform reliability).

The rationalization of Soviet economic policies and planning that has ensued from these developments should not be exaggerated. Nevertheless, by the end of the first subperiod the erstwhile neglect of the chemical industries was reversed (May 1958), the fascination with gigantic hydroelectric projects was seriously questioned (August 1958), the development of petroleum and natural gas was given emphatic priority over coal, the dieselization and electrification of railroads was sharply speeded up, and automation was pushed forward with a much heightened sense of urgency. Soviet industry took on an aspect consonant with the Fifties and Sixties of this century, rather than with the Twenties and Thirties.

In sum, as the last of the 1958 harvest was reaching the government's collection points and the year waned, Mr. Khrushchev and his lieutenants had reasons for satisfaction and even self-congratulation. The "anti-Party group" and Marshal Zhukov had been removed from positions of power the year before, and Mr. Khrushchev's domestic authority was at its apogee. The East European revolts and ferment of 1956-1957 had been brought under control, leading to a new and quite stable *modus vivendi* within the European part of the Soviet bloc. For a year the Soviets had been enjoying a new world prestige thanks to their rocketry and space exploration. In July 1958, Baghdad fell out of the Baghdad Pact. The last of the imperial holdings of the West European powers were disintegrating, Latin America was growing more restive, and many new opportunities seemed to be opening up for Soviet foreign policy.

But it was the domestic economic front that may have given Mr. Khrushchev the greatest feeling of gratification. Agriculture, which he had taken under his own close tutelage, had done very well during the preceding five years, total output rising, as we have seen, some 50 percent. In this sphere at least Khrushchev's revision of Stalin's policies seemed to be paying off handsomely, although the extremely favorable weather in the new lands in 1956 and 1958 also had a good deal to do with the quick success. Per capita incomes, in both town and village, had risen sharply, too. Buoyed by the success in agriculture and by the unlocking of resources in the course of the 1957 reorganization, and benefiting by a continued large flow of resources into it, industry also expanded its output rapidly. And the new technological and investment policies, coupled with prospects of rapidly growing capital formation, bore promise of further vast gains in the productivity and efficiency of industry and other modern sectors of the economy.

This optimism is fully reflected in the current Seven-Year Plan (1959-65), adopted by the 21st Party Congress, January-February 1959.[19] The plan inaugurates "the full construction of the Communist society," that is, the ideal society of the future, with economic abundance and full social harmony, foreseen by Marx as the ultimate stage of human history. The plan also aims to take the Soviet economy most of the way to catching up with the United States and overtaking it in per capita production and consumption, which is predicted for around 1970 and which is to clinch the "historic victory of socialism over capitalism" on our planet. The 22d Party Congress in October 1961—perhaps best remembered for its "de-Albanization"—adopted a new Party program which calls for the "building of the foundations of Communism" over the next two decades and outlines certain major production targets for 1970 and 1980. The program, however, carefully avoids stating that the Communist society will come into existence in the USSR by 1980.[20]

But to return to the Seven-Year Plan: its aim to increase gross industrial output by 78 percent over the seven years is ambitious but not clearly unrealistic; but its goal of raising agricultural production by 70 percent, above the record 1958 level at that, is entirely fanciful. As these lines are written, four of the seven years have already passed. The Soviet authorities claim to be appreciably ahead of schedule in fulfilling the industrial portion of the plan, namely: to have raised industrial output by 45 percent instead of the 39 planned for the four years. At the moment, this claim cannot be accepted without careful scrutiny, though there is little doubt that industrial production has been rising quite rapidly. In agriculture, however, there has been hardly any progress towards the 70 percent increase—a problem that has lately been attracting the most serious attention of Mr. Khrushchev himself.

V

From the latter part of 1958 on, the upward momentum of the Soviet economy began to slacken. Some of the once-for-all benefits (such as those stemming from the industrial reorganization of 1957, or from the mass release of prisoners) were exhausted; the overall labor supply became much less favorable for demographic reasons; the new plans and investment policies, as well as the various international and scientific commitments, placed additional pressure on resources; and the recently introduced institutions and modes of operation led to new difficulties and problems. Compared with the first post-Stalin subperiod, the four years from 1959 through 1962 can be characterized as a period of reduced rate of growth and a more moderate rise in living standards, of patchwork remedial measures intended to close loopholes, safeguard or bolster incentives, and tighten—especially, recentralize—the organizational structure.

The retardation is especially noticeable in agriculture, where total output has been marking time, fluctuating with the weather, and at best keeping up with the population. True, the extraordinarily favorable weather conditions of 1958 have not recurred, and this is hardly to be expected over the short run. Weather apart, the chief reasons for the very limited progress (if any) in agriculture seem to be (a) the continued imposition of overambitious plans, which often operate perversely; (b) unwillingness or inability to allot sufficient resources to this sector and to supporting activities (fertilizer production, roads, distribution facilities); (c) continuing ineptness in planning, management, distribution, supply, etc.; and (d) a possible sag in incentives. As to the last, it should be noted that peasant incomes may have dropped significantly after 1957-58, at least up to 1960, owing to a renewed squeeze on the peasants' private plots and livestock and to the financial burden that fell on the collective farms for tractor and machinery purchases following the dissolution of the MTS.[21]

The rate of growth of industrial production, though still high, declined substantially after 1957.[22] Given this, and the failure of agricultural output to rise significantly after 1958, we are not surprised that the rates of growth of the national product as a whole and of urban real incomes fell substantially.[23] As we have just seen, peasants' real incomes actually declined, at least during 1958-60. In mid-1961, the budgeted outlays for defense were sharply raised, so that by 1962 and 1963 the nominal appropriations for this purpose increased some 50 percent from the level of early 1961. It is, how-

ever, not certain that in real terms defense outlay rose as much as
the budget figures suggest.[24]

As the Seven-Year Plan progressed, it also became increasingly apparent that the various reforms and reorganizations of the preceding five years had not been sufficient to improve fundamentally the
"qualitative" aspects of the economy's operations, such as adherence
to plans ("plan discipline"), the articulation of supply and demand,
the quality of manufactured articles, the speed and effectiveness of
construction, the satisfaction of the consumers' needs, and, definitely
not least, the propensity to innovate. In some of these matters, such
as industrial innovation, the new institutions seemed to have aggravated the economy's chronic problems and defects. We shall return
to these "qualitative" matters a little later, after we take note of the
remedial steps taken in the years 1959-62.

On the organizational plane, these remedial steps have been generally of two sorts: the elaboration of the administrative hierarchy
in the economic sphere, and the recentralization of planning and
economic administration. Both were perhaps to be expected; they
are a natural response of any formal organization that is faced with
serious problems of operating effectiveness and—for reasons good
or bad—is not ready for a more fundamental overhaul. In this
sense, as well as in some others, the recent organizational changes
have been essentially conservative.[25]

To mention merely the more important of these: In June and
July of 1960, republic-wide sovnarkhozes were created in the three
largest republics (Russian, Ukrainian, and Kazakh) to administer
the many smaller sovnarkhozes of 1957 vintage. In November 1962
an all-union sovnarkhoz (SNKh SSSR) was established, apparently
on the organizational ruins of the old State Planning Commission
(Gosplan), which was suddenly discredited for its incorrect policies
and bungling by Mr. Khrushchev at the Central Committee Plenum.
In the meantime, the main all-union supply administrations, attached to Gosplan following the 1957 reorganization, steadily acquired greater powers. At the same time, by all signs, the (lower)
sovnarkhozes steadily lost power to the various republican and all-
union bodies. The sovnarkhozes themselves are being reduced, at
this writing, to something less than half their previous number by a
process of amalgamation, following the resolution of the November
1962 Plenum. (In the Russian Republic the reduction in the number

of sovnarkhozes has been particularly sharp, from 67 to 24.) The same Central Committee Plenum also decreed the vertical cleavage of the Party structure into two parallel hierarchies, one concerned primarily with industry and related branches, the other with agriculture.

In agriculture, the major organizational innovations during the second subperiod, i.e., following the abolition of the MTS, were the establishment of (a) a separate organization to supply agriculture with equipment, spare parts, and various essential materials (Sel'khoztekhnika) in early 1961, and (b) a full-fledged hierarchy of territorial production and procurement administrations, to which now both collective and state farms became subordinate, paralleled by a structure of territorial councils and (at higher levels) agricultural boards. The latter measure is notable, inter alia, for establishing a definite administrative machinery responsible for agricultural production, and for virtually abolishing the distinction between state and collective farms in this regard.

On the planning side the changes have been equally substantial. The product-line ("branch") State Boards,[26] established primarily in the defense industries at the time of the 1957 reorganization, have been gradually increased in number until now they cover construction and nearly all branches of industry. They are responsible for planning and carrying out technical progress and investment policy in their respective branches. But planning must be coordinated territorially as well within individual industries. Hence, in May 1961, the country was divided into seventeen so-called large economic regions, each comprising an average of six sovnarkhozes, and each with a "coordinating and planning council." In November, 1962, came the turn of the highest planning organs to be revamped once again. The newly created SNKh SSSR, the organizational successor to the previous Gosplan SSSR, was charged with short-term planning functions as well as with overall managerial duties. At the same time, and adding to organizational and terminological confusion, the State Scientific-Economic Council (Gosekonomsovet SSSR) was renamed Gosplan USSR while retaining its long-term planning functions. Further, in March, 1963, a Supreme Economic Council of the USSR (VSNKh SSSR), a cabinet-level body, was created to coordinate the activities of Gosplan, SNKh SSSR, and the numerous State Boards, and to be the "supreme state organ in charge of industry and construction in the country." Thus, a novel and rather logical structure for the planning and management of the Soviet economy has been erected step by step. Yet this structure is also so complex and cumbersome that its longevity ought not to be overrated.

The cumulative effect of these reorganizations of the past four years, as well as of various other changes, has been to further centralize planning, management, and administration. Agriculture and investment are two good examples. The conception, widespread in the West, that the Soviet economy today is in some overall sense less centralized than at the end of Stalin's regime, is very dubious; indeed, the opposite could probably be convincingly argued. Certainly, with regard to one of the most crucial criteria of decentralization, the enhancement of the autonomy of the individual enterprise, the changes in the past decade have been minute. The Soviet enterprise continues to be closely, continuously, and in great detail, directed and controlled from above. In fact, this virtual lack of autonomy, the irritating and often incompetent "petty tutelage" over enterprises, the frequent changes in plans, the continuing and seemingly ever growing supply difficulties, and, more recently, the multiplication of superordinate authorities, each with its directives and audits, have been causing more frequent and vocal complaints, sometimes bordering on cries of desperation, from managers and some economists.[27]

It may be noted here, however, that this "creeping" recentralization rests ultimately on two underlying factors: the chronic overcommitment of resources (the haste, in historical terms), and the divergence between the goals, values, and interests of the regime's leadership and those of individuals and groups within the Soviet society.

Of special concern to Soviet leaders in recent years has been the sluggishness of innovating efforts, despite constant and heavy pressure toward greater dynamism. This phenomenon derives from a powerful combination of "conservatism" by management, which often stands to lose financially by upsetting production routine, and the cumbersomeness of the bureaucratic apparatus.[28] A particularly complicated and thorny matter, it is intimately related to the whole institutional structure, to the nature of the plans and of performance criteria ("success indicators"), and to the price pattern. Much attention has been lately devoted to the problem at the highest levels (for instance, the Central Committee Plenums of

June 1959, July 1960, and November 1962). Some steps have been taken to give the individuals concerned a direct material stake in innovation, but no major resolution of this matter seems to have taken place.

VI

Nearly double in size (in terms of national product), far more advanced technologically, and somewhat reformed organizationally, the Soviet economy today has left the grim and bleak days of the winter of 1953 far behind. But its most pressing problems still bear a striking resemblance to those of a decade ago. They are four, in sum:

(a) The constant pressure on the economy's resources, owing to the regime's "world-historic" goals, the cold war, the internal problems of the "socialist camp," the scientific and technological race with the West, and the ever-rising economic aspirations of a fairly rapidly growing population.

(b) The very slow increase (if any) of agricultural production since 1958, severely retarding overall economic growth as well as the rise in living standards.

(c) In other sectors, a welter of problems: poor planning, widespread and large-scale waste of resources, all too frequent production of the wrong things and at the wrong time, resistance to innovation, and so forth. Construction is faring particularly badly in this regard, with the volume of so-called incomplete construction (due to poor planning and management) rising every year.[29]

(d) The Soviet man's imperfect tractability to remolding in accordance with "Communist morality." Even if he abides more by moral and juridical laws than his prerevolutionary grandfather, as Soviet ideologists would have us believe, there are today so many more laws to break at every turn. In fact, there is probably a good deal of dedication and idealism, especially among the young; but cynicism and callousness prevail as well, assured of handsome material rewards by disequilibria in the economy. If the Soviet press is to be believed, economic crimes and transgressions of all sorts and degrees—from petty pilferage of state property, through systematic deception of superiors, to large-scale "speculation" and bribery—are widespread and may be on the increase. Time will tell whether the new series of severe penalties enacted in the past two years, including capital punishment, will turn the tide.

With all its ills and problems, the Soviet economy could undoubtedly continue for a good time yet in the present manner. Neither paralysis nor explosion is in question; nor do serious students of the Soviet economy expect them. But this is not the issue, of course. What is significant is that the limits of patching over the essentially Stalinist structure of the economy are being approached; that this fact is being increasingly recognized by many persons in various positions and walks of life; and that a great deal of rethinking on all levels, from abstract political economy to down-to-earth subjects, is under way. "Anyone who is at all familiar with planning and economic reality [in the USSR] can see that it [i.e., this reality] is presently undergoing an important, if not a crucial, stage—a time of profound thinking, of reexamination of habitual concepts, of the appearance of new problems which only yesterday raised no thoughts, and of the seeming disappearance of other problems which only yesterday looked very important." Thus read an editorial in the *Economic Gazette* of October 13, 1962. Very similar sentiments were aired simultaneously in an editorial in *Planovoe khoziaistvo*,[30] the official organ of the highest planning authorities of the USSR. It is difficult to believe that Mr. Khrushchev's tinkering with the economic-administrative structure and his reshuffling of planning bodies a month later offered a fundamental and durable solution. On the other hand, the simultaneous splitting of the Party into parallel industrial and agricultural pyramids is a radical step that carries more of a ring of desperation than a tone of conviction. To torture a metaphor—it seems to throw good politics after bad economics.

In brief, the Soviet economy today faces an enormous organizational and institutional problem, a problem of finding a workable degree of centralization (or decentralization) under new and changing conditions. Unlike the difficulties in agriculture, which at least bear reasonable hope of alleviation as the economy grows richer and can afford to pour in more resources to rescue that sector, the organizational problem promises to grow worse by dint of the economy's very success. The planning job, as it is now carried on in the Soviet Union, is roughly proportional, in its sheer bulk, to the square of the number of commodities and of the number of economic units. As these multiply with the economy's growth, the task of planning swells much faster. Thus, in 1960, the all-union Gos-plan and the supply administrations attached to it "planned" (drew up material balances for) 12,000 commodities; in 1962, 18,000 com-modities. (Many more commodities are planned at lower levels.) In the words of *Planovoe khoziaistvo,* "If the present methods of planning and rates of economic growth persist, by 1980 the whole adult population of the country will be required for planning and administration." [31] The topheaviness of the economic structure is, of course, not only, or not primarily, costly because of the resources it so engages; it is eminently costly by dint of its inimical adaptations to demand and to changing technology, and effects on efficiency and morale.

One possible way out is to preserve or even enhance the degree of centralization, but to render its operation more supple and swift with the aid of mathematical economics and electronic computers. An ideologically and politically palatable course, especially after the purging of the worst dogmas from Soviet economics, it now at-tracts a very large amount of attention on the part of Soviet econ-omists, mathematicians, and planners. It is very likely to forestall the need for other solutions; that it will prove to be a lasting solu-tion, one would be rash to assert. Another possible course, with politically and ideologically opposite implications, is a thorough de-centralization, which in its extreme form would amount to some sort of a socialist market economy. (The last is not to be confused with the much-publicized Liberman proposal,[32] which, at least at its face value, would have increased slightly the autonomy of management while otherwise preserving the present organizational structure.) But the bars to thorough decentralization are not only ideological in some proximate sense. They are also imposed by the severe pres-sure on the economy's capacities, and the consequent need to mobi-lize resources and enforce priorities.

Here we abut on the international scene. The pressure on Soviet resources is, directly and indirectly, a function of the way the regime conceives its relation to the rest of the world. Should this conception change so that some major part of the resources now going into military and related activities could be directed to other uses, we would probably see a greater effort to lift agriculture from its pres-ent level, a significant increase in the volume and share of resources devoted to investment, and some more immediate benefits to the consumer. In short, such a release of resources from defense would, in the near term, give a push both to the rate of economic growth and to living standards. However, we may also ask whether in the event of a fundamental improvement in the international relations (with China, too?) and in conjunction with domestic tendencies and aspirations, the Soviet regime of that moment might not relax its sense of haste and tension, whether the pressure on resources might not slacken, and the bars to a fundamental decentralization of the economy might not sag. Should the economy be greatly de-centralized, the effects on its performance and efficiency would be much more far-reaching and profound than a simple reallocation of several percentage points of the national product from defense to other uses.

But this is largely conjecture. The converse view would also seem to be plausible—namely, that in the present state of international tension, we can surely expect the Soviet economy to maintain a high rate of investment, and hence to continue to grow fast, even if not quite so fast as in the mid-Fifties. We can expect living stand-ards to continue to rise at some significant rate, even if agricultural difficulties persist. But it is more problematical to expect any funda-mental decentralization of the organizational structure, unless the international climate changes no less fundamentally.

FOOTNOTES

[1] According to the index calculated by Norman M. Kaplan and Richard H. Moorsteen (*American Economic Review*, June 1960, p. 296), total civilian industrial production, exclud-ing munitions, in 1952 was 67 percent above the 1940 level, and that of manufactured consumer goods, 30 percent.

[2] Abram Bergson, *The Real National Income of Soviet Russia Since 1928* (Cambridge: Harvard University Press, 1961), p. 256; Naum Jasny, *The Soviet 1956 Statistical Hand-book: A Commentary* (East Lansing: Michigan State Univer-sity Press, 1957), p. 41.

[3] See the estimates of Timothy Sosnovy in *Soviet Studies* (Glasgow), July 1959, p. 4, and in the collection of essays sub-mitted to the Joint Economic Committee of the U.S. Congress under the title of *Dimensions of Soviet Economic Power* (Washington, D.C.: U.S. Government Printing Office, 1962),

p. 331. The latter volume (hereafter cited as *Dimensions*), contains a wealth of information on the postwar Soviet economy but unfortunately reached me too late to be fully taken into account in this essay.

[4] For these and other agricultural production data see the contribution of D. Gale Johnson and Arcadius Kahan to U.S. Congress, Joint Economic Committee, *Comparisons of the United States and Soviet Economies* (Washington, D.C.: U.S. Government Printing Office, 1959), Part I (hereafter cited as *Comparisons*), and the contribution of Joseph W. Willett to *Dimensions*, pp. 95ff.

[5] This rough estimate finds support in the just-published calculations of Stanley H. Cohn (*Dimensions*, p. 75), which show an average annual increase of GNP of 6.8 percent for 1950-1960, implying a slightly lower rate than this for the period referred to in the text, 1952-1962.

[6] *Cf.* the calculations of *civilian* industrial output by Rush V. Greenslade and Phyllis Wallace (*Dimensions*, p. 120), who find an annual rate of 9.4 percent over the nine years 1952-1961. Other Western estimates (*ibid.*, p. 162), generally come close to theirs.

[7] See the estimates (to 1961) of net agricultural production, weighted by 1958 Soviet prices, by Joseph W. Willett in *Dimensions*, p. 98.

[8] The reader is referred to the contribution of James W. Brackett to *Dimensions*, pp. 487ff., for a wealth of up-to-date data on Soviet population and for projections to 1981.

[9] *Cf.* Sosnovy, *Dimensions*, p. 331.

[10] These estimates are in "ruble factor cost" *à la* Bergson. For more detailed data, see Nancy Nimitz, *Soviet National Income and Product, 1956-1958*, The RAND Corporation, Santa Monica (Calif.), RM-3112-PR, June 1962; Norman M. Kaplan, *The Stock of Soviet Capital on Jan. 1, 1960*, The RAND Corporation, P-2248, March 15, 1961; Abram Bergson, *The Real National Income of Soviet Russia since 1928*, p. 245; Stanley H. Cohn, *Dimensions*, p. 72; and, regarding defense, J. G. Godaire, *Dimensions*, p. 42.

[11] See the contributions of Nicholas DeWitt and Seymour M. Rosen in *Dimensions*, pp. 235ff., 273ff.

[12] With regard to population and the labor force, see the

contributions of Brackett and of Weitzman, Feshbach, and Kulchycka in *Dimensions,* pp. 493ff.

[13] On the last point, it must be added that enterprises were required to maintain man-year labor productivity as a condition of shortening the work-week. This undoubtedly brought about or hastened many rationalizing measures that otherwise would have been ignored or postponed. It is therefore moot to what extent the reduction in the work-week was unfavorable to growth.

[14] *Cf.* Bela A. Balassa, "Success Criteria for Economic Systems," *Yale Economic Essays,* Spring 1961, p. 13. My definition is very similar to but not identical with Balassa's.

[15] These figures derive from official data, which however may not be very well based in this case. See J. A. Newth, "Soviet Agriculture: The Private Sector, 1950-1959," *Soviet Studies,* October 1961. Note that the enormous discrepancy between output and area in this instance stems partly from much higher yields in the private sector as compared with the socialist sector, and partly from the former's concentration on livestock products, utilizing in part feed obtained from the socialist sector.

[16] Jasny estimates that per capita peasant incomes from all sources rose between 1952 and 1958 by as much as 55 percent, but it must be borne in mind that 1952 incomes were catastrophically low. Naum Jasny, *Essays on the Soviet Economy* (New York: Praeger, 1962), p. 155; *cf.* Alec Nove, "The Incomes of Soviet Peasants," *Slavonic and East European Review,* June 1960. For discussions of the various post-Stalin measures in agriculture, see Lazar Volin, "Reform in Agriculture," *Problems of Communism,* January-February 1959; his and Nancy Nimitz's contribution to *Comparisons,* Part I; and my "Soviet Agriculture since Stalin," *Annals of the American Academy of Political and Social Science,* January 1956. See also Alec Nove, "Soviet Agriculture Marks Time," *Foreign Affairs,* July 1962.

[17] For details and interpretation see Alec Nove, "Toward a 'Communist Welfare State'?", and discussion thereof, in *Problems of Communism,* January-February 1960; also, the contribution by Edmund Nash to *Dimensions,* pp. 393ff., which contains a convenient chronology of the measures.

[18] For description and analysis of the reform see especially Alec Nove, "The Soviet Industrial Reorganization," *Problems of Communism*, November-December 1957; Michael Kaser in Gregory Grossman, ed., *Value and Plan* (Berkeley: University of California Press, 1960); and Oleg Hoeffding, "The Soviet Industrial Reorganization of 1957," *American Economic Review*, May 1959.

[19] Mr. Khrushchev's "Draft Theses" for the Seven-Year Plan were first published in the Soviet press on November 14, 1958. For the English translation of the final text of the "Directives for the S.Y.P.," see *Current Digest of the Soviet Press*, April 1, 1959. For analyses of the plan see Oleg Hoeffding, "Substance and Shadow in the Soviet Seven-Year Plan," *Foreign Affairs*, April 1959; Leon Herman, "The Seven-Year Haul," *Problems of Communism*, March-April 1959; and Naum Jasny, "The Soviet Seven-Year Plan: Is it Realistic?," Institute for the Study of the USSR (Munich), *Bulletin*, May 1959.

[20] A liberally annotated English translation of the program will be found in Herbert Ritvo, ed., *The New Soviet Society* (New York: New Leader, 1962). An unannotated translation of the preliminary text appears in *Current Digest of the Soviet Press*, August 9, 16, and 23, 1961. For an extensive discussion of the program see, *inter alia, Survey* (London), October 1961.

[21] See Arcadius Kahan, "Recent Trends in Soviet Farm Incomes," *Problems of Communism*, November-December 1961. I have also benefited on this score from conversations with Professor Jerzy F. Karcz.

[22] According to the Greenslade-Wallace index, the average annual increase of *civilian* industrial output was 10.7 percent during 1952-57 and 7.7 percent during 1957-61 (*Dimensions*, p. 120).

[23] *Cf. Dimensions*, p. 75, with regard to national income, and, with regard to real disposable wages, the calculations by Rachel E. Golden on p. 354.

[24] On the magnitude of the Soviet defense effort see the contribution of J. G. Godaire in *Dimensions*, pp. 33ff.

[25] They are discussed at some length in Alec Nove, "The Industrial Planning System: Reforms in Prospect," *Soviet Studies*, July 1962; Herbert S. Levine's essay in *Dimensions*,

pp. 47-65; and my article "The Structure and Organization of the Soviet Economy," *Slavic Review*, June 1962.

[26] Often and less exactly rendered into English as "State Committees."

[27] The Soviet press has been increasingly candid on these matters in recent years. An especially valuable source of such information, as well as sensible analyses of their causes and proposals for remedial action, is the weekly *Ekonomicheskaia gazeta* (Economic Gazette), organ of the Central Committee of the Communist Party of the USSR.

[28] Some of these problems are discussed more fully in my "Soviet Growth: Routine, Inertia, and Pressure," *American Economic Review*, May 1960.

[29] It may be worth dispelling here the myth that, "at least," the Soviet economy fully utilizes its productive capacity. In fact, this is not so. While no general statistics on the subject are available, the Soviet press frequently reports idle capacity, including whole factories, major underutilization of nominally employed assets, stoppages, and a large and growing backlog of equipment awaiting installation or repair, sometimes for many years. Production of unwanted goods is yet another common problem.

[30] No. 10, 1962, p. 2.

[31] *Ibid.*, p. 5.

[32] *Pravda*, September 9, 1962. See also the *New York Times*, October 15 and 20, 1962.

Soviet Society Since Stalin:
Changes and Continuities

Paul E. Zinner

Khrushchev's Russia is not Stalin's Russia. The old dictator bequeathed to his unchosen successors a legacy of personal rule which they could not have assimilated even had they wanted to. He left behind him a society frozen, or nearly frozen, in its tracks, approaching general paralysis: the pervasive terror so withered the people's senses as to make them incapable of responding properly even to coercion. It was to be expected that Stalin's death in March 1953 would bring changes, in form if not in substance, to alleviate the incredible pressures under which all the society had been laboring, and to avoid possible breakdown or insurrection. The Soviet leaders, concerned about their country's and their own welfare, saw that rapid adaptations were necessary. They devised a crash program to forestall untoward developments and to gain time to adjust relations among themselves. They made concessions to the people in the form of amnesties and material palliatives, and to the outside world in the form of gestures toward an international *détente*.

Under the circumstances they could not have done less and still hope to survive. Yet the emergency measures of the period immediately following Stalin's death did not reflect panic. Nor did they presage a structured program of changes in the management of the affairs of Soviet society. They provided the rulers and the population with an essential breathing spell to take stock and strengthen flagging energies. In a longer perspective, the basic issue was—who would succeed Stalin? Pious references to collective leadership, which for a while abounded in Soviet media, were a convenient cover for the struggle for supremacy among individuals and factions. As long as collective leadership was hailed as the time-honored Leninist norm, one could be reasonably certain that forces at the top were divided and that no one had sufficient power to oust his rivals. The Party line was a barometer of the atmosphere in the ruling hierarchy.

This struggle for power dominated Soviet politics for about three years. While it lasted, no clear pattern of adjustments emerged, except that overt terror and the formidable police apparatus were decreased. The contours of these processes are well known. Lavrenti Beria, the Stalinist police chief, made a bold bid for power in the spring of 1953, utilizing the avenues of authority and communications at his disposal to place his supporters in prominent regional control posts. He was cut down in July 1953, reportedly at a meeting of the Party Presidium. Following his disappearance, the police apparatus was quickly neutralized and then gradually divested of its extraordinary and extralegal prerogatives. In March 1954, control over security matters was vested in a State Committee, under collective leadership, attached to the Council of Ministers, while normal police duties continued to be under the jurisdiction of the Ministry of Internal Affairs.

The action against the secret police apparatus, though undoubtedly motivated by the political leaders' desire to remove a threat to their own safety, also benefited the people greatly. It eliminated the major source of their personal insecurity, their unceasing anxiety, their dehumanization. It was a significant and welcome development in a totalitarian state that had depended so much on coercion to suppress opposition and attain its social goals.

In 1955 the possible lines became discernible as to how the succession struggle would be settled. Georgi Malenkov, who had been the heir apparent, was unceremoniously dismissed from the leading government post, the Chairmanship of the Council of Ministers. It was he who had delivered the keynote address at the Party's 19th Congress in October 1952—an honor traditionally reserved for the leading personage of the Party, and thus the ruler of Soviet Russia, but on this occasion, since the task was too onerous for the aging Stalin, passed on to a substitute. Immediately after Stalin's death, Malenkov seemed to be taking over direction of the government as well as the Party. But in a matter of days he was shorn of his Party post, which went to Khrushchev as perhaps the most innocuous contender for power.

Malenkov's demotion was followed by a blow at the prestige of another old Bolshevik, Vyacheslav Molotov, the former Chairman of the Council of People's Commissars and long-time manager of Soviet Russia's foreign affairs. He had been closely associated with Stalin's excommunication of Josip Tito, the Yugoslav Communist chief, from the Communist family, and on both ideological and personal grounds he continued to oppose any rapprochement with the Yugoslav Party. Khrushchev's ostentatious courting of Tito indicated that Molotov had lost control over his particular field of competence.

The major turning point of the post-Stalin era was the speech Khrushchev delivered before a closed session of the 20th Party Congress in February 1956.[1] He roundly condemned Stalin, substantiating many of the evils of which the West had long accused the dead despot. He denounced Stalin's "cult of personality," a euphemism for personal tyranny. He specified transgressions of legality and decency that had cost the lives of untold thousands of honest Soviet citizens, including some of the best sons of the Party itself, and retarded the construction of socialism in Russia. The tarnishing of the idol that had dominated Soviet society for twenty-nine out of its first thirty-six years unmistakably marked the end of an era.

II

Although the anti-Stalin speech was meant for home consumption, it had greater repercussions abroad than in the Soviet Union. More or less accurate reports of its content circulated throughout the world, and within a few months the U.S. State Department released a translation whose authenticity Soviet authorities have never challenged. Consternation spread among Communist Parties, especially in Eastern Europe, where the ruling Stalinist regimes found it very difficult to adapt to the new line.[2] In Poland, the most populous of Russia's East European satellites, an incipient civil war was averted. There was a bloodless transfer of power to Wladyslaw Gomulka, a "nationalist" Communist who for many years had been in prison because of his deviationist views, and was rehabilitated only weeks before he became the leader of the Party. Hungary was less fortunate. There the obstinacy of Stalinist diehards prevented reforms and an orderly transition to a more moderate Communist government, and a popular uprising swept out the Communist regime. Since Hungary's defection threatened the stability of the entire Soviet-controlled salient in Europe, the Russians entered and in a bloody counterrevolution restored Communist power.

These upheavals caused Khrushchev to suffer a temporary setback, but he recovered rapidly. By the spring of 1957, he was able to meet the last serious threat to his authority from disgruntled members of the Party Presidium. These old-timers, many of whom were senior to Khrushchev in high Party councils, disapproved of de-Stalinization, if only because it was directed in part against themselves. They could neither break their ingrained habits of work nor alter their hardened views of society. They would have maintained Stalin's image, had they been able to, and put down the dangerous innovations for which Khrushchev now began to show a marked propensity. Their fears were well founded: Khrushchev's anti-Stalinist jibes encompassed activities and attitudes with which the Party's old guard could be easily identified.

What impelled Khrushchev to set a new course of de-Stalinization cannot be stated with certainty. As we have noted, he undoubtedly perceived a necessity to clear the air and prepare for a comprehensive series of internal reforms. The anti-Stalinist campaign was, in Party language, "forward-looking"—to be done with the past, to write off its legacy of horror, and to start the Soviet Union moving again along a "glorious path of socialist conquests," with new ideas and new, young cadres. De-Stalinization was the spearhead of Khrushchev's campaign to breathe new life into Soviet society, to reopen clogged channels of communications, to cleanse the whole body politic of the surfeit of muck that weighed upon it and threatened to smother it completely. Khrushchev set himself at the head of the youth movement, ostentatiously separating himself from his cronies, casting them into the ashcan of history as unredeemable relics of a bygone era. Although he could not foresee all the consequences of his actions, he must have been aware of some of the risks, and he must have felt enough confidence in his own ability to ride out whatever storm he might provoke and to enhance his leadership in the process.

His gamble, if it was that, paid off handsomely. By the summer of 1957, he was undisputed boss of the Soviet Union. References to collective leadership gradually disappeared from the Party's vocabulary. In the spring of 1958, Khrushchev discarded even the pretense that responsibilities for Party and government were divided; he concentrated all authority in his hands by assuming the post of Chairman of the Council of Ministers while remaining First Secretary of the Party. For what the comparison is worth, one might note that Stalin did not formally unite in his person the leadership of Party and state until the spring of 1941.

Despite incontrovertible evidence, some Western observers have persisted in interpreting Khrushchev's position as precarious, seeing him threatened by a vestigial Stalinist faction. Paradoxically, his jovial manner and his demonstrated magnanimity toward his enemies, all of whom save Beria have remained alive and even at formal liberty, have helped perpetuate this erroneous view. Khrushchev's behavior has betrayed no concern whatever about his hegemony. He has traveled freely in the Soviet Union and abroad, unafraid that his absence from Moscow would encourage his opponents to wrest control from him, or that the temporary delegation of responsibilities to one or another of his intimates would diminish his own stature. He has shuffled and reshuffled the Party Presidium and the Council of Ministers, displaying a consummate ease that would be beyond his reach were he not sole master. With the image of the dour and merciless dictator that the world has now learned to associate with Stalin, it is hard to impute to this smiling and apparently relaxed person the iron qualities of a supreme ruler. Yet Khrushchev is that in every sense of the word. The demolition of the cult of personality has not entailed relinquishing the reality of the single leader. As it has been since its inception in 1917, apart from the two struggles for succession, the entire Soviet system came again under the control of one man.

The whole evolution of Soviet society since 1957 has reflected Khrushchev's guiding hand. Halting and haphazard adjustments gave way to a broad sweep of purposeful reorganization and changes in social relations. Even when the development was inharmonious, it revealed deliberate orchestration. Repeatedly Khrushchev has turned to organizational problems in industry and agriculture, attempting to give the Soviet economy more elasticity in planning and production without relinquishing the state's central control over all economic endeavor. At the same time he has continually recast the administrative apparatus of the Party and the government, reallocating functions, delegating responsibility to regional bodies without impairing the central authority of Moscow, and generally streamlining the cumbersome system of checks and controls. He has also carried out a large-scale reorganization of the police and the judiciary, abolishing old institutions, creating new ones, and initiating long-overdue criminal and civil codes.

Perhaps in order to ensure a permanent influence on the form and content of Soviet society, Khrushchev laid down general guidelines over the next two decades or so, until full Communism is attained. This twenty-year plan was in the form of the new Party program adopted by the 22nd Party Congress in October 1961,[3] the first general statement of purpose since 1919. While conditions had certainly changed sufficiently to warrant a new programmatic statement, Stalin put it off for almost three decades. To give the Party a new charter is the act of a self-confident man and of one in a hurry to fix his place in history. The new Party program was to have been followed by a new constitution, but the commission appointed to replace the antiquated Stalinist constitution of 1936 has not yet submitted a public draft.

The measures initiated by Khrushchev were implemented in part through an unrelenting campaign of de-Stalinization, which, far from abating, gained in intensity. The additional momentum was the mainspring of reform and innovation in many areas of government, administration, education, science, literature, and art. The defamation reached unprecedented proportions at the 22nd Party Congress, when Khrushchev and a well rehearsed claque again and again returned to attack the dead tyrant, specifying many of his crimes in detail. Stalin's embalmed body, lying next to Lenin's on display in a glass coffin outside the Kremlin, was moved to just behind this mausoleum, the resting place of such minor saints of Bolshevism as Frunze, Kalinin, and Zhdanov. No gesture could have made the point more strongly to the Soviet public.

Taking heart from the official sponsorship of de-Stalinization, people began probing the limits of tolerance of the new Party leaders. Using de-Stalinization as a shield, writers published unusually forthright and strongly derogatory accounts of life under Stalin, including even some about the heavily populated labor camps.[4] As it had been during periods of relaxation of the tsarist autocracy, literature became the most significant medium of social and political criticism, since nothing like direct political opposition was imaginable.

Another motive for Khrushchev's persistence in his anti-Stalin campaign, for the vehemence of his diatribes against Stalin at seemingly every opportunity or provocation, may well be that the new Vozhd wants to aggrandize his stature by cutting down the measure of his predecessor. Stalin casts a monumental shadow. As his successor, Khrushchev might have become less a ruler in his own right than a mere caretaker. Khrushchev has a greater than average lust for power, for otherwise he could not have bested this group of highly power-conscious, skilled politicians and climbed to the top. As a good Bolshevik he must have a well-developed sense of history and desire to leave his mark on it. One way to achieve this objective is to establish a direct link of succession from Lenin to himself, with Stalin as a long aberration. Thus, Khrushchev has assiduously fostered the notion that the legitimate line of descent from Lenin, the great apostle of Communism, is to himself, a worthy disciple and creative innovator.

At times, Khrushchev seemed to carry his attack on Stalin to an unnecessary extreme, thus opening himself to justified criticism if not by his contemporaries then by his successors, who will regard Stalin and his crimes with some measure of detachment, never having experienced them, and who might well feel that a deserving leader of Soviet history had been needlessly maligned. At other times, Khrushchev himself seemed to retract some of his harsh judgments and to modulate his criticism. The scope and limit of de-Stalinization have not yet been firmly and explicitly set; error is possible in either direction. Khrushchev is not jettisoning the entire past and inaugurating, however cautiously and circumspectly, an era of liberalism; he himself does not equate de-Stalinization with genuine liberalization. He means to keep a firm control system, by means different from Stalin's. While the transformation of Soviet society at Khrushchev's behest is still too fluid to permit any final inferences about the ultimate purposes and consequences of de-Stalinization, examining some of the institutional and social changes can shed light on these problems.

III

Together with the preeminence of the single leader, the outstanding place of the Party as the instrument of control over the society has been preserved. In fact, the Party's prestige, influence, and direct responsibility have been strengthened, first of all because Khrushchev relied on its apparatus to establish his ascendancy over his rivals. As First Secretary he could determine the composition of Party cadres and, as Stalin had done before him, he used this simple yet effective device to entrench himself unassailably at the center of the society's most important institution.

But Stalin had, in fact, allowed the Party's authority to lapse somewhat; so arbitrary and so personal did his rule become that no institution aside from the secret police maintained clear supremacy over competing bureaucracies. Under Stalin the totalitarian structure, far from monolithic, had on the contrary a peculiar artificial pluralism. It consisted of more or less isolated, narrowly circumscribed hierarchies of administrative officials defined by such functional specialties as the military, economic management, and the like. In this manner Stalin effectively prevented the accumulation of too much vested power in any single institution, and he used the police to interfere arbitrarily in all of them in order to prevent any office-holders from establishing security. Eventually the Party, although formally it remained the repository of decision-making and control over all other institutions, itself was affected by this division and restriction of functions.

Khrushchev elevated the Party again above the competing networks of functional specialists. While the intensity of the struggle between it and other bureaucracies has not been fully revealed, it would appear that no major difficulties were encountered in dispersing their key personnel and subordinating them to the Party. The process has, however, not been completed, and its self-contradictory features have tended to obscure the observable results. In order merely to continue operations if not to improve efficiency, the vast corps of "civil servants" had first to be assured of far greater certainty of tenure and rewards than under Stalin. At the same time, it was imperative to prevent the functional bureaucracies from taking advantage of the new circumstances and thus to forestall open struggle among them.

Khrushchev achieved this goal by playing off one interest group against another and whittling down each in turn. Immediately after Stalin's death, he relied heavily on the armed forces to check the power of the police and to maintain order in the country. Many officers hated the secret police, which had ravaged their ranks, and they were eager to retaliate. As an added incentive, Khrushchev relaxed the system of political control in the armed forces and, as a symbolic gesture of their newly won prestige, appointed Marshal Georgi K. Zhukov, a popular war hero whom Stalin had cast into near oblivion, to be Minister of National Defense and made him a member of the Party Presidium. No sooner had Zhukov served this purpose than, in the fall of 1957, he was purged and completely eliminated from public life, while the Party's control over officers was simultaneously strengthened. There was no indication of a significant resistance to these moves.

Having done with the secret police and the armed forces, Khrushchev turned on the economic managers, a large, sprawling administrative elite with a greater potential for resisting orders than for asserting its preferences. Decentralization from Moscow of the government offices that planned for and directed the increasingly complicated economic machine occasioned the transfer and replacement of tens of thousands of officials, and effectively broke up any managerial clique. Meanwhile, Khrushchev amalgamated leading Communists into other organizations and on an unprecedented scale assigned to the Party day-to-day operational responsibilities. Through twin managerial hierarchies of industry and agriculture, the Party now directly administers the economy, exercising control over economic activities through a joint Party-government inspectorate.

The separation of the Party from management had been both a tradition and an anomaly in the Communist system. The Party, as ideally conceived, was meant to play the part of a central nervous system, receiving all the impulses from the sense organs, integrating them, making decisions either in direct response to or independently from sensory perceptions, transmitting orders to various specialized organs, and checking on their performance. In practice this proved to be an excessively cumbersome arrangement, with much duplication of functions, numerous jurisdictional disputes, and frequent confusion. At crucial points of transmission the Party sometimes delegated too much authority and often assumed too much direct responsibility, so that the Soviet system worked less because of its efficient organization than because of the informal arrangements that local officials made in contravention of regulations.

Khrushchev has tackled this mammoth reorganization in a seemingly reasonable manner, though how successful he will be remains to be seen. According to some observers, the Party's role as guardian of political-ideological interests is likely to be undermined by its involvement in day-to-day technical-managerial functions. This is not a necessary consequence, and it is certainly not what Khrushchev intended. He has repeatedly emphasized that in the period of transition to "Communism" (whatever the term may mean in practice), the state will indeed begin to wither, with a concomitant gradual transfer of responsibility for "self-government" to social organizations. The Communist Party, as the outstanding "social organization," will thus acquire an even more important part to play. The obliteration of strict divisions of responsibility between Party and government is a conspicuous step toward the withering of the state, intended to make a Marxian prediction, reaffirmed by Khrushchev, come true. It also attacks the perennial problem of reconciling political-ideological with technical-managerial interests. Given the character of the Soviet system, which precludes competitive politics, this is probably *the* central issue for the political leadership to resolve; and there are no pat answers. If Khrushchev succeeds in fusing the country's technical-managerial talent with its political-ideological elite, he will realize the ideal form of totalitarian party-state more than at any previous time in Soviet history, without lessening the Party's extraordinary formal prerogatives. In short, the Party remains the prime mover of society and the source of all authority. It stands outside and above the law, and while it now rules with judicious restraint, it alone determines the limits of its legitimate actions.

No institutional reform has taken place, and none is contemplated, that would effectively restrain the Party from the wanton, capricious use of its power. The need for such guarantees has been recognized, for the population is obviously wary of a repetition of Stalinist arbitrariness. As a corollary to de-Stalinization, therefore, Khrushchev solemnly vowed that violations of "legality" cannot and will not be repeated. He has gone so far as to introduce into the Party statutes provisions limiting the number of times office-holders may be "reelected" and providing that at each "election" a certain proportion (from one-third to one-fourth) must be replaced; and he has promised the same type of rotation system for elected government bodies. Thus, he maintains, individual leaders will be unable to entrench themselves in power by perpetuating their term of office indefinitely. Of itself, of course, a mechanical rotation of office-holders is meaningless; it does not make them responsible during their term of office, and it does not give the electorate, whether it be the Party membership or the population at large, anything like a choice of candidates. Under Stalin the turnover rate of officials exceeded the modest figure Khrushchev suggested, for thousands upon thousands were peremptorily dismissed, imprisoned, or killed. For example, of the 139 members of the Party's Central Committee duly "elected" in 1934, only twenty-four still held their jobs five years later. Khrushchev guarantees one outward manifestation of democracy, but he passes over in silence the substance of democracy, which alone makes rotation in office a significant index of freedom. The guarantees, in any case, must be taken as meaningful only as long as he wishes to abide by them, and in principle this is no different from the Party's place under Stalin.

As another verbal reform of the government, the Party program has proclaimed the termination of the period of proletarian dictatorship and the onset of socialist democracy. The Soviet state henceforth is an "all-people's state" *(obshenarodnoe gosudarstvo)* devoid of class dictatorship, a formulation that merely eliminated an anachronism from Soviet terminology. The Stalin constitution of 1936 made the term "dictatorship of the proletariat" obsolete, since by its description the Soviet Union no longer had antagonistic social classes. The workers, the peasants (working on state farms or in collective farms), and the working intelligentsia made up the social matrix of the USSR, and with these cooperative strata there was no necessity for a class government. The adoption of the constitution, however, coincided with Stalin's theory that, as the construction of socialism progresses, the class struggle becomes sharper, so that the socialist state has to maintain eternal vigilance and mercilessly purge Communists and non-Communists who have fallen prey to alien class ideologies. Now this dictum of Stalin's has been declared mistaken and proletarian dictatorship has been relegated to the past.

In practice the shift to socialist democracy has encompassed only minor, formal institutional and procedural changes. For example, there have been hints in Soviet scholarly journals of "strengthening Soviet parliamentarism," [5] though what this means is hard to determine. So far, all one can say is that the bicameral Supreme Soviet (the federal legislature of Russia) has met regularly twice a year and that some of its commissions have participated in the preparation of draft legislation. The sessions of the legislature, however, have averaged only three to five days, and the commissions, as far as we know, have had no more than two or three weeks to consider pending legislation. This does not suggest a working parliamentary system, especially when the composition and method of electing the deputies are kept in mind. Once again, Khrushchev is deftly manipulating appearances in an attempt to create a mood of solidarity, to increase confidence in the government, to draw people into political participation on the government's terms.

IV

Indeed, Khrushchev's major political effort, it would appear, has been to engage the population in government-sponsored, self-policing, and sustained social functions. In other words, he is promoting a sort of continuous, controlled national vigilantism to ensure strict observance of norms of moral conduct (particularly in relation to public property), and to apply appropriate sanctions against transgressors. The instruments through which the population is expected to police itself are the people's volunteer corps, an auxiliary of the regular uniformed police, with full police power while on duty; the comrades' courts, tribunals of one's peers, established at places of work as well as in residences, which decide cases involving misdemeanors and petty violations of the social and economic code; and since November 1962, the Party-state control committee, an inspectorate charged with auditing and spot-checking in all economic establishments to circumvent and detect criminal acts on the part of management that damage the public weal.

The last of these institutions—on whose activities there is no information at the time this is being written—may elicit the most favorable public response, although the ultimate success of an undertaking involving tens of thousands of nonprofessional, technically unqualified snoopers and informers may be doubted. In 1923, in an attempt to cut down the bureaucratic excesses associated with the country's early economic growth, Lenin had united the Workers' and Peasants' Inspection with the Central Control Commission of the Party. Under Stalin, the Workers' and Peasants' Inspection itself became a bureaucratic, professional instrument, losing all semblance of spontaneity and popular participation. In 1934 it gave way to a Commissariat of State Control, which in one form or another survived until the establishment of the new inspectorate.

The people's volunteers first appeared in 1958, and their status was formalized by decree in 1959. They are unpaid, auxiliary policemen who perform patrol duties in their off-hours, usually under the guidance of the regular police. Organizationally, however, they are under direct supervision of the Party. They wear no uniform apart from a red armband on their left sleeves. According to official Soviet claims, there were 2.5 million organized volunteers by the end of 1960, and two years later close to 4 million. How many of these totals are active is a matter of conjecture, as is the manner of enforcing government regulations. Theoretically, the organized volunteers can intervene in a large variety of situations, with the right to reprimand and detain persons whose actions are contrary to loosely defined "norms of public behavior." They may question loafers suspected of "shirking honest labor," or break up street fights, or attempt to right such categories of misconduct as drunkenness, the use of foul language, matrimonial quarrels, and the improper upbringing of children.

The comrades' courts serve as public forums for exposing petty infractions of the social and economic code. Their primary purpose is not to mete out punishment, but rather to bring the force of social pressure to bear upon offenders and thus to teach the community an object lesson in proper "Communist morality." These lay tribunals also function on a voluntary basis, after working hours. Their jurisdiction extends over a great variety of offenses, which can be classified in four major categories: labor discipline; hooliganism; social relations (e.g., nonfulfillment of parental duties, negligent attitudes toward one's elders or neighbors); and minor civil disputes (i.e., disputes over property valued at less than 50 rubles).

Khrushchev himself, urging the expansion and strengthening of the network of comrades' courts in 1959, stressed their prophylactic or preventive function. With "still . . . not a few cases of violation of public order," he recommended that the maintenance of order and security "should be performed by social groups, as well as by the militia [regular police] and the courts." [6] The time had come to pay more attention to comrades' courts, which should aim mainly "to forestall (preduprezhdat) . . . various types of deviation from the norms of communal order."

Although social organizations are being utilized to enforce the observance of a proper code of conduct, they have not replaced the regular, professionally staffed institutions of government entrusted with the maintenance of order and the dispensation of law. If anything, the position of the regular police and especially that of the judiciary have been strengthened. Stalin had relied on terror to achieve his purposes, working through the secret police and covert administrative processes. He largely ignored the regular police and the courts, both of which fell into disrepute as a result of the gross violations of legality; Khrushchev has attempted to cleanse their reputation and build up a new respect for them.

Khrushchev is no less aware than Stalin was of the constant necessity of imposing outward norms of behavior on the Soviet people. But his methods, diametrically opposed to Stalin's, sometimes create an erroneous impression.

The change in status of the secret police has been accompanied by the decentralization of the regular police apparatus. In 1960, the Ministry of Internal Affairs of the USSR was abolished, and the powers vested in it were transferred to Ministries of Internal Affairs in the fifteen constituent republics. Whether or not this reshuffling actually caused a loss of central direction over police activities, it was probably meant to create that impression and at the same time to increase efficiency. In the fall of 1962, these fifteen Ministries of Internal Affairs changed their titles to Ministries for the Protection of Public Order, or MOOP (Ministerstvo Okhrani Obshestvennovo Poriadka).[7] With the disappearance of the MVD, a significant symbol of universal fear was withdrawn from circulation—but this was perhaps the sixth time since 1917 that a face-lifting had taken place.

As another example of Khrushchev's skillful manipulation of appearances, of his attempt to create a favorable image of institutions that the Soviet people distrust, one can cite the effort to build up the militia as a traditional defender of the people's welfare. In 1962, for example, the government proclaimed November 10 as National Militia Day to commemorate its exploits and to celebrate the unbreakable bonds between it and the people. Indeed, the militia has enjoyed little prestige among the people; there have even been murderous attacks on militiamen and isolated station houses, in part because the corps has lacked enough arms to defend itself. In legislation enacted in 1962, penalties of utmost severity were imposed for "attempts on the life, health, and dignity of the militia and the people's volunteers." [8] Steps have also been taken to supply the militia with the "modern equipment of all sorts" that it needs, though what type and quantity of weapons were not specified.

Putting the judiciary in shape to perform the functions now expected of it has also been an arduous and protracted endeavor. The judiciary under Stalin, whether or not it itself violated the norms of legality, was too often superseded by the terror apparatus which, whenever it invaded the courts' sphere of competence, rode roughshod over them. Khrushchev, at pains to transform the judiciary into an effective instrument of "Communist construction," has tried to restore "socialist legality" to its rightful place. "Socialist legality," however, does not connote what the West means by the rule of law, which induces the courts to administer justice, if not infallibly, then impartially and independently. While the rule of law is clearly inconsistent with individual license, it works to the benefit of individual citizens by protecting their inalienable rights against a capricious government. The rule of law is more than its expression in the judicial process; it reflects the underlying philosophy of Western governments which subordinates rulers and ruled alike to firm and clearly enunciated norms of social behavior. The ideological foundations of the Soviet system preclude any *a priori* limitations of power, and Khrushchev has shown no propensity to undermine these theoretical pillars. Like other branches of government, the judiciary is part of a unified power structure designed to enforce the political will of the "sovereign"—that is, the Party personified by its leader. No Soviet official enjoys independence or even autonomy, without which the impartial administration of justice is inconceivable. By the procedure of Soviet courts, all participants from judge to defendant play a part in the unified proceedings under the overall supervision and direction of the state prosecutor (procurator), who acts as the chief agent of the political authority in judicial matters. He is presently described as the guardian of "socialist legality": that is, it is his duty to prevent outside agencies from encroaching on the courts and thus to make certain that justice is done. The crux of the matter is the meaning of "justice."

In Soviet law the interests of society as a whole, as the Party defines these interests, have absolute primacy over the interests and rights of individuals. The rights of individuals derive from the duties imposed on them: they are entitled to enjoy their rights only to the extent to which they fulfill their obligations. According to articles 130 and 131 of the Soviet constitution, it is the duty of every citizen "to maintain labor discipline, honestly perform public duties, and to respect the rules of socialist intercourse; . . . to safeguard and fortify public, socialist property as the sacred and inviolable foundation of the Soviet system, as the source of wealth and might of the country, as the source of the material prosperity and cultural life of all the working people." [9] "Justice," therefore, means principally the protection of "socialist property." Any act that can be construed as damaging socialist property or failing to promote its unfettered growth is an infraction of constitutional obligations, which is by definition punishable.

While laws are drafted in this perspective, providing suitable punishment for the infraction of rules is not the only, or even the main, function of Soviet legislation. As seen by Soviet lawmakers, legislation is an "educational instrument" that helps instill the proper civic virtues in the population and shape the morality of the "new Soviet man." The law courts, similarly, are institutions peculiarly suited to carry through this "educational function." While the reform of the Soviet judiciary must be judged against this conceptual background, this does not lessen the importance of procedural changes that have been introduced. At least for the time being, extralegal prosecution of innocent people has been suspended, and this in itself is a tremendous advance from past practices. But it is rather a far cry from the protection of what in the West are termed inalienable rights.

In 1956, as part of the reform of the judiciary, the central Ministry of Justice was abolished, and its functions were transferred to republican Ministries of Justice. A large number of decrees that sanctioned administrative procedure against presumed offenders were annulled, and the Supreme Soviet adopted guiding principles for new criminal and civil codes in 1958 and 1961, respectively.[10] These new legal codes do not adequately safeguard the defendant against gross miscarriages of justice, but they do cautiously advance his rights to counsel and they define transgressions of the law much more precisely than ever before. They certainly do not conform to the time-honored Western principle: no crime and no punishment without law, without guilt, without cause *(nullum crimen, nulla poena sine lege, sine culpa, sine causa)*. But at long last the Soviet citizen knows more or less when he is committing a crime, and the total legal insecurity under Stalin is relieved.

What have been, broadly defined, the social implications of the new legal codes and court practices? Clearly the paramount concern of Soviet lawmakers is no longer political disloyalty, but rather socialist discipline and property regulation. The new codes are concerned primarily with the regulation of socialist attitudes toward public property and the limitation of personal-property rights. They are a response to behavior common in the late 1950's, when many disregarded the sanctity of public property and showed a profound interest in the pursuit of private gain. This widespread pattern poignantly demonstrated the failure of the system to instill "socialist virtues" in the people. Indeed, so serious is the aberration that after the adoption of principles of criminal legislation in 1958, each of the republics of the USSR has had to enact stringent, so-called "antiparasite" decrees, which catalog a long list of social and economic crimes.[11] For less serious infractions, the offender may be remanded to "work settlements" (in effect, labor camps) for a period of two to five years. The worst of the offenses are punishable by death. In 1962, hardly a week passed without the execution—duly noted in the Soviet press—of persons found guilty of large-scale embezzlement of government funds, illicit trade and marketing operations, speculation in foreign currency, and similar crimes.

At the same time, the new legal codes reflect the determination of Soviet leaders to hold fast to their charted course toward Communism, which they equate with the abolition of all private property, the curtailment of personal property to the barest essentials, and the distribution of the product of public property in accordance with presumed needs. "Personal property derives from socialist property and serves as one means of satisfying citizens' needs. As we move toward Communism, the personal needs of citizens will be satisfied to an ever greater extent through public resources." [12] Legislation has been devised to force people to earn their living through "honest labor"—that is, in public employment at going wage rates —and to prevent them from supporting themselves by profits derived from private property. To this end, at least for the present, private property is sharply differentiated from personal property, which is defined as material goods, primarily consumer durables, owned for personal use. For example, an automobile or a house may be owned for personal use subject to certain restrictions, but if the home is rented out or the car hired out as a taxi, it becomes private property, whose owner is liable to prosecution.[13]

The ownership of automobiles has not been, of course, the subject of an extensive special legislation, because the government has a simpler way of coping with this type of property. It simply allocates materials for the manufacture of only a very small number of passenger cars—approximately 150,000 in 1961, and in 1962, when no separate figures for cars and buses were released by the statistical office, possibly even fewer. By fiat of its rulers, the Soviet Union—

a mighty industrial power second only to the United States—shall not enter the automobile age.

The problem of home-ownership is somewhat more complicated. In 1957, reacting to the continuing gross housing shortage, the government permitted and even encouraged private-home construction. The consequent housing boom not only competed with public-home construction, but more important, gave rise to an incipient "class" of rentiers, capitalists of the worst sort, who have let their homes at usurious rents and have, in some cases, gone on to acquire whole strings of dwellings. To forestall further speculation in home-ownership, under the civil code the area of any privately owned dwelling is restricted to a little over 600 square feet. Any person or family is prohibited from owning more than one home and from using that as a source of unearned income. After mid-1962 no further plots of land could be allocated for private-home building in the major metropolitan areas of the Soviet Union (all land is owned by the state and is only leased to individuals); [14] and in several republics homes are to be confiscated that are used in violation of these restrictions or that have been built from unearned income.[15]

Khrushchev has frequently expressed his personal disdain for private ownership. Eventually he means to deprive peasants even of their private garden plots, now a legitimate source of income. These presently spell the difference between a tolerable food supply for the cities and serious shortages. They are only an infinitesimal percentage of the total area under cultivation, but they furnish a disproportionate amount of marketed potatoes, vegetables, poultry, eggs, and dairy products. In his fond expostulations on the virtues of communal ownership, Khrushchev has also confidently forecast the day of plenty when apartments will be available in abundance and ample taxi pools will cater to those desiring (temporarily) to get away from it all.

The population of the Soviet Union gratifies its long frustrated drives as well as it can. Demonstrating a remarkable survival of capitalist, acquisitive instincts after nearly half a century of socialist indoctrination, the people are giving vent to dissatisfaction with both the amount and the quality of consumer goods. Although much has been made of rising levels of living in the post-Stalin era —and indeed definite, if selective, improvements have taken place— the appetite of the Soviet people has far surpassed the ability and willingness of the authorities to meet their demands. Instead of being grateful for what the party has done for them, the people tend to grumble and satisfy themselves at the expense of public property, extracting a sort of tax-in-kind from the government. These attitudes are shared by young and old alike. According to Khrushchev, speaking at the 14th Congress of the Young Communist League (Komsomol) in April 1962:

> Even now . . . there are certain young people, and not young people alone, who . . . without working . . . want to dress better, to have the smartest and best suits and shoes—and to have as many suits and shoes as possible, so as to change them frequently, to eat as well as possible, to have a good apartment and television set, and other fine things, . . . [and] some even dare to grumble: Why, they say, . . . is there a shortage of some goods, why is the quality poor? But they themselves do not lift a finger to do anything for the good of society. . . . Yes, comrades, we still have parasitical elements in our midst. . . . They want to live only at the expense of others, and some steal and sometimes even kill.[16]

The very fact that social and economic "crimes" have become prevalent indicates how substantially conditions have improved: under Stalin few dared oppose the control system. Under Khrushchev, with a relaxation of terror, discipline has deteriorated if not broken down. What percentage of the national wealth is pilfered each year can hardly be estimated. While it is unlikely that what the people manage to steal seriously damages the Soviet economy, the persistence of predatory acquisitiveness must profoundly disturb the Soviet leadership, the few who set the standards on the basis of their political ideology; for they now see themselves engaged in a war of attrition of monumental dimensions against the many whose purpose apparently is no higher than a humdrum pursuit of individual happiness.[17] Since economic rationality is in direct conflict here with dogma and vested power, the outcome of the struggle cannot be predicted.

V

A decade after Stalin's death, when this is being written, the Soviet Union has barely begun to shed the fetters of his rule. Khrushchev has tried valiantly to undertake a steady controlled decompression, and he has had some success. Obviously, the day-to-day existence for the majority of citizens has improved. Pervasive fear no longer stalks the country, and some of the most wretched material conditions of life have been alleviated. There is some evidence that many people are grateful to Khrushchev, but there is also evidence that they do not trust him and especially his government, that they are dissatisfied with the rate and scope of improvement. The memory of the Stalinist era is still vivid, and few reassuring institutional safeguards have been introduced to give people hope of staving off the resurgence of tyranny. They are conscious that their well-being depends on the party's good will. The people crave for intellectual and political freedom, but no one thinks seriously of organizing against the ruling minority.

The economy suffers from serious chronic ills. Agriculture is the "sick man" of Soviet society, and the gulf grows between the cities—which are being modernized in every respect, albeit slowly—and the stagnating countryside, the home of almost half the total population (100 million out of a total of 220 million). Khrushchev's panaceas have repeatedly failed; his predilection for organizational solutions for human problems cannot instill confidence that the agricultural lag will be overcome. The rural population, still dreadfully underprivileged, with little hope of bettering itself, has small incentive for cooperating with the Soviet state. To increase that incentive—that is, to attack the major problem in Soviet agriculture and probably in the Soviet economy—means tampering with collectivized agriculture, the fundamental of the whole system.

Industry also has its characteristic major ailments. The technical problem of central planning grows more and more complex with each success of the economy. Consumer satisfaction is as great a difficulty as agricultural production: the totalitarian welfare state is nowhere near in sight, and it may be a contradiction in terms. Some Western observers have suggested that with increased economic well-being the totalitarian controls will inevitably loosen. It may well be that the opposite is correct—that the party intends to keep the population permanently in relative impoverishment precisely because enrichment would lead inevitably to increasing political discontent and thus threaten the regime's very existence.

In short, Soviet Russia ten years after Stalin's death is very much a totalitarian system, but one that has shed many of its police-state characteristics. The ingredients of totalitarian control (coercion, persuasion, and incentive) are mixed in different proportions from those of that bygone era. A more subtle means of totalitarian control is emerging, with a heavy reliance on administrative maneuver and psychological manipulation, with unchanged essentials combined with numerous adaptations to changing conditions and requirements.[18]

It is as difficult to forecast the shape of Soviet society ten years hence as it was to foresee the decade that followed Stalin's death in 1953. The future course of Soviet society will be profoundly influenced by events that we know will take place but whose effect is more or less problematic. Among the most significant will be the struggle to succeed Khrushchev when he dies or is incapacitated. Another important factor will be the social changes concomitant with the country's continuing urbanization and the yet greater growth of the number of white-collar jobs. To suppose, however, that this white-collar middle class will assert itself politically against totalitarian dictatorship, somewhat as the entrepreneurial middle class once threw off royal absolutism, is not in my opinion well based. The bureaucratic middle class has neither economic independence nor a strong sense of self-reliance. It is imbued with deference toward the authority upon which its status depends. Still, one cannot write off in advance this so-called embourgeoisement of Soviet society as an inconsequential social development without any profound effects on the state's power relations. The social composition of the leading Party cadres will be a valuable index of the change that takes place.

Whatever its internal developments, Soviet society is bound to be affected by international relations. As one of the world's two superpowers, the Soviet Union heads a bloc of militant regimes ideologically dedicated to nothing less than world revolution, so that the interdependence between external and internal policies is great. The government has to be mindful not only of the terms of struggle with hostile powers but also of the terms of cooperation with Communist countries and with parties impatient to seize power. The drains upon Soviet resources for the conduct of the external struggle are very heavy, but it is difficult to see how the Soviet Union can avoid many of these obligations. And while it would be far-fetched to imagine outside forces that could significantly reshape the Soviet leadership itself, external pressures could quite conceivably retard or promote various internal trends and thus affect in important ways the future system of political control.

FOOTNOTES

[1] *The Anti-Stalin Campaign and International Communism* (New York: Columbia University Press, 1956), pp. 1-89.

[2] Paul E. Zinner, ed., *National Communism and Popular Revolt in Eastern Europe* (New York: Columbia University Press, 1956).

[3] Herbert Ritvo, ed., *The New Soviet Society* (New York: New Leader, 1962).

[4] Yurii Bondarev, *Tishina* (Stillness) (Moscow, 1962); Alexander Solzhenitsyn, *One Day in the Life of Ivan Denisovich* (New York: Praeger, 1963).

[5] See, for example, I. S. Senin, "Some Questions of the Activities of the Budget Commission of the Soviet of the Union of Supreme Soviet of the USSR," *Sovetskoe Gosudarstvo i Pravo* (Soviet State and Law), Moscow, no. 11 (November 1962), pp. 26-37.

[6] *Pravda,* January 28, 1959.

[7] *Current Digest of the Soviet Press,* 14:36, October 3, 1962, p. 21.

[8] *Ibid.,* 14:7, March 14, 1962, p. 4.

[9] See Herbert McClosky and John E. Turner, *The Soviet Dictatorship* (New York: McGraw-Hill, 1960), p. 630.

[10] "Principles of Criminal Legislation of the USSR and the Union Republics," *Current Digest of the Soviet Press,* 11:4, March 4, 1959, pp. 3-7; "Principles of Civil Legislation of the USSR and the Union Republics," *ibid.,* 14:4, February 21, 1962, pp. 3-13.

[11] *Ibid.,* 13:17, May 24, 1961, pp. 8-9.

[12] *Ibid.,* 14:4, February 21, 1962, p. 3.

[13] A pertinent paragraph of the decree of the Supreme Soviet of the RSFSR, *On Intensifying the Struggle against Persons Who Avoid Socially Useful Labor and Lead an Antisocial, Parasitic Way of Life,* reads as follows: ". . . able-bodied legally adult citizens who do not wish to perform a major Constitutional duty—to work honestly according to their capabilities—and who avoid socially useful work, derive unearned income from the exploitation of land plots, auto-

mobiles or housing, or commit other antisocial acts that enable them to lead a parasitic way of life are subject, upon the order of a district (or city) people's court, to deportation to specially designated localities for a period of from two to five years, with confiscation of property acquired without labor, and to mandatory enlistment in work at the place of deportation." *Current Digest of the Soviet Press,* 13:17, May 24, 1961, pp. 8-9.

14 *Ibid.,* 14:32, September 5, 1962, p. 17.

15 *Ibid.,* p. 25.

16 *Ibid.,* 14:16, May 16, 1962, pp. 13-14.

17 Officially, any manifestation of individualism and pursuit of self-interest is designated as a "survival of the past." Among the more troublesome of these "survivals" are: (1) a disdainful attitude toward labor, (2) a desire to sponge off society, (3) private-ownership tendencies, (4) misconduct at work and at home, (5) religious prejudices. Report by F. R. Kozlov, Secretary of the Communist Party Central Committee, October 28, 1961. *Ibid.,* 13:57, December 20, 1961, p. 9.

18 Khrushchev believes implicitly in the value of total planning. His ideal is that of an engineered society. In an exchange with President Sukarno of Indonesia he maintained, "Socialism should mean that every minute is calculated, a life built on calculation." *New York Times,* March 2, 1960.

The East European Satellites:
Variations on a Soviet Theme

Paul Kecskemeti

At the end of the second World War, a vast tract of East-Central Europe, running from the Baltic to the Adriatic and the Black Sea, came under Soviet political control, based mostly upon military occupation. Ever since then, the political history of the countries or country fragments involved (East Germany, Poland, Czechoslovakia, Hungary, Rumania, Yugoslavia, Albania, and Bulgaria) has been a set of variations on a common theme.

The unitary, common theme was the gradual imposition of totalitarian political regimes closely modeled upon Stalin's Soviet Russia. But there were also variations, departures from mechanical uniformity. This was inevitable. The process of sovietization started from initial conditions that differed widely from one country of the region to another, and also differed from those prevailing in Russia during the formative period of the Soviet regime itself. Moscow's pressure toward uniformity, massive as it was, did not succeed in effacing these initial differences. Thus, political developments in each country of the region proceeded along specific lines, reflecting variations in social structure, the degree of industrial development, national-political orientation, indigenous Communist strength, and so on. Because of these variations, no two countries of the region experienced the ordeal of sovietization in exactly the same manner. I shall briefly outline the various patterns of sovietization that emerged, the stresses generated by them, and the physiognomic differences now prevailing among the Communist regimes of the region as a result of the divergent historical paths they followed.

II

The withdrawal of the German forces from East-Central Europe in 1944-45 brought about the collapse of the German occupation regimes, puppet regimes, or Axis regimes [1] that existed there, and gave the signal for the introduction of a new political order. This process took place under the general guidance of the Soviet Union. Nominally, the political transformation of the liberated areas was a joint responsibility of all the Allies, but this principle remained on paper. The decisive voice was Stalin's, and the execution of policy rested with the Soviet military authorities where Soviet forces were in occupation. In Yugoslavia and Albania, where local Communist partisan forces rather than the Soviet armies had displaced the Germans, Moscow exercised only remote control over political developments. The local partisans were nominally under Communist Party discipline, but they tended to ignore restraining counsel from the center.

In undertaking the political reorganization of East-Central Europe, Moscow deliberately ruled out the introduction of the integral Soviet form of government and instead adopted the "People's Democracy" [2] as the standard pattern. Its main feature was shared power. Governments were to be formed by coalitions consisting of several parties certified as "antifascist" and "democratic." It was understood that such certification would be withheld from the parties of the Right, but the "democratic" coalitions were supposed to include, in addition to the Communists, non-Communist workers, peasants, and "national bourgeois" parties. In other words, the expansion of Communist control beyond the confines of the Soviet Union was started on a dualistic basis, providing for two distinct forms of rule—the Soviet system proper within the USSR, the People's Democracy elsewhere. This distinction is still being maintained in name, although in all People's Democracies as they exist today, the original multiparty coalitions have long given way to exclusive Communist control.

The Soviet leadership's reasons for sponsoring People's Democracy were manifold and complex. To begin with, no full-blown one-party regime could be created at once in countries where the Communists had no organized mass following and hardly even any cadres—and this was true throughout most of East-Central Europe. Moreover, it was important for Stalin to convince the Allies that he was satisfied to share power with non-Communists in the areas liberated from the Germans. Any indication that exclusive Communist power was his ultimate goal risked provoking a strong Western reaction, barring the door to Communist expansion. In Western

Europe, notably in France and Italy, this risk was particularly serious. There the Communists could enter the precincts of power by joining coalitions, but it was necessary for them to convince their partners of their democratic reliability. Playing the coalition game also in Eastern Europe, where the Soviet presence would have permitted a more ambitious course, served to clinch the point.

Other factors, too, made for gradualism and moderation. In economic matters, quick recovery took precedence over everything else; in their eagerness to get production under way again, the Soviets inhibited proletarian militancy concerning wages and workers' control, and adopted a cautious approach toward such basic institutional reforms as nationalization. In the field of agriculture, the overriding initial objective was to gain peasant goodwill. Moscow therefore promoted land reforms giving the land to the peasants, disclaiming any intention to collectivize agriculture.

All these considerations made it imperative to stress the contrast between the Soviet regime and the People's Democracy, and to present the latter as a version of Western-type, pluralistic rule. Actually, however, the coalition of "democratic" parties as the basic feature of the People's Democracy fundamentally differed from the multiparty coalitions familiar in Continental Europe. The key feature of multiparty parliamentary democracy is the mechanism of *shifting* majorities. The People's Democracy concept, however, called for a *permanent*, indissoluble coalition, a "front" supposedly uniting like-minded parties for a common policy. Following the "front" principle, the Communists treated any dissent within the coalition as betrayal of the "democratic" principles to which all partners were committed. The initially heterogeneous "fronts" could thus be transformed into more and more homogeneous ones, until all opponents were absorbed or squeezed out and the ruling coalitions included only Communists and fellow-travelers completely subservient to them. Far from representing a distinct species, intermediate between the Soviet system and Western democracy, the People's Democracy was merely a pluralistic initial stage of a dynamic process that led to exclusive, totalitarian Communist control. The initial stage could be more or less far removed from the homogeneous end state; the People's Democracy concept was flexible in this respect. Stalin, at any rate, favored a good deal of initial diversity. Only Poland was singled out for special treatment.

Poland's case indeed was special: the wartime Polish government-in-exile, established in London, had repeatedly clashed with the Soviet Union over territorial and other issues. Hence Stalin insisted upon an integrally Communist-controlled Polish-front government from the beginning, and the Allies had to exert a considerable effort to induce him to lift his ban upon including representatives of the government-in-exile in Poland's first postwar government. But elsewhere, in Czechoslovakia, Rumania, and Hungary, for example, Stalin accepted genuinely heterogeneous multiparty coalitions, including "bourgeois" elements, as a starting point. He supported a similar policy for Yugoslavia; Tito was instructed to form a coalition government together with Šubašič, the King's spokesman, but Tito disregarded these instructions. Using police terror, he made it impossible for the non-Communist parties to contest the elections set for November 1945. A single, Communist-sponsored front list was elected, so that Yugoslavia achieved the one-party regime already toward the end of 1945. In Albania and Bulgaria, developments followed a similar course. In the other East-Central European countries, however, the evolution of the Popular Democracies from permanent coalitions of independent parties to exclusive Communist control took several years.

III

The uniformity of the pattern of sovietization, then, was broken up right at the beginning by Balkan Communist leaders, notably Tito. Clearly, the tempo set by Stalin was too slow for them, and they saw no justification for Stalin's accommodating attitude toward the Western powers. Tito behaved as truculently as possible in dealing with the West, quarreling with Italy over Trieste and Venezia Giulia, aiding Greek Communist guerrillas, and shooting down American planes. All this amounted to open defiance of Stalin's foreign policy. The first rift in the Communist bloc was caused by Tito's radicalism.

It is noteworthy that Tito, the exponent of the radical, maximalist line, had spent the war years as an underground leader. Other local Communists with a background of underground activity, cut off from Moscow and unfamiliar with Stalin's political style and outlook, had generally taken it for granted that "liberation" by the Soviet army could mean only the rapid imposition of the dictatorship of the proletariat. They were disabused when the Soviet military authorities, more or less ignoring them, organized coalition regimes instead, and gave the leading positions in the reconstituted Communist Parties to émigrés who had spent the past decade or two in the USSR. These "Muscovites"—Gottwald in Czechoslovakia, Rákosi in Hungary, Bierut in Poland, and so on—imposed the coalition policy over the radicals' objections.

Moderation vs. radicalism, however, was a self-liquidating issue in the Communist movement. Having secured control over the police, the courts, and other key positions, and sure of the backing of the Soviet authorities, the Communists lost no time in starting to wreck their coalition partners. Details varied, but by the spring of 1947, the movement toward exclusive Communist control was in full swing. At the same time, Soviet policy toward the West was stiffening. Communist expansion in the West was making no headway: the French and Italian Communists were forced out of the government in May 1947, and the Soviets were denied control over the West German economy. Since the results of Stalin's early postwar policy of cooperation had been disappointing, Soviet foreign policy and bloc policy veered toward radicalism, with Zhdanov as the chief spokesman of the new course.

The new forward policy was officially launched at the conference of Communist Parties held in September 1947 at Szklarska Poreba in Poland; this conference established the Cominform, an inter-Party bureau for publicizing joint ventures. Fittingly enough, the seat of the new bureau was Belgrade, the stronghold of Communist militancy. Barely restored on a radical basis, unity in the bloc collapsed over a different issue: Tito challenged Soviet organizational control within the international movement.[3]

Having won his point on radicalism, Tito engaged on an ambitious empire-building venture: together with Dimitrov, the Bulgarian Communist chief, he undertook to confederate all East-Central European states. Greece, where the Communists, supported from Yugoslavia and Bulgaria, sought to seize power by force of arms, was to be added to the new empire.[4] To Stalin, such a concentration of power in the hands of foreign Communists was anathema. To make things worse, Tito ejected the Soviet police agents planted in the Yugoslav apparatus. Stalin reacted with fury. He secured Yugoslavia's expulsion from the Cominform and sought to engineer an upheaval in the Yugoslav Party and put conventional Stalinists in control. But Tito was able to maintain himself by ac-

cepting help from the West. Yugoslavia, the erstwhile spearhead of
Communist militancy, quickly adopted a neutralist course in foreign policy, still maintaining a "socialist" orientation but supporting only the most moderate policies advocated by Moscow. The first
result of this startling reorientation was the collapse of the Communist forces in the Greek civil war. Deprived of Yugoslav support,
they had to give up the struggle in 1949.

IV

The initial stage of postwar political developments in East-Central
Europe, characterized by multiparty People's Democratic coalitions,
was liquidated in 1948-49. Communist intimidation and terror had
broken up the existing "bourgeois" parties, and the Social Democrats had been forced to merge with the Communists. In most cases,
the destruction of the multiparty system was a protracted, gradual
affair, characterized by what Hungary's Stalinist boss, Mátyás
Rákosi, called "salami tactics." In Czechoslovakia, however, the
change was effected in an abrupt and violent manner: a *coup d'état*
backed by armed factory guards imposed a Communist government
on February 25, 1948.[5]

Thus the stage was set for integral sovietization. This "second
revolution," to use Seton-Watson's term, followed identical lines
everywhere: the nationalization of all means of industrial production, the forced build-up of heavy industry, and the beginning collectivization of agriculture; terroristic regimentation of culture,
education, and public life; and a hard line in foreign policy, reflected in stepped-up defense programs. New constitutions adopted
throughout the region abolished political pluralism in all but name
and made the Communist-controlled form of People's Democracy
mandatory.

This virulent stage of sovietization caused enormous hardships
and stresses. Forced industrialization drew manpower away from
the countryside, and industrial workers were driven to exhaustion
by constantly raised work norms. Rising industrial output, however,
did not benefit the economy, because the biggest projects were
planned without regard for economic needs, available sources of
raw materials, or profitability. In the agricultural sector, the collectivization drives met with the peasants' determined passive re-

sistance, which was so strong that by 1956 the socialized sector ordinarily ranged between only one-fifth and one-third of the area under cultivation. In Poland, where the regime did not push collectivization, the percentage was below ten; only in Bulgaria did the Communists succeed in bringing the collective sector up to nearly 80 percent by this date.[6] In fact, the collectivization drives had to be kept within limits because contrary to all theory small peasant farms consistently turned out greater marketable surpluses than the large collective units. But even so, the countryside was not able to provide enough food for the increased urban populations.

These economic problems were particularly acute in Poland and Hungary, where the Communists undertook to create a huge heavy industry overnight. The Czechoslovak and East German economies were not overtaxed to the same extent, because a large base of heavy industry had already existed there before the Communists took over. But even in these highly developed parts of the bloc, Communist economic policies caused great dislocations and inflationary stresses.

The ordeal of sovietization was peculiarly aggravated by the fact that the onset of the "second revolution" (1948-49) coincided with the Yugoslav crisis. This conflict, besides exacerbating the cold war and stimulating inflated defense expenditures, split all Communist Parties down the middle. Suffering from severe psychopathological delusions, Stalin concluded that Tito was in league with the West and sought to destroy him. Every Communist who had been friendly with Tito or leaned toward his side in earlier debates automatically became an enemy, and a colossal purge of Titoist "traitors" got under way. In the Soviet Union, Zhdanov's "Leningrad circle" was doomed;[7] in the now-satellitized East European countries, the Stalinists started to liquidate "Titoist" deviants, notably including the former domestic underground. This campaign brought about the downfall of Gomulka in Poland, Rajk in Hungary, Kostov in Bulgaria, Patrascanu in Rumania, and innumerable lesser-known figures. Many were executed or sent to prisons and concentration camps on forged evidence and extorted confessions purporting to show that they were Western agents and spies. The purge was particularly fierce in Hungary, where the victims included not only the former underground cadres but former Social Democrats and Communist and fellow-traveling intellectuals with a Western background. This internecine warfare in the Party, which provided a lurid backdrop for the sovietization campaign, had critical political consequences in the sequel.

V

By early 1953, the satellite regimes' radical industrializing and collectivizing drives had led to a severe economic crisis over the entire region. Chronic shortages and inflationary stresses made it imperative to cut back sharply from the overambitious goals set for the satellites by the Stalinist leaders. Yet Marxist dogmatism, personified by Stalin, prevented any reconsideration and modification of policy: forced industrialization and collectivization was the only "correct" way to "build socialism," regardless of the consequences. Then, in March 1953, Stalin died.

Stalin's disappearance changed the course of bloc politics. Governmental power passed to a small group of oligarchs, Stalin's most powerful lieutenants, who were anxious to prevent any single member of their select company from eclipsing the rest and achieving one-man rule. Moreover, the successors had enough practical sense to recognize that the tempo of "building socialism" had to be reduced. The result was the proclamation by Moscow of a "New Course," stressing "coexistence," the relaxation of international tension, a retreat from unrealistic and overambitious economic goals, and the mitigation of terrorism.

In most of the satellite countries, the New Course was implemented without fanfare, but in East Germany and Hungary the incumbent Stalinist regimes were forced by Moscow to engage in public self-criticism, condemning their earlier radical course and announcing far-reaching changes. The East German regime demonstratively lifted a number of repressive measures that had been directed against the middle strata. In Hungary, the Stalinist boss Mátyás Rákosi was forced to abandon the premiership to Imre Nagy, known for his opposition to the collectivization of agriculture and to other harsh Stalinist policies. The result of this reshuffling was dual rule, for Rákosi remained leader of the Party.

The frank and abrupt introduction of the New Course in East Germany and Hungary had unexpected consequences. Seeing that the Communist leadership, discredited by its own admissions, made concessions to the middle strata while still insisting upon increased work norms, the workers rose in open revolt in Berlin and other centers (June 17, 1953). In Hungary, the peasants took the regime's self-criticism as a signal for a violent assault on collectivization. The East German revolt was put down by Soviet military force, and order was restored in Hungary by a mixture of repressive measures and concessions. But the Hungarian regime remained divided between Stalinists and moderates; the Party headed by Rákosi and the government led by Nagy were working at cross purposes.

This internal division was exacerbated by a policy that Moscow now strongly pushed, the rehabilitation of the victims of the Hungarian mass purges of 1949 and subsequent years. Official recognition that the entire purge had been based upon fictitious charges was a tremendous shock precisely to believers in the Communist ideology. Such admissions of error and mismanagement spread total disaffection among Communist intellectuals, who came to feel that Rákosi's continued presence at the head of the Party was morally intolerable. The opposition began a relentless campaign against the Stalinist Old Guard, denouncing its treachery against the Party and its alienation from the people. The writers succeeded in securing some public outlets for their charges, notably the *Literary Gazette,* the organ of the Communist Writers Union.

In other satellite countries, the New Course also led to ferment among Communist intellectuals, but where for one reason or another the purge could be kept quiet (that is, in East Germany, Czechoslovakia, Rumania, and Bulgaria), intellectual critique lacked a cutting edge. Outside Hungary, this issue produced a similar shock only in Poland. There, Moscow had not insisted upon rehabilitation, but the sordid truth about the framing of Gomulka and a host of other members of the home underground became known when revelations by a former high police official who had defected were broadcast from the West. In Poland, too, a campaign began within the Party to purify the regime and to remove the Old Guard. Radical opposition thus set Poland and Hungary apart from the rest of the bloc.

VI

The New Course came to an end both in Soviet Russia and in the satellite countries with the fall of Malenkov early in 1955; thereafter, the Communist regimes were engaged in tightening controls. But a new shock was not long in coming: in February 1956, in a closed session of the 20th Congress of the Soviet Communist Party, Khrushchev aired Stalin's crimes against the Party, and his revelations were soon made public by the U.S. State Department. In Poland and Hungary, the speech gave new impetus to the Party opposition, starting a chain of events that culminated in the revolutionary outbreaks of October 1956 in Warsaw and Budapest.

The two revolutions cannot be discussed here in detail; [8] in the present context, they serve to point up the new, post-Stalin differentiation within the Communist bloc. While earlier the Balkan regimes had broken Communist uniformity by following a militant "Left" course, after Stalin's death Poland and Hungary drifted away from the other satellites in the "Right" direction. This differentiation still persists, although after a brief flurry of independence in October 1956, both Poland and Hungary were brought back into line.

The Polish revolution was less radical than the Hungarian: in Hungary, popular passion swept away the Communist regime and forced the revolutionary government to denounce the Soviet alliance, whereas the Poles were content with reforming the regime and preferred to stay within the bloc as their mainstay against the German threat to their new western boundary. The Hungarian revolution was suppressed in blood, and Communist restoration followed under Kádár. In Poland, the internal reforms inaugurated in October were gradually whittled away. Eventually, basic political institutions both in Poland and in Hungary reverted to the standard totalitarian type. In fact, Hungary in one respect carried sovietization further since 1956 than the earlier Stalinist regime had been able to do: now all the land is collectivized. Yet, the two post-October regimes stand in a clear contrast to those which had had no October experience.

In what does this contrast consist? The basic institutions, as indicated, are similar everywhere, and the post-October regimes cultivate no deviant ideologies. On the other hand, the personal backgrounds of the leaders deviate markedly: both Gomulka and Kádár had been in prison during the Stalin era, while the other satellite leaders are former Stalinists. But this difference in background has scarcely any relevance today: former Stalinists and anti-Stalinists have found common ground in Khrushchev's de-Stalinization policy. What really differentiates the post-October regimes from the others is not so much the leaders' outlook and basic orientation as the Party's standing within, and relation to, society as a whole. In the satellite countries which had no October, the Party, never having been seriously challenged, can still pretend to speak for the entire community. There, the "building of socialism" and the "transition to Communism" are presented as concerns shared by the whole people, and dissent is treated as an antisocial phenomenon, while the post-October regimes cannot put forward such claims. As the theoretical organ of the Hungarian party put it in a discussion of the new Soviet Party program: "It must be admitted that our country stands at a lower stage of social evolution than the Soviet Union." [9] Since with the completion of Kádár's collectivization drive the Hungarian "social base" is about as "socialist" as in the rest of the bloc,[10] the social "backwardness" noted by the Party organ must be understood to relate to the "superstructure," or, in this instance, to a lag in popular thinking. What is meant is that the people are by and large indifferent to the cause of socialism. Before October, such a diagnosis could not have been made public without a call for strong remedies: the intensification of the class struggle, the eradication of the remnants of bourgeois thinking. But the post-October regime just notes widespread popular indifference as a fact, for the time being unalterable. The same is true of Poland, as indicated by the regime's cultural, religious, and agrarian policies. In both countries, dissent is ignored as much as possible, rather than being treated as an antisocial phenomenon calling for stern rebuke and suppression. Isolated within their societies, the post-October regimes know they must trim their sails in order to keep things under control. Thus they make no issue of widespread deviant attitudes, as long as these are not expressed in overtly defiant manner. In Soviet Russia and the other satellite countries, Communist controls are more relaxed than under Stalin, but they have a far wider scope than in the post-October regimes: the Party is less hesitant to set the line in politically sensitive cultural matters.

Another curious differentiation remains to be mentioned. Albania, the smallest and weakest satellite, is actively opposing the "coexistence" line standard in the European bloc, aligning herself with the militant Chinese position. It would be hard to explain this in terms of ideological preferences; Albania is not concerned with "building socialism" in the Chinese manner. Nor do the Albanian Communists have any stake in Chinese expansion *per se*. They do, however, feel threatened by their big neighbor, Yugoslavia, and this seems to be why they prefer a bloc policy that would, among other things, perpetuate the rift between Yugoslavia and the bloc. Behind Albania's condemnation of Yugoslav "revisionism," we may perceive a defensive reflex against Yugoslav expansionism.

VII

In this paper the varying patterns of sovietization in East-Central Europe have been analyzed primarily in terms of happenings within the ruling circles—policy decisions made in Moscow, compliance or noncompliance by local Party leaderships, conflicts and rivalries within Communist groups, and the like. This emphasis is not meant to imply that such other factors as cultural traditions, national cohesion and self-assertion, and popular resentment of Communist regimentation, had no significance. In fact, as we have seen, popular resistance to collectivization has been prolonged and effective. It is also noteworthy that the two "October" countries are the only ones in the area with a strongly anti-Russian national tradition. National self-assertion and security are the basic reasons for such developments as Tito's defiance of Stalin, Gomulka's success in keeping Poland within the bloc, and even Albania's pro-Chinese orientation. But the key to variations in Communist policy and in the degree of stability of the Communist regimes must be sought in the vicissitudes of the top Party layer. Had popular resentment been the dominant factor, we should have seen the most violent outbreaks around 1951-52, and this not only in Hungary and Poland but elsewhere, too. Actually, disturbances occurred only after controls were relaxed, and then mainly where the ruling group had become severely divided. Popular resentment broke through with elementary force once an opening was provided by division within the Party. Failing this, it remained contained. Czech, Rumanian, and Bulgarian quiescence after the 20th Congress, as contrasted with the Polish and Hungarian ferment, does not necessarily indicate a much higher degree of popular acceptance of Communism. Had a conflict within the leadership opened a crack in the protective wall of control, there would have been disturbances in those countries, too.

What does this imply for the future? Unity within the leadership remains a critical factor, and it is vital for the regimes within the Moscow orbit to close ranks against the Chinese heresy as long as the conflict between Peking and Moscow is not healed. Also, unity at the top will be endangered, with possible critical consequences for the stability of the Communist regimes, when the Soviet leader's position again falls vacant. Not that we can simply extrapolate from the succession crisis following Stalin's death: after Khrushchev, things will not look the same. Still, we can draw some tentative conclusions from the above analysis. A succession crisis involving mere personal rivalries need not undermine the stability of the Communist systems, but it would be different if the contenders were to invoke fundamental moral issues. In the past, terror was the most explosive moral issue, and this will not be relevant unless there is a resurgence of police terror. But less dramatic issues might also lead to deeply divisive splits.

In the satellite countries, political stability is guaranteed, first and foremost, by Soviet military power. The lesson of Hungary has sunk in: one cannot reckon with future attempts at self-liberation. But if the satellite governments are guaranteed by external pressure, it follows that they are isolated within their national communities, not only as an oppressive but also as an alien element. While the subject peoples cannot break loose from Soviet control by their own efforts, any internal weakening of the Soviet power system would release the centrifugal force of national self-assertion.

FOOTNOTES

[1] Occupation regimes were in charge in Bohemia-Moravia, Poland, Yugoslavia, and Albania; Hungary and Slovakia found themselves under illegitimate puppet (Quisling) regimes; Bulgaria and Rumania still had the monarchies that had joined the Axis early in the war. Austria (not to be discussed here) and East Germany, of course, formed part of the Nazi Reich itself.

[2] On "People's Democracy," see Hugh Seton-Watson, *The East European Revolution* (2d ed.; London: Methuen, 1952), pp. 167ff.; Zbigniew K. Brzezinski, *The Soviet Bloc, Unity and Conflict* (rev. ed.; New York: Praeger, 1961), pp. 45ff.

[3] Robert Bass and Elizabeth Marbury, eds., *The Soviet-Yugoslav Controversy, 1948-1958: A Documentary Record* (New York: Prospect Books, 1959).

[4] On the Balkan confederation scheme, see Boris Meissner,

Das Ostpaktsystem (Frankfurt a.M. and Berlin: Alfred Metzner Verlag, 1955), pp. 15ff.

[5] See Hubert Ripka, *Czechoslovakia Enslaved: The Story of the Communist Coup d'Etat* (London: Gollancz, 1950).

[6] For figures, see *Economic Survey of Europe in 1956* (Geneva: United Nations, 1957), ch. 1.

[7] Robert Conquest, *Power and Policy in the USSR* (New York: St. Martin's Press, 1961), pp. 95ff.

[8] On the Polish revolution, see Konrad Syrop, *Spring in October: The Polish Revolution of 1956* (New York: Praeger, 1958). The Hungarian revolution is analyzed in Ferenc A. Váli, *Rift and Revolt in Hungary* (Cambridge: Harvard University Press, 1961); Paul Kecskemeti, *The Unexpected Revolution* (Stanford: Stanford University Press, 1961); and Paul E. Zinner, *Revolution in Hungary* (New York: Columbia University Press, 1962).

[9] *Társadalmi Szemle,* January 1962, p. 8.

[10] Peter Kende in *Hungary Today,* by the editors of *Survey* (New York: Praeger, 1962), pp. 74ff.

Communist China–
The First Fourteen Years

Robert A. Scalapino

The People's Republic of China will shortly celebrate its four-
teenth anniversary. On October 1, 1949, in the shadow of Peking's
historic Imperial Palace, Mao Tse-tung formally inaugurated a new
national government and a radically new era. Ten days earlier, the
Communist-sponsored People's Political Consultative Council had
ratified the Common Program, the first blueprint for Communist
rule. For the Communists, these were both hectic and exhilarating
days. The hour of triumph had followed nearly thirty years of
struggle. The civil war was drawing to a close, with the Kuomintang
forces disastrously defeated and Chiang Kai-shek already brooding
in exile on Taiwan. Mao's New Democracy now dominated the land.
A small group of veteran Communist revolutionaries stood at the
apex of power, in supreme control over nearly 600 million Chinese,
one-fourth of the world's population. And how many of these 600
million could realize that they were about to experience the greatest
upheaval in the 4,000-year history of their civilization?

An accurate, balanced analysis of Communist China today is a
truly formidable task. In the first place, one must deal with a huge
and diverse society. In size and population, Communist China is
nearly one-half of Asia. Its people, who presumably number between 700 and 750 million at present, are spread over an area of
nearly 3,660,000 square miles. Within the boundaries of greater
China, moreover, exist a variety of subcultures, each containing elements of uniqueness that cannot be quickly or easily leveled, even
by Communism. Another problem lies in the fact that China is currently undergoing massive and extraordinarily rapid change. Nor is
the change always in a single and predictable direction. Lenin's
phrase, "Two steps forward, one step backward," captures in some
measure the Communist mode of operation, although it does not

suggest sufficiently the factors of confusion, experiment, and drastic alteration.

In broad terms, this is still the opening era of Chinese Communist rule, comparable in some respects to the Lenin and early Stalin periods in the Soviet Union. To obtain further perspective on China, therefore, let us recall briefly the remarkable succession of events that took place in the first fourteen years of Bolshevik rule. The opening phase of Soviet rule has been called the era of War Communism, a relatively short but very harsh and chaotic period, marked by bloodshed and bitterness. Civil war, property seizure ("land reform"), the liquidation of "class enemies," and mass suffering were prominent characteristics of this era. It was followed by a temporary retreat, the period of the New Economic Policy. NEP represented an effort to cover excesses, to restore morale and productivity. As one authority has phrased it, it was a period marked by "groping, experimentation, and a measure of freedom." [1]

In 1928 came the First Five-Year Plan, during which agrarian collectivization was advanced on a massive scale. Its speed and harshness led to intensive peasant resistance. On March 30, 1930, Stalin himself took account of the mounting costs. In a speech entitled "Dizzy from Success," he ordered a relaxation, another temporary retreat. The bad harvests of 1931 and 1932, however, combined with the sabotage, killings, and general chaos in rural Russia to produce a major crisis. By 1933, a large area had been affected by famine and destruction. Yet industrialization continued to advance at a rapid pace. The Soviet Union had now entered its Second Five-Year Plan, and the foundations of heavy industry were being swiftly constructed. Whatever the cost and the mistakes, Soviet pioneering in state planning and mass mobilization for purposes of modernizing created a deep and lasting impact upon those people of the "backward" world who yearned to catch up, who dreamed of a one-generation industrial revolution.

It is not necessary at this point to indicate the precise parallels between Soviet and Chinese experience, or to suggest the differences. It is sufficient to assert that in both cases, the opening years of Communist rule were characterized by a series of sharp thrusts that penetrated to the very core of the social structure, followed by periods of regrouping and consolidation. In some degree, no doubt, this is the essence of war and revolution in any form. Under such conditions, however, analysis and prediction are rendered especially hazardous.

There is one final problem involved in an analysis of contemporary China that should be mentioned. One is confronted with a paucity, sometimes total absence, of reliable information on matters of supreme importance. The Western observer must often grope his way along, with minimal statistics and a series of "eye-witness" accounts that are wildly contradictory. Even the Chinese Communist leaders themselves have not always been accurately informed about conditions in their society. It is now abundantly clear that with respect to agrarian production, for example, they were badly misled for a time by cadres anxious to please and fearful of missing assigned quotas. No one can know all of the "facts" about China today, not even those men at the summit of power. Thus, most statements about Communist China must be advanced as tentative hypotheses susceptible to correction and change.

II

The broad strategy of Chinese Communism can best be introduced by quoting one oft-repeated sentence of the Chinese Communists themselves: "Under the correct leadership of Chairman Mao, the universal truths of Marxism-Leninism have been integrated with the particular requirements and capacities of Chinese society." [2] In these few words is contained the essence of Chinese Communist thought and practice. In them, one can sense the mixture of faith and science, dogmatism and pragmatism, uniformity and deviation, internationalism and nationalism, that are involved in this fantastic new era.

On the one hand, the Communist leaders are "true believers," men who take doctrine seriously and who have sacrificed much for their beliefs. These are first-generation revolutionists who have fought for a lifetime on behalf of a cause to which they are totally devoted, gun in one hand, Marxian scriptures in the other. They have discovered ultimate truth and consequently, they have the same fundamental self-assurance, proselytizing zeal, and fixation toward ends that mark all men who have been fully converted to a cause. But by the same measure, these leaders are practicing revolutionaries who by a painful process of trial and error are continuously discovering what will work in China and what will not. They have succeeded—indeed they are alive—only because they are pragmatists, because they have been able to adjust to the necessities of their situation, often by means of dramatic policy shifts. Moreover, these men are *Chinese,* and as such, men who have a deep cultural and political bias in favor of their own society. There is no way in which to make the two broad forces described above compatible. One must simply recognize their coexistence within the Chinese Communist movement, and seek to discern the balance that prevails between them at any given moment on any particular issue.

III

It is appropriate to look first at the Chinese economy under Communism, and initially at agriculture. The Chinese Communists claim to have come to power because of their ability to understand the peasant, and to mobilize him effectively on behalf of revolution. Communism in China, as in much of the world, has had an intellectual head and a peasant body. With over 80 percent of the Chinese people living in rural areas before 1949, and the great bulk of these belonging to the peasant class, it is not surprising that men like Liu Shao-ch'i would call the peasant question "the central question in our democratic revolution." [3]

After the Kuomintang-Communist coalition broke apart in 1927, the Communist Party was forced to retreat from the urban centers into the hills of Kiangsi. For the next two decades, first in the South and then in the North, the Communists operated from rural bases, almost totally separated from urban industrial life. It was under these circumstances that the Maoist strategy of encircling the cities was born. Peasants had to be mobilized; manpower and material supplies had to be acquired for Party use; rural bases had to be made as self-sufficient as possible. For these purposes, both terror and persuasion were employed, and the sources of persuasion were various promises of economic betterment and nationalist appeal. Initial Communist policy and techniques had already been firmly established long before the Communists came to full power in 1949.

In their hour of final victory, the Communists employed the famous Leninist cry, "Land, Bread, Peace," with minor variations. They played first upon the fervent desire of the Chinese people for an end to war, both international and civil. They also promised relief from the rampant inflation and other economic burdens that were weighing heavily upon all people, but especially the urban residents. For the peasant, their primary slogan was "land reform." During the Anti-Japanese Patriotic War, the Communists had generally followed a moderate policy, concentrating upon rent and interest reduction rather than land confiscation, in order to induce maximum unity. Now they returned to their historic demand, "land to the tillers."

The agrarian policy of the Chinese Communists after 1949 can be divided into three major phases: the era of "land reform," which was consummated between 1949 and 1952; the era of "advanced agricultural cooperatives," which reached its climax in the winter of 1955-56; and the era of the communes, which was launched with extraordinary intensity during the latter part of 1958. Each of these eras deserves some attention.

During the three years up to 1952, a managed and far-reaching agrarian revolution was conducted throughout the whole of China. According to Communist authorities, some 47 million hectares of arable land were taken from landlords and "rich" peasants, and redistributed among 300 million peasants who had previously owned little or no land.[4] In this era, the Communist leaders were determined to level the rural gentry, to remove the "feudalist" element, regarded as impossible to reform and dangerous in its effect upon the masses, an obstacle blocking contact between the regime and the peasant.

The revolutionary government thus sponsored open-air accusation meetings in every area, involving millions of peasants. In these meetings, landlords' crimes were recited and punishments assessed. This constituted the most bloody, ruthless phase of the revolution. The exact number killed may never be known, although the Communists themselves talked about liquidating over a million "reactionaries," "criminals," and "Kuomintang agents." The widespread use of terrorism served both to level the gentry and to commit, in some fashion, the peasantry. Once one had accused one's former landlord or neighbor of crimes, and obtained some of his possessions, one's ties were with the future, not the past.

Land redistribution was regarded as a step necessary to complete the "bourgeois-democratic" revolution, but Communist leaders had always seen this measure as a purely transitional phase. On two counts, "land reform" could not be allowed to remain in effect:

according to Communist theory, the small peasant economy could never be as efficient as a system of collectivized agriculture; moreover, private ownership, long continued, would lead to capitalism. Thus, in agriculture as elsewhere, the Communists thought in terms of a continuous revolution. The transition to socialism was to begin immediately upon completion of the bourgeois stage. Indeed, argued the Communists, if the proletariat seized power in the course of the bourgeois revolution, as in China, it would thereby be able to control its final stages and bring about a smooth transition to socialism.[5]

In accordance with this theory, a second phase of Chinese agrarian transformation under Communism began after 1952, reaching its climax in 1955-56. "Advanced agricultural cooperatives" were established, involving the common ownership of all means of production, including land, draft animals, and farm implements. By the spring of 1958, some 740,000 such cooperatives existed throughout China, with an average membership of 160 families.[6] Certain intermediate stages had preceded the advanced cooperative. The most rudimentary form of collectivization had been the mutual-aid team, developed during the period of land reform. These teams, both of a seasonal and of a year-round type, had been created for the purpose of assisting in production, but the principle of private ownership had been maintained intact.

The next stage in the Communist timetable of collectivization was the "semisocialist cooperative." Land was pooled and a "unified management" established, with extensive state control over production and marketing. Moreover, the harvest was now distributed in accordance with the work credit given each peasant, not on the basis of land ownership. In theory, however, the land remained privately owned, and some private production was allowed. It was a relatively short step to the "advanced cooperatives" noted above. Within five years or less, millions of Chinese peasants had had land given to them and then taken away from them as a part of the march toward socialism.

The third significant era in the Communist agrarian revolution began in 1958 with the establishment of the communes. In April 1958, the first commune—with the significant name of Sputnik—was created in Suiping County, Honan Province. Within a few months, the whole of rural China had been communized. Ultimately, some 24,000 communes were developed, containing an average of about

5,000 families, or between 25,000 and 30,000 individuals. What were the nature and the purpose of the communes? In the words of the Communists themselves, the commune was intended to be "a basic unit of society" with the responsibility of managing all industrial and agricultural production, conducting its own trade, cultural, and educational work, running its own local political affairs, and developing its own defense force in the People's Militia.[7] Mao himself is given credit for suggesting the name "commune," and for suggesting the functions of the new administrative unit; in his discussions with peasant leaders during the summer of 1958 he is supposed to have urged the creation of a more comprehensive organization than the state farms, one that would encompass industry and trade as well as agriculture.

The Communists have insisted that the commune movement developed spontaneously, as a product of peasant demands. In reality, of course, the movement was state-sponsored and directed, although it is possible that once the word had been received, it was pushed by zealous cadres at a more rapid rate than Peking had anticipated. The fundamental purposes of the communes were these: the maximum utilization of peasant manpower, under a system that would ensure full-time labor for both men and women; the development of rural industry, operating with a low capital input, with the objective of moving toward rural self-sufficiency; optimum efficiency in the distribution of foodstuffs and other necessities, together with the prevention of hoarding, thereby ensuring the state the largest possible revenue; and large-scale farming on a basis that would encourage more rapid mechanization and the development of "scientific agriculture."

This was the "big leap forward." In the spring of 1958, a decision was made to launch an economic forced march that would dwarf earlier efforts. The campaign banners bore the inscription, "going all out, aiming high and achieving greater, faster, better and more economical results to build socialism." The main theme was the simultaneous development of industry and agriculture, or in the picturesque Chinese vernacular, "walking on two legs." There is ample evidence that the Politburo approved this policy only after heated debate. Numerous references were subsequently made to "Right-wing opportunists" who doubted the economic validity or political soundness of the new program, some of them quite possibly from as far west as Moscow.

The big leap forward was undoubtedly the product of both problems and progress. China's leaders recognized that agriculture was the key to rapid industrialization, and agrarian productivity was lagging in comparison with industrial gains. The peasant had to be driven harder if the industrial process was to be speeded up. Moreover, the full range of techniques had to be employed, "indigenous" as well as modern, both in industry and in agriculture, and the masses had to be more fully committed to industrialization. At the same time, however, the new forced march was conceived during a period of considerable optimism on the part of the hierarchy. Production in heavy industry, as we shall later note, had been encouraging. And in 1958, the harvest was exceedingly good, with almost ideal weather conditions prevailing.

Originally, the government claimed that 375 million metric tons of grain (including potatoes and yams) were produced in 1958, a fantastic gain over the 185 million tons claimed for 1957. The quota for 1959 was set at 500 million tons. Then came a shock. Confronted with evidence of gross exaggeration by local and provincial authorities, the central government was forced to scale down the 1958 figures to 250 million tons. Even this figure was probably too high, although the 1958 harvest was good. Agrarian production after 1958 was quite insufficient to sustain the tempo of industrialization projected by Peking. Indeed, even the minimal consumption needs of an expanding population could not be satisfied. A grave food shortage developed, jeopardizing both the economic and the political programs of the regime. By 1962, drastic alterations in economic planning and organization had been effected. Some observers asserted that the big leap forward had become the big retreat.

How serious was the problem and what were its causes? As of early 1963, no basic agrarian statistics have been published by the Communists since their famous "revised figures" of August 1959. Peking has merely stated that conditions in 1961 were "slightly better" than previously, and that 1962 also represented a "slight improvement" over the preceding year.[8] The best estimates would appear to be as follows: as of 1963, the worst of the food crisis is over and conditions, while by no means good, have improved. Possibly the 1961 yield was 165 million tons and that of 1962 about 180 million tons, some 10 to 20 percent above the figure of the previous year. If these figures are correct, the 1962 crops would be approximately equal to the 185 million tons supposedly produced in 1957. But meantime, by how many millions has the population increased? As is well known, the Communist government was forced to import large quantities of grain from Canada, Australia, and other non-Communist countries in 1961-62, and these imports are continuing. It would appear, however, that the downward agrarian spiral has been halted at least temporarily.

No one should underestimate the ordeal through which millions of Chinese have recently passed. The combination of excessive labor and meager rations became almost unbearable. During the long period of acute food shortage, the average official ration was just over one pound of food per day, sometimes less. Only a few special groups such as miners and soldiers obtained more. Caloric and vitamin intake naturally varied greatly, depending upon both the amount and type of food, but one independent source has estimated that the average 1962 diet represented no more than 1700 calories a day, with some regions unable to achieve even that average.[9] Generally, a minimum of 2,000 calories per day has been considered necessary over a protracted period to maintain good health. While conditions varied considerably from region to region, it seems reasonably clear that this minimal requirement was not met for many millions of people.

The less fortunate had to supplement their diet with grass and other "natural foods" that could be rendered edible. The most fortunate individuals received food parcels from relatives living abroad. From Hong Kong alone, more than one million parcels a month flowed in during 1961-62. The cloth ration also was extremely scanty: four and one-half feet per person per year, and cloth coupons had to be used for the purchase of shoes as well.

The common story of recent refugees has been that of a gray, grim life filled with hardship and toil. In 1962, an estimated 140,000 additional refugees flooded into Hong Kong, more than half of them coming during a brief period in May when the Communists allowed relatively free exit. These refugees were overwhelmingly "economic" rather than "political" in motivation. For the most part, they were simple peasants, fishermen, or urban residents who had been ordered to the communes for farm labor. They were fleeing a life of scarcity. Their concern was with food and clothing, not Marxism-Leninism or "political freedom." [10]

At the same time, it should be emphasized that there has been no evidence of large-scale famine in China. The Communists enforced a rough equity of distribution through a strict rationing system, although differences existed both because of local food conditions and because rations were adjusted in accordance with occupation in some cases. Nevertheless, the general picture has been one of "shared meagerness" rather than the pools of starvation and plenitude that have often characterized China in the past. Moreover, whenever possible, medical attention has been given to those suffering most seriously from malnutrition and special care has been directed toward children. Sanitation and health, it might be noted, have been given heavy stress by the Chinese Communists since 1949, following lines pioneered by the Soviet Union. The anti-fly and rat campaigns were intensive and sustained; vaccines and other prophylactics have been developed on a large scale; calisthenics have been made a regular part of the daily regimen. (How can one perform effectively on behalf of the state if one is not healthy in body and in mind, the Communists demand.) In many respects, Communist China has represented the same spartan, puritan qualities associated with many revolutionary societies in their earliest phases—qualities, it might be added, that have been severely strained since 1959 because of the growing economic crisis.

Ultimately, Peking had to probe the causes for this crisis and undertake corrective measures. Initially, Party leaders placed the blame almost exclusively on the weather. Adverse weather conditions, they exclaimed, affected some 40 million hectares of productive land in 1959, 60 million hectares in 1960, and in 1961 an even greater acreage. Weather did help reduce recent harvests, but the Communists themselves have now admitted the existence of other vitally significant factors. During 1960-61, the central government conducted a series of intensive field investigations, sending some of its leading representatives into the rural areas. Among other things, they reported that with incentives minimal and pressures exceptionally high, peasant resentment had swiftly mounted, much of it directed against the local cadres.

These cadres (the Chinese term *kanpu* means literally to get things done) have served as the vital instruments of the Party at local levels, charged with implementing and developing the basic directives issued in Peking. It is natural that resentment would be directed against them in many cases, because they have represented the most important locus of immediate authority. The commune system involved a substantial amount of local autonomy with respect to such matters as the allocation of available resources. Quite literally, the average peasant's fate was in the hands of the cadres and local Party officials: his rations, his work schedule, his entire pattern of living.

In line with Peking directives and in their desire to please superiors, the cadres in many communes set a pace impossible to sustain. At the height of the big leap, many individuals were working fourteen to sixteen hours a day in field or shop and, in addition, being forced to drill in the people's militia and attend innumerable discussion groups and mass meetings. Unreasonable production quotas were assigned, and when it was duly reported that these quotas had been overfulfilled, the central government, bursting with pride, sent out higher quotas.

Meanwhile, all incentives had been taken away from the peasant. No significant private plot or personal livestock was left him. He did not even work the same parcel of land continuously, and hence he had no opportunity to know its special qualities or benefit from any intensive efforts that he might devote to it. He was an anonymous part of a large production brigade and anything gained was shared with thousands of others. Thus morale and efficiency declined. Intensive labor combined with inadequate food cannot long be sustained. Weariness, hunger, and apathy spread over the land.

Fundamentally, the agrarian crisis was caused by the attempt to drive the peasant too hard and too fast while at the same time taking from him both incentives and sustenance. And these errors were implicit in the overambitious plans that emanated from Peking. In the final analysis, the top Communist leadership, not "overzealous cadres," had to assume basic responsibility. For a time after 1957, the Communist leaders believed that China could accomplish a massive one-generation thrust toward modernity that would encompass the entire economy. In fifteen years, China would surpass British steel production and concurrently double or treble agrarian production. The overriding principle was the simultaneous development of industry and agriculture, walking on two feet. But China lacked the necessary skills, developed resources, and mechanization to accomplish this goal at the rate projected. A retreat became imperative.

The new slogan is "All for Agriculture." [11] By 1962, the central government had executed a number of basic changes designed to raise agrarian productivity. In the first place, drastic alterations

have been made in the commune system. The planning and allocation of resources have been centralized again; local autonomy has
been sharply curtailed. An attempt is under way to eliminate the
irregularities, waste, and "mismanagement" involved in commune
administration, to patrol more closely the cadres and local party
leaders. At the same time, smaller working-level units have been
given greater importance and a number of incentives have been
built back into the agrarian economy. Today the emphasis is upon
the production team rather than the production brigade or total
commune. The teams, composed of twenty-five to thirty individuals,
now benefit when their group production rises; they do not have to
share all gains with the entire commune. Moreover, they are assigned land on a quasipermanent basis, enabling them to become
familiar with "their" land and benefit from continuous labor upon
it. Even more important, each family has been assigned a small
private plot of land and the right to keep some poultry and livestock. Once again, private produce can be sold on the "free market"
for extra income.

In addition, the tempo has been cut, some of the pressure reduced. Cadres are being exhorted to avoid "commandism," to give
special heed to the voice of "the wise, experienced farmer." There
has been a reduction in the hours of work, a sharp curtailing of compulsory meetings, and in general, a more normal pace of life. The
regime has promised to pay increased attention to necessary consumer goods. It has recognized that the peasant can only sacrifice so
much for rapid industrialization, and that his limits were exceeded
during the frenzied era after 1958. It has seemingly accepted the
fact that the modernization process must be spread over a longer
period of time than was earlier envisaged.

Thus, basic reforms have also been necessary with respect to the
commitment of capital, resources, and manpower. The changes were
publicly signaled by Premier Chou En-lai in his speech before the
National People's Congress in April 1962.[12] Chou presented a ten-
point economic program that strongly emphasized measures to
raise agrarian productivity and to meet some of the immediate,
minimal needs of the people. Industry has been informed that for
the present, it must get along with what it has in the way of
machinery, manpower, and materials—or operate with less. Excep-
tions are made for those industries engaged in production for
agrarian use. Heavy emphasis is being put upon increasing the pro-

duction of chemical fertilizers, farm machinery, and irrigation equipment.

Since 1961, at least 20 million workers have been returned from urban areas to the countryside, and more are being sent. All segments of Chinese society, including the young educated class, are being urged to participate in farm work. Scientific institutes are being assigned such tasks as improving seed strains and developing new insecticides. Handicraft cooperatives and artisans, according to Communist authorities, produced more than 500 million small farm tools in the first ten months of 1962. Meanwhile, the 1962 target for chemical fertilizers was declared to have been surpassed, with 50 percent more fertilizer produced than in 1961. In line with the campaign for maximum self-sufficiency, the steel industry reportedly is now able to produce all but 30 of the 450 parts involved in the production of medium-sized tractors.[13] Reclamation and irrigation work, as well as rural electrification, are being strongly pushed.

At this stage, it is impossible to predict the success of the present drive to modernize and improve the agrarian sector of the economy. On the one hand, rural collectivization has yet to prove itself an efficient operation in any Communist society. Indeed, as Nikita Khrushchev can ruefully testify, agriculture continues to be a severe drag upon the economy of "the most advanced socialist state," after nearly half a century of Communist rule. The problems of Chinese agriculture, moreover, are exceptionally difficult. Nowhere in the world does the combination of numbers, minimal living standards, and backward technology constitute such an adverse starting point as in China. On the other hand, if the Communist leaders do make major commitments of capital, resources, and manpower to agriculture, and if they are able to win, or regain, sufficient peasant support, substantial gains in productivity are by no means impossible. Modern Japan has indicated what a combination of "scientific agriculture" and incentives to the peasantry can do in raising productivity. The question is whether agriculture under a Communist system can emulate those gains. The fate of the Communists in China probably hinges upon the answer.

IV

In his report on the occasion of the tenth anniversary of the Chinese People's Republic, Chou En-lai claimed that from 1949 to 1959

Chinese industrial production had increased 11.7 times. In the earlier year, moreover, industrial output represented only 30 percent of the gross national product, compared with 63.6 percent a decade later. It is advantageous, of course, to use the period around 1949 for comparative purposes, because at that time, China was wracked with rampant inflation, civil war, and massive dislocations. Nevertheless, it cannot be doubted that in their first decade, the Chinese Communists scored some impressive results in the drive for industrialization, especially in the field of heavy industry.

Premier Chou claimed in his 1959 report that in the nine years between 1950 and 1958, Chinese industrial production had risen at an average annual rate of 28 percent. At the end of that period, according to his figures, China had moved from 26th to 7th place in steel production, from 9th to 3d place in coal production, from 25th to 11th place in the production of electric power, and from 5th to 2d place in cotton-yarn production.[14] On the basis of these gains, fantastic targets were projected for the opening years of the big leap.

The history of industrialization under the Communists can be divided roughly into three phases: the era of economic rehabilitation, the era of the First Five-Year Plan, and the era of the big leap and its immediate aftermath. In the first era, which lasted approximately three years, emphasis was placed upon restoring production. Order was reestablished. Inflation was swiftly brought under control, and rigorous measures were taken against those engaged in black-market activities or other illegal operations. The enterprises owned by "bureaucrat-bourgeois" elements (many of whom had fled) were confiscated. Private enterprise, however, continued to exist, albeit under increasing supervision and control. Appeals were made to the entrepreneurial class to cooperate in the liquidation of capitalism, with the promise that those who demonstrated their loyalty would be converted into managers of state property. Both carrot and stick were extended to the "national bourgeoisie" from the outset of the People's Republic.

In the course of the First Five-Year Plan, the socialist transformation of Chinese industry was accomplished. By 1959, 87.9 percent of state revenues came from the state-owned sector of the economy, 11.3 percent from the rural communes, and only 0.8 percent from private sources.[15] Initially, control over industry was established by state allocation of raw materials, supervision of the labor market, and strict control over sales and marketing. Gradually, industries were converted into so-called "joint state-private enterprises." By 1956, all major industries had been socialized by this method, or by outright state ownership. Capitalists participating in joint enterprises receive a fixed rate of interest on their shares as compensation.

Thus was the Maoist principle of simultaneously uniting with and struggling against the national bourgeoisie applied. Those entrepreneurs who dedicated themselves to cooperation with the New Democracy remained in many cases as managers or officials in their state-controlled plant. The Communists needed their technical knowledge and administrative experience. At the same time, by means of such drives as the *wu fan* (Five Anti) movement, industrialists or businessmen involved in "economic crimes against the state" were severely punished. Political thoughts also had to be carefully patrolled. No class was put under closer surveillance than the commercial-industrial class. A person of bourgeois background cannot join the Communist Party. In sum, he is a man always on parole.

From all indications, the First Five-Year Plan, which began in 1953 and ended in 1957, was a marked success in quantitative terms. Industrial productivity in these five years increased at an average annual rate of 18 percent, with heavy industry averaging an increase of 25.4 percent.[16] Clearly, the Chinese Communists are indebted to the Soviet Union for substantial assistance in this era. While Russian aid was not massive (possibly no more than 3 percent of total capital investment) and not free (almost all aid was in the form of low-interest loans), that assistance was concentrated mainly upon the large-scale projects that formed the backbone of Chinese industrialization. Moreover, it is impossible to measure in monetary terms the value of such aid as the training of scientists and technicians, the presentation of blueprints, and the loan of experienced personnel. The Chinese Communists also made effective use of confiscated capital, and the talents of those who had been trained in the West.

Then came the Second Five-Year Plan, and the era of the big leap and the simultaneous development of industry and agriculture. Mao himself is given credit for having initiated the idea of accelerating the pace of development. In the winter of 1955, he supposedly put forth the slogan "achieving greater, faster, better and more economical results in developing socialist construction," which, as noted earlier, became the chief slogan of the big-leap era.[17] What were the basic principles the Peking authorities sought to apply to industrialization in this period? First, priority to heavy industry was to continue since this was regarded as the necessary foundation for any industrialization program (and a requirement for state power). Both modern and indigenous methods of production were to be employed, however, and encouragement was to be given to small and medium as well as large-scale enterprise. With limited capital and technology, China could develop rapidly only if it made maximum use of its built-in resources, and harnessed all possible manpower and methods to the task. Thus commune-based industry was powerfully appealing. It promised to provide the countryside with a new degree of self-sufficiency and to involve the great peasant masses in the industrial process, gradually moving them forward, and with minimal capital outlay involved. The so-called "backyard hearth furnaces" were based upon the same principles. To the Communists, these tactics had proved successful not only in Japan but in their own past—in the period when they were almost wholly dependent upon remote rural bases.

The initial year of the big leap was 1958. In that one year, according to Chinese authorities, overall industrial production increased by 66 percent, with heavy industry scoring a gain of 103 percent and light industry increasing by 34 percent. Nonagricultural employment reportedly went from 40.9 to 58.3 million in a single year.[18] Even if these statistics are inaccurate, there can be little doubt that this incredible year witnessed one of the most massive thrusts ever attempted by any regime seeking rapid development. The dislocations produced in the economy by such an extraordinary drive can be imagined. In the headlong quest for quantity, quality was given scant heed. Transport and raw-material bottlenecks were often critical, and much waste occurred; products deteriorated awaiting shipment or completion, and half-finished factories stood idle. Machinery was overused or mistreated by workers not yet skilled, and the paucity of spare parts became a most serious problem. Then came two added blows: adverse weather conditions and increasingly strained relations with the Soviet Union.

The latter problem had a direct bearing upon China's economic crisis. The Soviet Union, clearly disapproving of the big leap and the communes, and involved in an acrimonious dispute with China over basic policies, began to apply economic sanctions as early as 1958. Some two thousand Soviet technicians were abruptly withdrawn, all forms of assistance were sharply curtailed, and the volume of Sino-Soviet trade declined. Perhaps the Soviet Union bears a greater responsibility for the ensuing crisis than has been commonly recognized, although the decisions that precipitated trouble both with Russia and in the economy were made in Peking. Certainly, it is significant that from this period Chinese leaders repeatedly asserted that modernization through one's own efforts is both necessary and possible. But self-sufficiency put additional strains upon a society already strained to the breaking-point.

At last a retreat was signaled. Officially, the three Red Banners are still in effect: socialist construction, the big leap forward, and the people's communes continue to be proclaimed as the basic goals of the People's Republic of China. As noted earlier, however, each of these goals has undergone substantial alteration since 1961. An industrial retrenchment has accompanied the greater emphasis upon agriculture. According to reports, in such areas as Shanghai, Canton, and the general Kwangtung area, industrial production has been cut back as much as 20 to 30 percent.[19] The great Anshan steel complex supposedly has been operating at only about half its capacity. It is significant that the government has not released any figures on industrial production recently, and that there has been no announcement of a Third Five-Year Plan some months after the supposed conclusion of the Second Plan.

As previously mentioned, only in those segments of industry directly related to agrarian productivity or vital consumer goods, is there a full commitment of resources. The urban unemployed have been shifted in huge numbers to the countryside. Officially, this is the era of "readjustment, consolidation, filling out, and raising standards." In more direct language, it is a period when the Chinese leaders are seeking to correct the excesses and mistakes of recent years, returning to a more rational allocation of available resources. The commitment to rapid industrialization remains, and the Peking leaders fully expect to resume their march after a few years. How long will it take to restore confidence in the economic policies of the present leadership, to rebuild morale at the all-important cadre and managerial levels, and to realize the present thesis of "developing the national economy with agriculture as *the foundation* and industry as the leading factor"?

Because there has been real concern on the part of China's leaders about the declining morale, it is not surprising that the pendulum has swung, temporarily at least, to the side of conciliation and concession. The slogan "Politics in command," pushed so forcefully in the mid-1950's, has undergone some alteration. In the continuing battle over whether it is more important to be Expert or to be Red, expertise is once again given heavy emphasis. The peasants were not alone in obtaining certain concessions during the recent era of hardship in an attempt to mollify public opinion. Toward such important groups as the entrepreneurs and intellectuals, the government once more has proffered its "encouragement and support." An extension of interest payments to ex-capitalists for three more years was announced in 1962. Again, an appeal has been made for free speech and candid criticism. The policy of "letting a hundred flowers blossom and a hundred schools of thought contend" has been echoed. With the "Rightist" purges of 1957 which followed the first hundred-flowers era still fresh in their memory, however, the intellectuals and other "bourgeois" elements are not likely to become too adventurous.

V

In surveying the Chinese economy under Communism, we should include a final word about foreign trade. According to available data, the "three bad years" (1959-61) have resulted in a decline in total Chinese foreign trade and an important change in its composition.[20] In the mid-1950's, as much as 70 percent of China's foreign trade was conducted within the Communist bloc, mainly with the Soviet Union. Since that time, trade has been increasingly with non-Communist countries. Sino-Soviet trade may have been cut by as much as half, with the drastic decline taking place from 1960 to the present. It has been estimated that 20 percent of current imports from the Soviet Union are essential military items and another 33 percent are petroleum and petroleum products; perhaps 25 percent is local trade between border areas, with the remainder in such items as machine parts and lubricating oils.[21] It is clear that currently China is exporting more to the Soviet Union than she is importing from it. In 1962, the export surplus may have been as high as $200 million, as the Chinese reduced debts earlier contracted to Russia.

Petroleum imports from the Soviet Union continue to be critical to the Chinese economy, and would be even more important, of course, in the event of any prolonged war. Currently, the Russians furnish China with about 40 percent of her oil. But the Soviet Union has not been able (or willing) to make up Chinese grain deficiencies, so that China turned to Canada, Australia, and other non-Communist countries. As long as China needs food—and presumably as long as her relations with the Soviet Union are strained —economic rather than ideological considerations are likely to dominate trade patterns despite the difficulties of shifting trade as long as the West retains its ban on the sale of strategic goods. Even so, China has increased its machinery purchases from such countries as Great Britain and West Germany (ordering jet transport aircraft from the former), and has recently signed a five-year trade agreement with Japan providing for expanded commercial relations. The extension of such trade is likely to be difficult because of the shortage of hard currencies and internal production problems, but the new trend has already attracted widespread attention throughout the commercial world.

VI

The current retreat is indicated by more than the new economic policies. It has influenced such diverse factors as population theories and higher education. The Chinese Communist attitude toward birth control has undergone several shifts in the past fourteen years.[22] Initially, the Communists took the orthodox Marxian position that a dynamic socialist society could absorb an infinity of people and hence they showed no interest in population control. In the mid-1950's, however, the Party, presumably alarmed by the results of the 1953 census and current rates of population growth (2.2 to 2.4 percent?), sponsored an active birth-control program. Clinics were opened; posters and other means of propaganda employed. Then came the big leap and, in another mood of wild optimism, the Chinese leaders concluded that their real problem was a shortage of manpower and that productivity could easily race ahead of births. The lean years that followed 1958, however, have caused another policy reversal. By press, radio, and other means, the government is again urging the people to postpone marriage and use various forms of abstinence and control, so as to "preserve their health," "advance their studies," and "improve their efficiency." That a socialist society cannot cope with an expanding population is not admitted, but there can be little question about the objectives now being sought.

Will this campaign succeed? It is probable that the recent years of hardship have reduced the birth rate, quite apart from government policy. Nevertheless, the population of Communist China may be over 700 million, the figure that some Chinese authorities are now using. Unchecked, it could easily reach one billion by 1980. Under those conditions, however successful the modernization campaign, relief from the grinding poverty that is the lot of the common man would be slight. Population is thus one of the most crucial determinants of China's future, a problem that the Communists, despite their Marxist training, have had to half-recognize.

Educational policy has also been affected by the retrenchment.[23] The number of students allowed to enter high schools and universities in 1962 was reportedly 20 percent below the 1961 figure and 40 percent below that for 1960. If these reports are correct, enrollments are once again close to those in 1958 in spite of the increase in school-age population. The Communists have admitted that the big leap forward produced grave deficiencies in educational quality: teachers, texts, laboratories, and all other facilities were grossly inadequate. For the present the emphasis is upon quality in higher education and there is some indication that the time allotted for politics and political indoctrination has been reduced. The stress upon vocational, technical, and scientific training continues, in the hope of turning out large numbers of agronomists, engineers, physicians, and scientists of all types during the next decade. Students turned away from institutions of higher learning are told to swallow their disappointment and take up productive work in agriculture at once. Some Chinese "peasants" are frustrated would-be scholars —but this, of course, has been true since the enthronement of the scholar-bureaucratic class at the beginning of the Confucian era.

VII

The political-military aspects of Communist China are at least as complex and as susceptible to change as the socio-economic factors. Once again, hard data are scarce, and most concepts must be advanced as tentative hypotheses. China is governed today by a small group of veteran Communists, most of whom have fought and worked together for more than thirty years. As in all Communist societies, the men holding supreme power are those occupying positions in the Political Bureau of the Communist Party. The top seven leaders are unquestionably those who serve on the Standing Committee of this Politburo: Mao Tse-tung, Liu Shao-ch'i, Chou En-lai, Chu Te, Ch'en Yun, Lin Piao, and Teng Hsiao-p'ing. These are the men who make the basic decisions determining the destinies of one-quarter of the human race.

How should we characterize them? Generally speaking, they derive not from the proletariat but from what might loosely be called the middle class. They are predominantly intellectuals, but somewhat parochial intellectuals who gained most of their knowledge and experience within China. Not one of them has spent any substantial time in the West in recent years; few of them have been in the West at all. Occupationally, they are practicing revolutionaries who fought on the barricades (more accurately, in the hills) for nearly three decades. Until the end of their lives, they will speak and think largely in military terms. These are first-generation Communists.

From every indication, Mao Tse-tung, now nearing seventy years of age, occupies an unassailable position within the Party. Mao's supremacy dates from 1935-36, but the Communist victory in 1949 strengthened his position in a variety of ways. A cult of personality is so useful to a new nation or a new era that it can scarcely be avoided. Clearly, it has prevailed in the Chinese People's Republic. Mao is hailed as father of the nation, foremost Marxist-Leninist theorist, and beacon-light for the oppressed peoples of the world. His policies are always correct, his words always omniscient, his attitude always proper. To attack Mao, whose image has been built up to such extraordinary heights before the masses, would be fantastically dangerous for any Communist rival at this point. In a certain sense, therefore, the presence of Mao in itself is the best guarantee of unity within the Party, and as long as he lives, an open struggle for power at the top Party levels seems very unlikely, whatever his mistakes. According to recent interviews with refugees, even dissidents often do not hold Mao responsible for their woes, blaming others for the excesses and errors of the regime that he heads.

Communism, of course, has not been able to work out a method of peaceful succession. Can Mao pass on his mantle successfully to

Liu Shao-ch'i, the heir apparent? Or will Chou, or a man like Teng Hsiao-p'ing, holding the vital post of Secretary-General of the Party, suddenly move forward? Or will it be some man presently as unknown to the world as was Nikita Khrushchev in 1950? No one can answer these questions, but recent trends within top Party echelons should be noted. On the whole, purges or demotions at the Politburo level have been few during the first fourteen years of Communist power. Some observers believe that the Party leaders, however vigorously they may debate policy, have long since worked out a division of labor and a mutual respect, and recognize in true Marxist-Leninist fashion that the future of each is dependent upon the unity of all, so that any decision made at the top must be faithfully followed by those who disagree. Others believe that rivalries are more serious, that men within the Politburo symbolize different styles as well as different policies, and that their respective factions are engaged in a continuous, albeit subdued, rivalry.

The evidence is not sufficient at this point to prove either hypothesis. It should be remembered, of course, that the Chinese Communist Party had a long history before the victory of 1949, and that the present leadership had been established in that era only after serious and repeated intra-Party struggles. Since 1949, there have been two significant purges involving top-level Party personnel. The first purge was conducted against Kao Kang and Jao Shu-shih. Kao was the first Chairman of the Northeast People's Government, comprising the six Manchurian provinces (where the Russians were especially active); Jao was the first Chairman of the East China Military and Administrative Committee, the highest governmental body of the East China area. Both men were prominent Politburo members. In 1954, the purge of both men was announced. According to the Central Committee, they had been guilty of separatist plots and an attempt to seize power from the present Party leadership.

In 1959, Marshal P'eng Tu-huai was removed as Minister of Defense, and subsequently, in 1962, it was announced that two of P'eng's supporters, Huang Ke-cheng and Tan Cheng, had been removed from the Party's Central Committee. It is thought that the ouster of P'eng and his supporters is closely related to the internal struggle over the validity of "big leap forward" policies. Sino-Soviet relations may also have been involved: P'eng saw Khrushchev in Albania shortly before his removal. Huang and Tan were replaced by Lu Ting-i, veteran Communist propaganda expert; Kang Sheng, former Central Intelligence Director; and Lo Jui-ching, Chief of the General Staff and also a top secret-service man.

While these events are important, they do not appear to have the same significance as the political changes that have occurred in the Soviet Union during the Khrushchev era. In China, contrary to the USSR, there has as yet been no public break within the inner circle, among the six or eight men who are at the very top. At the same time, the frequent references to "Rightist opportunism" within Party ranks suggest that the policy struggles of recent years may have left their mark. In addition, it appears that some provincial and sectional rivalry continues to exist despite Party efforts at the total unification of China. Regional loyalties die hard, and they are deeply implanted in Chinese culture. This may well be a problem more serious in terms of relations between local and central units of the Party than has commonly been recognized. Party-army relations will be discussed shortly. Here it is sufficient to note that the most serious top-level political crises since 1949 have directly or indirectly involved the Red Army.

VIII

Governmental organization in China is strongly patterned after the Soviet model, but there are some important differences. As in the USSR, the formal structure of national government is capped by an elected body. This National People's Congress, or NPC, is "elected" every four years by the citizenry at large. It has generally been composed of over 1200 delegates, many of the "model workers," peasants who broke production records, and other individuals chosen to give the body occupational, regional, or nationality balance. The NPC is supposed to meet annually to discuss and determine basic policies. In reality, it ratifies rather than makes decisions. It is a forum from which Party policies can be enunciated and given governmental sanction. In 1962, however, when the NPC met in secret session, it was reported that some genuine discussion did take place, even some debate.[24] If the NPC were to evolve into something more than a convenient propaganda outlet, its seventy-member Standing Committee would presumably play the more important role.

Unlike that of the Soviet Union, the executive-administrative structure of the People's Republic of China is bifurcated. One line is represented by the fifty-five-member State Council headed by Premier Chou and including all the Ministers of State. The other line is headed by the Chairman of the Republic, two Vice-Chairmen, and a Secretariat, with the important National Defense Council and Supreme State Conference responsible to them. Mao was Chairman of the Republic until April 1959, when the position was given to Liu. The Vice-Chairmen are currently Tung Pi-wu and Soong Ch'ing-ling, widow of Sun Yat-sen and sister of Madame Chiang Kai-shek.

The one-hundred-member National Defense Council is headed by Liu, and he also heads the more important Supreme State Conference. This latter body is a special council of varying composition which the Chairman can call into existence to discuss "important matters." It is the leading deliberative body which includes non-Party individuals and helps to formulate substantive policy for the Chinese state.

Behind every state organ, however, stands the Party. Mao is China's No. 1 man despite the fact that he holds no formal state office at present. He is Chairman of the party's Central Committee, Chairman of the Politburo, and senior member of the Politburo Standing Committee. In China as in the USSR, these positions represent the summit of power.

Today, the Chinese Communist Party claims approximately 17 million members, or about 2 percent of the total population.[25] An additional 25 million persons belong to Communist Youth organizations. From Liu, we learn that 80 percent of the current Party members have joined the Party since 1949, 70 percent since 1953.[26] Membership has increased substantially, from 12,720,000 in 1957 to 14 million in 1959.[27] The fluctuation in membership is much larger than these figures alone would indicate. "Unfit members" are continuously weeded out, and the turnover at local levels in recent years must have been very high. According to Teng Hsiao-p'ing, numerous Party members were found guilty of bureaucratism, sectarianism, and subjectivism during the rectification campaign of 1957, and some were guilty of more serious crimes.[28] "Bourgeois individualism," he asserted, was rife in a section of the Party, and all subsequent Party pronouncements have indicated that the primary problem is "Rightist opportunism."

Party leaders are quick to ascribe these difficulties to the socioeconomic composition of their membership, and to the inadequate political training acquired by many new members. As late as 1957, more than two-thirds of all Party members had a peasant background. Intellectuals comprised about 14 percent of Party membership, and workers only 13 percent.[29] Leaders admitted that a certain number joined the Party for personal and careerist reasons rather than as a result of conviction, and that others had lost their revolutionary zeal. How to build a "pure, dedicated, and efficient Party" to set the example before the people, to tutor the masses in the New Democracy, remains a critical problem for the Chinese Communists. Naturally, many ambitious individuals want to join the Party because it is the most promising route to position and power. But perhaps the true political elite are the veterans of the Long March, that small remnant who joined the Party in its early days and who managed to survive the harsh decades that followed. In short, the great bulk of Communist China's political elite are new and relatively insecure. Only a handful have established their role and position firmly.

Against the fact of Communist Party power, one must juxtapose the theory of the Revolutionary United Front. *De jure,* Communist China is not a one-party state, but a state operated by a coalition of parties and nonparty elements led by the Communist Party. The strategy of the Party in its quest for power had been "to unite with 90 percent—the people—and to fight the 10 percent—their enemies." In class terms, this meant two alliances, the worker-peasant alliance and the alliance between the working class and the national bourgeoisie.[30] By means of these two alliances, the first "fundamental," the second "auxiliary," it was possible to "isolate and split up the big bourgeoisie and the feudal landlord class." The national bourgeoisie is to be considered a patriotic class, susceptible to being won over, yet at the same time, fundamentally weak and wavering. Hence Party strategy must be simultaneously to unite with and to struggle against this class, ultimately to liquidate it.

The Maoists always considered it essential for "the proletariat" (the Party) to come to power *in the course of* the bourgeois-democratic revolution, so that this revolution could be smoothly guided into socialism. Mao is heralded for having successfully synthesized the Leninist (Trotskyist) theory of uninterrupted (permanent) revolution with the Leninist theory of a two-stage revolution. In essence, the Communists assert that by means of a "managed" bourgeois revolution under the control of the Communist Party, the transition to socialism could take place without interruption and without further revolution.

In reality, the Party came to power in the aftermath of a national, patriotic war that had exhausted the country, greatly weakened the Kuomintang, and enabled the Communists in some measure to capture and use the nationalist movement.[31] The central political issues in China at the close of World War II had been how to stop the civil war and produce a United Front government. Both the Kuomintang and the Communist Party supported these objectives, while privately both retained their deep (and well-founded) suspicions of each other.

When the Communists came to power in 1949, they found it convenient to keep the United Front. Like the transitional People's Democracies of Eastern Europe, the new Chinese People's Republic used the United Front formula as a method of obtaining greater unity without jeopardizing the Party's ultimate and absolute control. Thus, Communist China not only permits the existence of certain non-Communist parties but commands them to exist, since they can help the "nonproletarian classes" accommodate themselves to Communism, thereby facilitating the unity of all under Communist leadership.

Maoism encompasses a fairly elaborate theoretical justification for continuing the United Front after the Party has come to effective power. So long as classes have not yet been eliminated, according to this argument, the bourgeoisie and other nonproletarian classes must be given representation. This can only be accomplished through parties other than the Communist Party, since the latter must represent the proletariat. Even after classes have disappeared, class remnants, vestiges of old class loyalties, will continue to create a need for parties subsidiary (and subordinate) to the Communist Party. Thus the United Front is now projected into the indefinite future.

At every level, state organs include representatives of such minor parties as the Kuomintang Revolutionary Association, the Democratic League, and similar groups, along with certain nonparty elements. Indeed, a great many ex-Kuomintang officials, both civil and military, made a successful transition into service for the regime. In the initial period particularly, and still today, the Communists have suffered from a serious lack of trained administrators, and this is another practical reason for the United Front. Those willing to pledge their loyalty can be used. The National Defense Council is studded with ex-Kuomintang generals. Many provincial and municipal authorities now in office served under the Nationalist government. Some of them were Kuomintang members. None of this, however, obscures the one essential fact: China today is controlled by the Communist Party, and the Party will brook no interference with its basic policies. A non-Communist can "cooperate"; he cannot oppose.

In certain important respects, the theory and practice of the United Front is related to the Marxian theory of contradictions as developed by Mao and his comrades. The Maoists see "the basic contradiction" in pre-Communist China as that between "the people" and "imperialism, feudalism, and bureaucrat-capitalism." The latter constituted the unholy trinity that had to be destroyed. There were other contradictions less fundamental or less pressing. It was important to distinguish between the principal enemy and nonprincipal enemies, and these categories changed with the circumstances. However, one should always concentrate upon destroying the former, while neutralizing, isolating, or winning over the latter.

Communist victory, moreover, did not resolve all contradictions existing in a society. Indeed, even after the classless society had been attained, the problem would continue in some degree. Contradictions between the Party and the governed were possible. Contradictions within the working class itself were bound to emerge. Such contradictions had to be handled differently from those involving the proletariat and its enemies. The processes of mutual discussion, conciliation, and rectification all had to be employed.

We stand now on the threshold of a most intriguing and complex subject, namely, the sources and nature of Chinese Communist power. It is highly doubtful whether terms like "police state" designate the "true" nature of Chinese Communist society. Certainly the Communists are not afraid of using power to the maximum—and in every conceivable form. Nor do they shrink from ruthlessness when they decide that this is necessary to gain their objectives. In Mao Tse-tung's words, a revolution is not a banquet. At the same time, however, Communist manipulation of power runs a wide gamut from coercion to persuasion, with a considerable element of voluntarism involved.[32]

Communist rule in China opened with a widespread purge of "reactionary elements." Terror was used most extensively against the old rural elite. As we have noted, several million individuals were probably liquidated or reduced to the lowest socio-economic level. The struggle to be classified as a "poor peasant" during this period, or at most, as a "middle peasant," was as intensive as any historical effort to achieve security and prestige.

For the Chinese Communists, the central route to power was control of the peasantry. The *first* essential revolution was the agrarian revolution. Mao and his comrades regarded the peasant as the main force in China's bourgeois-democratic revolution. Thus, the "feudal" elements of rural China had to be eliminated. Unlike the urban bourgeoisie and intellectuals, the rural gentry had very marginal utility to the Communists, and represented an entrenched power that was dangerous. Hence, the massive campaign to restructure rural China was given top priority. This was the most revolutionary, the bloodiest period of Communist rule.

By comparison, the Party's approach to the urban classes of affluence and prestige—the commercial-industrial leaders, professionals, and intellectuals—was generally more moderate. Properly reeducated, these groups could perform vitally important services for the state. The initial appeal, therefore, was for cooperation and support. Those who enlisted in the "patriotic" service of the New China were promised immunity from attack and even some privileges associated with the past. At the same time, however, the Party was quick to punish those who followed "old, corrupt practices," or who could not adjust sufficiently to the new order. Fundamentally, all elements of the "bourgeoisie" are supposed to undergo a self-induced metamorphosis: through a process of reeducation and remolding in which they themselves participate actively, the bourgeoisie must shed their old class character and emerge as classless servants of "the people" (read: the state).

After 1952, terror ceased to be a major instrument of Communist policy even in the rural areas. As someone put it, the Party stopped chopping heads and started shaping them. With remarkable speed, the Communists established a vast discussion-indoctrination network that, at least by intent, involved every individual. In this respect, the Communists were able to build upon the pervasive tradition of small-scale organization in China.[33] The Chinese has always been an organization man, a fact of signal importance to an understanding of recent events. The various street, factory, farm, and school units to which every person belongs, need not in themselves be considered a cultural aberration. But organization under the Communists is always public, never private. Moreover, it is a part of a chain of command that leads inexorably to the Politburo in Peking. In these respects, this is a new age. The purpose of small-scale organization in Communist China is to understand, execute, and if possible, "improve upon" state policies. In the course of pledging support, each individual explores in front of others his own actions and values. While the purpose of these grass-roots associations is essentially to ratify rather than to make decisions, the system does involve mass participation in politics—for the first time in Chinese history.

Not all individuals want to participate. Contrary to Aristotle, man is *not* a political animal. The most common complaint in Communist China has been that endless meetings and constant exhortations are both boring and exhausting. The ordinary man prefers under normal circumstances to be let alone, to participate in politics only when grievance moves him to action. This brings to mind Hu Shih's famous remark that not only is there no freedom of speech in Communist China, but there is no freedom of silence either.

Mass education through group discussion involves the use of introspection, group therapy, and many of the techniques associated with religious proselytizing.[34] First the individual is terrorized, shocked, or shamed. He is made to feel a deep sense of guilt or remorse for past sins. In this mood, he wants to be saved. To help in his reform, his friends or his group lend their assistance. In any culture, men have an emotional need *to belong,* and in Communist China, one can belong only if one has been "reformed." There can be little doubt that the so-called brainwashing techniques of the Communists derive both from certain universal principles and from certain specific aspects of Chinese culture. In the course of tearing down the individual's past, familial loyalties must be frontally assaulted, for this is often the cement that has held together his actions, attitudes, and values. But at the same time, the individual is caused to develop a new familial loyalty—to the state.

In many respects, nationalism has been the Party's most powerful weapon in its campaign to win support and consolidate power. The strong desires of the average Chinese, especially the youth, to participate in the building of a powerful state, to become a first-class citizen in a first-class nation, induce the greatest enthusiasm and loyalty. In Asia, Communism has succeeded only where it has been able to capture and use the nationalist movement. The Chinese Communists came to power in the context of "a great, patriotic war" in which they posed as the unifiers and liberators of the Chinese people.[35] Nationalism has not only survived the Communist revolution; it has flourished under it. To the younger generation in particular, the events of the last decade and a half can be and have been portrayed in strongly nationalist terms: the unification of the country under the most powerful government that China has ever known; the unity of all "patriotic" classes in the United Front; the struggle in the Korean War to "defend" China's northeastern frontiers against predatory American power; the unending campaign to "liberate" Taiwan; the fight to "defend" Chinese soil against Indian "aggression"; the general exhortation to stand firm against all manifestations of "American imperialism"; the continuous appeal to sacrifice oneself on behalf of the New China. China's nationalist revolution is being consummated under Communism, and the present stage of rough, raw nationalism cannot be obscured by any ritualistic homage to international solidarity.

In discussing Communist societies, it is customary—and in some degree appropriate—to use terms like "monolithic" and "totalitarian." Clearly, the object of the Chinese Communists is to operate without restraint upon every facet of the individual's life, permitting no organizational or personal opposition to its basic principles. The true Communists, like the true Confucianists, believe in the concept of the educative state and the tutelage of the masses by an elite born and bred to the task. Nor is there any distinction to be made between the state and society. Nothing must lie beyond Party power. At the same time, it is wise to distinguish between goal and accomplishment. No state and no party has ever attained a perfect totalitarian control. For their part, the Chinese Communists are still experimenting with various forms of centralization and local autonomy; the relationship between Party and non-Party elements is still undergoing change; the arena of permissive criticism is still unsettled.

In this connection, the hundred-flowers experiment warrants additional comment.[36] In January 1956, Chou En-lai delivered a speech urging greater freedom and more support for the Chinese intellectuals. In May, Mao issued his famous slogan: "Let a hundred flowers bloom, let a hundred schools contend." In the months that followed, a growing volume of criticism was heard, some of it extraordinarily bold. The Communist Party was openly attacked for various crimes and shortcomings, and by certain surprising sources: students, workers, and minor Party officials. It seems likely that the Party was both shocked and dismayed by trends. It was in this period that Mao wrote and delivered his speech: "On the Correct Handling of Contradictions among the People," in which he admitted that there could be cleavages between the Party and the masses.

The torrent of criticism increased, and finally the party was forced to act. A rectification movement developed into a full-fledged "anti-Rightist campaign" by the summer of 1957, and many hundreds who had earlier expressed forthright criticisms in accordance with Mao's injunction were sentenced to "reform through labor." The experiment in freedom—if that be its proper designation—ended in failure. Communist spokesmen pointed out that there was a difference between "constructive criticism" and those noxious weeds that seek to poison the socialist garden. Officially, the hundred-flowers thesis still holds, and, as noted earlier, it has recently been revived by a regime now anxious to cultivate the intellectuals more closely in the aftermath of economic troubles. It would be a bold—and foolish—man, however, who spoke his mind fully in China today. The Party has an ample supply of weed-killer.

How much dissidence exists in Communist China? What are the nature and extent of opposition to the regime? These questions cannot be answered at present. Dissidence is probably related to three factors: food and living conditions (this factor, of course, is subject to rather rapid change); age (all indications are that the older-age group is the most skeptical and maladjusted); and occupation (apart from the Party elite, the privileged classes have been the skilled workers and miners, the military, and other technicians, notably the scientists).

Serious deficiencies in food and livelihood have generated unrest, as the Communists themselves admit. The regime's attempt to meet this problem, as noted earlier, may or may not succeed. At present, however, there is no indication that a peasant revolt could be conducted, or that the current mood of the peasant is such as to harness him to revolution. The advantages given to youth no doubt add to the discomforts of the older generation in many cases, but power increasingly lies with the younger generation. The intellectuals and the businessmen, in particular, must find it difficult if not impossible to accept the regime. Here, an uneasy compromise prevails, based on their lack of effective alternatives and the state's need of their skills. In short, the likelihood of mass revolt is extremely slim. There is every indication that the Chinese People's Republic is here to stay.

IX

Whatever changes do take place in China are most likely to originate within the present government. Indeed, as noted earlier, many changes are taking place both in policies and in middle and lower personnel. But is there a possibility of some dramatic change at the top, say by a conflict between the Party and the military?

Historically, the Chinese Communist Party has prided itself upon having maintained rigid control over its army. The relation between Mao, Liu, and Chou on the one hand, and Chu Teh, Lin Piao, and military leaders of similar stature, may be regarded as support of that boast. Perhaps in part, however, Party supremacy is due to the fact that men like Mao must be regarded as paramilitary leaders who have contributed much to the theory and practice of Communist warfare.[37] It should be noted that in the last great struggle in the Party, that between Chang Kuo-t'ao and Mao Tse-tung in 1935-36, the Red Army was deeply involved. That struggle caused a major split within the army, and Mao emerged as the ultimate victor at least partly because Chang's forces were subsequently decimated by the Kuomintang and its allies.

There is no indication at present that the Party feels threatened by its military forces. At the grass-roots level, army morale seems reasonably good. In the punishing Korean War, the Chinese troops fought well and the percentage of deserters was small considering how recently the Communists had come to power. In recent years, moreover, the soldier has been glorified and, at least in a minor way, made a part of the privileged classes. His rations have been considerably better than those of the average civilian. There have been rumors that toward the end of the "three bad years," some soldiers were worried about the condition of their families. Yet during the brief period in 1962 when relatively free exit from Kwangtung province to Hong Kong was possible, there were almost no military defections. When the flow of refugees was stopped, moreover, in response to British appeals, the army enforced the new orders with promptness and efficiency. In brief, the Party probably does not need to worry about the peasant boys who march in the ranks—unless economic conditions again deteriorate and remain bad, in which case, it will have to worry about the morale and loyalty of almost everyone.

One cannot ignore such incidents as the dismissal of Marshal P'eng Tu-huai, or the fact that the "Kao Kang-Jao Shu-shih clique" had military connections. The Red Army is the one permanent organizational alternative to the Party. By its very nature, it can never be completely absorbed and hence must always be watched. Moreover, a certain transition is now under way that will ultimately produce a new Party-army relationship. The era of sole reliance upon guerrilla warfare or simple shock-troop tactics is over. The modernization of the Chinese military has commenced, and the young career officers who are now being trained must be strongly committed to the establishment of a highly professionalized military service. Mao and his generation will have a prominent place in military history, but they belong essentially to the past. And it is quite possible that they are considered privately as too old-fashioned to meet some of China's present military needs and problems. A rapid modernization program involves specialized academies, minimal political interference, and the maximum freedom for soldiers from such extraneous tasks as farm labor. To what extent will the demands for military modernization conflict with Party dogma, and to what extent will a modern, professional military force with its own *esprit de corps* betray separatist tendencies or aspirations for power?

Today, the Red Army numbers about 2,500,000, making it the largest, most powerful Asian army by a wide measure. Despite its dedication to modernization, it remains largely primitive, having only a few modern elements, such as paratroops, tank units, and rocket launchers. The Chinese military force also includes some 2,000 MIG jets and about 80 submarines. It is expected that China will shortly explode her first nuclear device. Even if this occurs, it will probably take five to ten years before China can be considered a nuclear power in military terms. That such is her goal, however, cannot be doubted. Party spokesmen have made it clear that under present circumstances, "socialist states" must have nuclear weapons. The Chinese Communists have also proclaimed that they will not be bound by any agreements relating to nuclear weapons to which they are not a party, nor will they participate in any negotiations if the Nationalists are represented. Peking intends to join the nuclear club, and to use her future atomic power as a bargaining weapon now.

Communist China is no match militarily for the United States, of course, nor will it be in the foreseeable future; and this adds to Chinese frustrations, anger, and fear. But Chinese military power cannot be ignored by any Asian country. The stalemate in Korea and the Chinese military victory in the Himalayas are now deeply ingrained upon the minds of all of the peoples who border this new and rising nation. How to contain China, how to bring it into the world of international law and order, will occupy the attention of diverse peoples throughout this century.

X

It thus remains to explore briefly Chinese Communist foreign policy. What is Communist China doing with its newly developed power? In the broadest sense, Chinese foreign policy is the product of *tradition*, buttressed by certain continuing geopolitical factors; *nationalism*, now reaching its crest; and *Marx-Lenin-Maoism*, the ideological expression of Chinese Communist beliefs and experience.[38] Each of these forces is significant in shaping Peking's foreign policy, but the most important is nationalism. In many respects, Communist China is behaving today like any other major state en route to power. Its first concern has been to define and defend its boundaries; to build Communist and neutralist buffer states around itself; and finally, to reach out for greater influence in the worlds in which it lives—the Asian world, the broader, underdeveloped world, and the Communist world. The quest for influence, even hegemony, in these worlds is discernible and disquieting not only to the West, but to the Soviet Union.

Sino-Soviet conflict is in very considerable measure the product of natural rivalries between two nation-states united by a common ideology but divided by differences in culture, a different timing of revolution, a different stage of development, and hence a different world outlook and sense of "national interest." [39] The basic issues between Russia and China are briefly these: what shall be the decision-making process within the bloc; what policy is appropriate toward the West, particularly the United States, and toward the developing nations; and what aid is proper among "fraternal social-ist allies"?

China poses today as the defender of the independence, equality, and integrity of each Communist state and Party against monistic Soviet power. According to the Chinese view, "democratic central-ism" is the principle governing relations *within* each Communist Party—majority decisions reached at the top level must be rigorously followed by the minority. But the basis for decisions *among* Parties is consultation, consensus, and unanimity. Clearly, the national sov-ereignty line is being defended by the Chinese, and the Soviet Union, more especially, "the Khrushchev group," is charged with "big-power chauvinism," an attempt to dominate and coerce vari-ous members of the bloc into accepting the Moscow line.

To the Chinese leaders, the United States—always written "Ameri-can imperialism"—is an implacable foe that must be eliminated before there can be peace. From the Chinese viewpoint, the United States represents the one power able and anxious to thwart China's aspirations. American bases surround China. American forces are involved, directly or indirectly, in the struggles now taking place in Vietnam, Korea, Laos, and India—areas on China's border. The United States prevents the "liberation" of Taiwan, and seeks to iso-late China from the world. Traditional xenophobia thus combines with modern nationalism and Marxism to define the United States as Public Enemy No. 1. The struggle for peace is inextricably con-nected with the struggle against "American imperialism."

Soviet talk about nation-to-nation competition has a realistic core. In a few decades, Soviet production and power may finally overtake and surpass that of the United States. But Communist China is very far from being in that position. Like Bolshevik Rus-sia four decades ago, therefore, the Chinese are prone to see world revolution as the shortcut to victory over the capitalist world. If China is to compete effectively with the United States today, it must be via revolutions in Guatemala, Somalia, and South Vietnam, not through nuclear parity and steel production.

Thus China violently opposes any signs of Soviet accommodation to the *status quo*, whether "coexistence" with the United States or lukewarm support to national liberation movements. There are cer-tain paradoxes or anomalies in Chinese policy, to be sure. While Peking exhorts Moscow to take major risks on such issues as Cuba and to stand firm for Marxist-Leninist principles, her own foreign policy is attuned to her power limitations and sufficiently flexible to encompass dealings with such "feudalists" as Mahendra of Nepal and Ayub Khan of Pakistan. Communist China cannot afford a direct and full confrontation with the United States, and she does not intend to be drawn into one. Her main weapons will continue to be political and economic: cultural missions and worldwide propaganda to undermine American influence; economic and technical "aid" to the developing world, especially its "progressive" elements; and temporary alliances with any group that supports China against her "principal enemies" of the moment. The alliance with Albania, the border and trade negotiations with Pakistan, and the aid to Cuba are all to be read in that light. Through these policies, China attacks the "modern revisionists" within the Communist movement, the Indian "reactionary group," and the "world imperialist camp led by the United States."

One must not overlook the close parallels between the theoretical formulations involved in Chinese Communist strategy for domestic power, and those involved in her assessment of correct foreign policy. The primary objective must be to unite with the "people" and struggle resolutely against their "enemies," to combine with 90 percent of the world's population and fight 10 percent. The bloc represents the proletariat, and current events indicate that there can indeed be contradictions within that class, especially when false leadership prevails or "bourgeois remnant thoughts" creep out. The developing world represents the peasantry—*the main force* at the present stage of the revolution, a force to be wooed and won, and ultimately to be led by the proletariat. Certain elements of the neutralist and Western worlds constitute the national bourgeoisie, whenever possible to be used and abused. Finally, there is the big bourgeoisie, *the primary enemy*—the imperialist world, led by the United States. One must not be frightened into appeasement by these paper tigers.

As noted earlier, Chinese leaders currently emphasize the importance of socialist development through one's own efforts. Nevertheless, it seems obvious that China views with some bitterness the current paucity of Russian aid to "fraternal allies." The Russian position is that the strength of the USSR must constitute the primary shield for world Communism. The Chinese view is that Russia could and should sacrifice considerably more on behalf of the weaker, less-developed Communist states.

Chinese Communist foreign policy, in short, comprises the following theses:

1. The struggle for control of world Communist policy must be continued, even at the risk of a total breach between Peking and Moscow, because Chinese national interest is at stake. The Chinese Party is currently in the minority, but that is a temporary position. With it stand a number of Asian Parties as well as a faction in almost every Party in the world. More importantly, with it stands *truth* and, hence, ultimate victory.

2. The momentum toward world revolution must be maintained, even at heavy cost in economic, political, and military terms. In one sense, China can ill afford such expenditures, but they are necessary both for defense and for offense. Special efforts in Cuba and Latin America are warranted, because this area lies close to the heart of "American imperialism." National liberation movements must be forwarded at all costs, and wherever possible, the capture of bourgeois nationalist revolutions by the proletariat must be accomplished.

3. At the same time, it is important to win over many of the existing "peasant" and "bourgeois" regimes of the Afro-Asian world, forming a United Front with them against imperialism. For these purposes, China is prepared to coexist with states having different social systems. Such states, however, must not challenge Chinese "nationalist interest," or they become enemies. Then, as in the case of India, they must be isolated and attacked.

XI

Future historians may decide that the emergence of Communist China was the single most important event of the 20th century. All calculations at present must be based upon the probability that the Communist regime will continue to survive, despite the many serious problems that plague it. In some degree, progress and poverty are certain to go together in China for the foreseeable future. State power will surely increase, while at the same time, mass poverty continues. Development will be uneven and often costly in terms of human sacrifice. No one can predict how much strain and travail will be imposed upon the Chinese people as the Party seeks to bring this vast backward society rapidly into modernity. Undoubtedly, the slogan, "Two steps forward, one step backward" will continue to mark the development of contemporary China.

It would be foolish to ignore the risks involved to the world, especially to the rest of Asia, by the rise of this dynamic new force. How to contain China—more precisely, how to foster her economic development but control her political excesses—is likely to be the most significant problem of our times. Meanwhile, China is eloquent testimony to an ironic fact: Communism, contrary to Marx's cherished belief, is not the result of modernization, but the hoped-for means. Perhaps, therefore, it should be viewed less as a sin, and more as a childhood disease, or alternatively, as one form of modern political adolescence—a particularly unpleasant form from the standpoint of those who cherish freedom.

FOOTNOTES

[1] Sir John Maynard, *Russia in Flux* (New York: Macmillan, 1949), pp. 252-253.

[2] See Liu Shao-ch'i, *The Victory of Marxism-Leninism in China* (Peking: Foreign Languages Press, 1959), pp. 38-39.

[3] *Ibid.,* p. 5.

[4] Tung Ta-lin, *Agricultural Cooperation in China,* 2d Ed. (Peking: Foreign Languages Press, 1959), p. 7.

[5] See Li Wei-han, *The Struggle for Proletarian Leadership in the Period of the New-Democratic Revolution in China* (Peking: Foreign Languages Press, 1962), pp. 80ff.

[6] Anna Louise Strong, *The Rise of the Chinese People's Communes* (Peking: New World Press, 1959), p. 11.

For a general study of agriculture under the Communists, see Chao Kuo-chun, *Agrarian Policy of the Chinese Communist Party, 1921-1959* (Bombay: Asia Publishing House, 1960). For diverse reports on the communes, see Richard Hughes, *The Chinese Communes* (London: The Bodley Head, 1960); and Edgar Snow, *The Other Side of the River* (New York: Random House, 1962).

[7] See the "Draft of the Sputnik People's Commune," dated August 7, 1958, in *People's Communes in China* (Peking: Foreign Languages Press, 1958), pp. 61-77.

[8] See the speech of Ch'en Yi of September 30, 1962, as re-

ported in *Peking Review*, No. 40, October 5, 1962, p. 7.

[9] UPI Report from Hong Kong, dated December 26, 1962, quoting "unconfirmed reports." These figures are similar to those used by other observers recently. See W.K., "Communist China's Agricultural Calamities," *The China Quarterly*, No. 6, April-June 1961, pp. 68-78 (W.K. suggests that the 1960-61 per capita average daily caloric intake may have been 1850-1900 calories); see also Edwin F. Jones, "The Impact of the Food Crisis on Peiping's Policies," *The Asian Survey*, 2:10, December 1962), pp. 1-11.

[10] UPI report cited above.

[11] See the article "Agriculture Heads the Agenda," *Peking Review*, No. 4, January 25, 1963, p. 17.

[12] For an abridged version of Premier Chou's speech to the 1962 National People's Congress, see "Press Communique on the National People's Congress, *ibid.*, No. 16, April 20, 1962, pp. 5-7.

[13] "Agriculture Heads the Agenda," *op. cit.*, p. 17.

[14] Chou En-lai, *A Great Decade* (Peking: Foreign Languages Press, 1959), pp. 1-3. For general evaluations of industrialization under the Communists, see Alexander Eckstein, *The National Income of Communist China* (Glencoe, Ill.: Free Press, 1961); W.W. Hollister, *China's Gross National Product and Social Accounts, 1950-1957* (Glencoe, Ill.: Free Press, 1958); T.J. Hughes and D. E. T. Luard, *The Economic Development of Communist China* (London: Oxford University Press, 1959); and Choh-ming Li, *Economic Development of Communist China* (Berkeley: University of California Press, 1959); and *The Statistical System of Communist China* (Berkeley: University of California Press, 1962).

[15] Li Hsien-nien, "The Great Financial Achievements of the People's Republic of China During the Past Ten Years," in *Ten Glorious Years—1949-1959* (Peking: Foreign Languages Press, 1960), pp. 170-171.

[16] Li Fu-chun, "On the Big Leap Forward in China's Socialist Construction," *ibid.*, pp. 132-133.

[17] *Ibid.*, pp. 129-130.

[18] John Philip Emerson, "Manpower Absorption in the Non-Agricultural Branches of the Economy of Communist China, 1953-58," *The China Quarterly*, No. 7, *op. cit.*, p. 76.

[19] See Richard Hughes, "The 'Great Leap' Is Now the 'Great Retreat'," *New York Times Magazine,* October 7, 1962, p. 27.

[20] See Takashi Oka, "Schism Cramps Peking Trade," *The Christian Science Monitor,* February 7, 1963, p. 1.

[21] *Ibid.,* p. 1.

[22] Among recent studies, see John S. Aird, "Population Growth: Evidence and Interpretation," *The China Quarterly,* No. 7, *op. cit.,* pp. 45-56.

[23] For a general study of education, see Leo A. Orleans, *Professional Manpower and Education in Communist China* (Washington, D.C.: U.S. Government Printing Office, 1960).

[24] For an interesting article, see A. M. Halpern, "Between Plenums: A Second Look at the 1962 National People's Congress in China," *Asian Survey,* 2:9, November 1962, pp. 1-10.

[25] See the speech of Liu Shao-ch'i on June 30, 1961, on the occasion of the 40th anniversary of the founding of the Chinese Communist Party, as republished in *The China Quarterly,* pp. 165-166, No. 7, *op. cit.*

[26] *Ibid.,* p. 166.

[27] For the 1957 figures, see Teng Hsiao-p'ing, *Report on the Rectification Campaign* (Peking: Foreign Languages Press, 1957), pp. 45-46; for the 1959 figures, see the introduction to Liu's speech, cited above, p. 165.

[28] Teng Hsiao-p'ing, *Report on the Rectification Campaign, op. cit.,* p. 45.

[29] *Ibid.,* p. 45.

[30] Li Wei-han, *op. cit.,* pp. 1-2.

[31] For a general survey of this era, see Robert C. North, *Moscow and Chinese Communists* (Stanford: Stanford University Press, 1953).

[32] For a perspective on questions like this, see Tibor Mende, *China and Her Shadow* (London: Thames and Hudson, 1960).

[33] See H. F. Schurmann, "Organization and Response in Communist China," *The Annals of the American Academy of Political and Social Science,* Vol. 321, January 1959, pp. 51-61.

[34] The most detailed study in English of this subject is Robert J. Lifton, *Thought Reform and the Psychology of Totalism* (London: Gollancz, 1961).

[35] See Chalmers A. Johnson, *Peasant Nationalism and Communist Power* (Stanford: Stanford University Press, 1962).

[36] For a study of this era, see Roderick MacFarquhar, *The Hundred Flowers Campaign and the Chinese Intellectual* (New York: Praeger, 1960); see also Mao Tse-tung, *On the Correct Handling of Contradictions Among the People* (Peking: Foreign Languages Press, 1957). See also Teng Hsiaop'ing, *Report on the Rectification Campaign* (Peking: Foreign Languages Press, 1957), and for more recent trends, see Dennis Doolin, "The Revival of the 'Hundred Flowers' Campaign, 1961," *The China Quarterly*, No. 8, October-December 1961, pp. 34-41.

[37] Among Mao's writings, many deal with military matters. See, for example, his *Problems of War and Strategy* (Peking: Foreign Languages Press, 1960—reprint of a November 1938 speech); also Lin Piao, *March Ahead Under the Red Flag of the Party's General Line and Mao Tse-tung's Military Thinking* (Peking: Foreign Languages Press, 1959).

[38] For an elaboration of this theme, see Robert A. Scalapino, "Tradition and Transition in the Asian Policy of Communist China" (Hong Kong Press, October 1961). For a general study, see A. Doak Barnett, *Communist China and Asia* (New York: Harper, 1960); also H. Arthur Steiner, *Communist China in the World Community* (International Conciliation, No. 533, May 1961), pp. 389-454.

[39] Among recent works dealing with the Sino-Soviet dispute, see G.F. Hudson, Richard Lowenthal, and Roderick MacFarquhar, *The Sino-Soviet Dispute* (New York: Praeger, 1961); Donald S. Zagoria, *The Sino-Soviet Conflict—1951-1961* (Princeton, N.J.: Princeton University Press, 1962); and Robert A. Scalapino, "Moscow, Peking and the Communist Parties of Asia," *Foreign Affairs*, 41:2, January 1963, pp. 323-343.

Trade Unionism and the Communists: American and International Experiences

John Hutchinson

Every movement has its leader, and every doctrine its scriptures. The impact of Communist ideas and actions on the American and international labor movements derive largely from Lenin. He was a contemporary observer of the rise of the modern trade unionism and also, as Marx was not, the supervisor of a revolution. His ideas on trade unionism, developed in the crucible of experience, guided the course of Soviet labor organization, and remain of great importance today.

Trade unions did not become legal in tsarist Russia until 1906, long after Lenin had become a professional revolutionist. But they did exist in rudimentary form, and during the 1890's Lenin and other intellectuals participated in union activities in St. Petersburg, forming the "League for the Emancipation of the Working Class," helping to conduct strikes, and using such occasions to spread revolutionary propaganda. From these and later experiences he developed a clear and generally consistent view of the role of trade unionism in a revolutionary age.

"The workers' organizations for carrying on the economic struggle," Lenin wrote, "should be trade-union organizations. . . . Let every worker who understands the necessity for organization, in order to carry on the struggle against the employers and the government, join the trade unions." [1]

Trade unions should attract as many members as possible. "The wider these organizations are, the wider our influence over them will be." [2] Trade unions should not be doctrinally selective, since "it would be far from being to our interest to demand that only Social Democrats [that is, Leninists] be eligible for membership in

164

the trade unions. The only effect of this, if it were attempted, would be to restrict our influence over the masses." [3]

There was the question of function. "Trade unionism and strikes, at best, can only enable the workers . . . to obtain slightly better terms of sale for their commodity—labor power. Trade unions and strikes become impotent when, owing to a depression, there is no demand for this 'commodity.' . . . To remove these conditions, it is necessary to conduct a revolutionary struggle against the whole existing social and political system." [4] The contribution of trade unionism to the revolutionary struggle was marginal but important. "Trade-union organizations may not only be of tremendous value in developing and consolidating the economic struggle, but may also become a very useful auxiliary to the political, agitational and revolutionary organizations." [5]

They had their place, and must learn to stay in it. Lenin was greatly perturbed that both Russian and West European unions tended to operate as independent organizations, uninformed by revolutionary doctrine, regarding themselves as essentially economic institutions devoted to the pursuit of immediate and short-run gains. "Revolutionary Social Democracy . . . subordinates the struggle for reform to the revolutionary struggle for liberty and socialism. . . . Any degrading of Social Democratic politics to trade-union politics means precisely to prepare the ground for converting the labor movement into an instrument of bourgeois democracy." [6]

It was a long controversy between those who believed in trade unions as economic institutions concerned primarily with collective bargaining, and those who wanted them to serve a superior political purpose; between those who believed that the spontaneous or internally derived policies of organized labor best satisfied the needs of both its members and history, and those who believed that history makes its own demands; between those who held that unions should be led by their own, and those who believed in their guidance by the historically anointed. Lenin was an interventionist on behalf of a supreme cause.

The only choice is either bourgeois ideology or socialist ideology. There is no middle course . . . for the spontaneous labor movement is trade unionism . . . and trade unionism means the enslavement of the workers to the bourgeoisie. Hence our task . . . is to combat spontaneity, to divert the labor movement from its spontaneous, trade-unionist striving to go under the wing of the bourgeoisie, and to bring it under the wing of revolutionary Social Democracy.[7]

It was the work of an elite.

> A small compact core, consisting of reliable, experienced and hardened workers, with responsible agents in the principal districts and connected by all the strict rules of secrecy with the organizations of revolutionists, can, with the wide support of the masses and without an elaborate set of rules, perform all the functions of a trade-union organization, and perform it, moreover, in the manner Social Democrats desire. . . . Our wiseacres cry out with the profundity of fools, "It is a bad business when the movement does not proceed from the rank and file." [8]

Stalin paraphrased it in later years. "Formally," he said, "the Party cannot give the trade unions any directives; but the Party gives directives to the Communists who work in the trade unions." [9]

Russian trade unions played an important role, without prompting from the professional revolutionaries, in the 1905 revolution. Over two million workers went on strike, forming in many cities the joint-action committees that bred the idea of the later city soviets. In response, Lenin made a temporary concession to the value of spontaneous action, but without giving up his position that trade unions must submit to the imperatives of the revolution and the discipline of the Party.

He also shifted ground slightly after the 1905 revolution on trade-union affiliation with the Party. Some Communists wanted both unions and Party to operate in secret. Others, when the government made some concessions on civil liberties, wanted open activity by both unions and Party. Lenin wanted open unions and a secret party, with the former acting as front organizations for the latter. He was no longer absolutely opposed to formal union affiliation with the Party, provided the unions admitted non-Communists and remained under Party control. It was a matter of tactical choice: the appearance of neutrality was acceptable; the reality was not.

Lenin also formulated more precisely at this time his concept of cell organization. Each factory must have a union cell, and each union must have a Party cell. Cells organized by trade must be joined to cells organized by territory, and Party policy must be followed by all Party members elected to union posts.

Thereafter Lenin wrote little on trade unionism until after the 1917 revolution. He returned to the subject in the early 1920's and disposed of three issues—the doctrine of increasing misery, the matter of Communist participation in reactionary unions, and the question of ethics.

It is Marxist dogma that, under capitalism, in the long run the poor grow poorer as the rich grow richer, or, according to some modern Marxists, that at least the relative share of workers in the national wealth always tends to decrease. Lenin, indeed, did not deny the possibility of limited or temporary improvements, but only fundamental ones. Important reforms could be initiated under capitalism, but revolution was needed to complete them. The danger was satisfaction, particularly in Western Europe. There the development of a bribed labor aristocracy, as Lenin called it, could corrupt the working class for a generation. "In countries more advanced than Russia," he wrote, ". . . the *craft unions, narrow-minded, selfish, case-hardened, covetous, petty bourgeois labor aristocracy, imperialist-minded, imperialist-bribed and imperialist-corrupted,* emerged as a much stronger stratum than in our country." [10] On the other hand, limited gains and small reforms could whet the appetite for revolution. Immediate advances were good if they brought greater freedom of action, attracted recruits to the cause, and developed the revolutionary spirit. The revolution was the criterion.

> We cannot and we will not in every way promote the improvement of the situation of the workers under existing conditions. . . . We struggle only for such an improvement of the situation of the workers as will increase their ability to lead the class struggle, that is, under which an improvement of the situation is not connected with a corruption of political consciousness. . . . We also struggle for reform . . . but . . . only in a revolutionary manner.[11]

Thus, the greatest service Bolshevism could render the bourgeoisie would be to leave the reactionary trade unions alone.

> The Party must more than ever in a new way, not only in the old way, educate and guide the trade unions, at the same time bearing in mind that they are and will long remain an indispensable "school of Communism." [12]

There was a final injunction on behavior.

> If you want to help, you must not fear difficulties . . . but must
> imperatively work wherever the masses are to be found. . . . We
> must be able to . . . agree to all and every sacrifice, even—if need be—
> to resort to various stratagems, artifices, illegal methods, to evasions
> and subterfuges, only so as to get into the trade unions, to remain in
> them, and to carry on Communist work at all costs.[13]

The task did not end with revolution. Soviet trade unions, as
Isaac Deutscher has observed, came to perform their tasks as "sub-
sidiaries of the state administration, not as autonomous social bodies
or working-class organizations in the accepted sense." [14] Lenin found
them useful and gave them praise.

> In its work, the Party relies directly on the *trade unions,* which
> . . . are formally *non-Party.* . . . Thus, on the whole, we have a
> formal, non-Communist, flexible and relatively wide and very power-
> ful proletarian apparatus . . . by means of which, under the leader-
> ship of the Party, the *dictatorship of the class* is exercised. Without
> close contact with the trade unions, without their hearty support and
> self-sacrificing work, not only in economic, *but also in military affairs,*
> it would, of course, have been impossible for us to maintain the
> dictatorship.[15]

In sum, Lenin believed that trade unionism is inevitable under
capitalism and necessary to the revolution; that unions and Party
might be separate in form but that the party must dominate in fact;
that the political struggle always has higher priority than immediate
economic gain, so that reforms achieved by union action must therefore be judged according to their contribution to revolutionary
goals; and that this alliance of labor and Party is as essential after
the revolution as before it. By organization or arms, by stealth or
in the open, at home or abroad, there was work at hand and glory
ahead. It was a powerful call.

II

Lenin's ideas were soon translated into practice. The Third International, intended to be a worldwide revolutionary party, was
established in Moscow in 1919. By formal action it assumed, among
other duties, the responsibility for guiding the work of organized

labor throughout the world. "The class struggle . . . demands that the general guidance [of trade unions] be united in one central organization. Only a political party can be such a unifying and guiding center. . . . In the execution of this duty the Communists must practically subordinate the factory committees and the unions to the Communist Party." [16] The Party's agent was the newly created Red International of Labor Unions (RILU), which gave special attention to the United States.

> In America as in no other country [its first conference report stated], the labor unions and their leading elements play the part of direct agents of capital. The American Federation of Labor serves as a most reliable tool in the hands of the bourgeoisie for suppressing the revolutionary movement. . . . Therefore the question of creating revolutionary cells and groups inside the American Federation of Labor and the independent unions is of vital importance.[17]

Communist infiltration came at an unfortunate time for American labor. During the 1920's trade unions were generally in decline; the temper of the decade, the open-shop activities of the employers, and a careless identification in some quarters of conservative trade unionism with revolutionary principles producing a substantial drop in union members and a defensive attitude by the leaders of labor. William Z. Foster, not widely known as a Communist but highly respected as an organizer of major campaigns in the steel and packing-house industries, launched the Trade Union Educational League (TUEL), affiliated it with the RILU, and began to "bore from within" existing unions. By 1922 the TUEL could muster about one-quarter of the votes for the presidency of the International Association of Machinists, and additional campaigns were undertaken in the building, railroad, printing, textile and garment trades. The TUEL failed to dislodge John L. Lewis as president of the United Mine Workers of America, but the Communists continued for a number of years to be a source of friction in the union. The TUEL was most successful in the New York garment industry. It captured the leadership of the New York Joint Board of the International Ladies Garment Workers Union, and by its conduct of the long 1926 strike almost bankrupted and destroyed the union. At that time both labor and management in the industry used professional mercenaries. Benjamin Gitlow, then the

Party official in charge of Communist activities in the needle trades, later wrote of the Party's typical behavior:

> While castigating the trade-union officials as gangsters and racketeers, we did not hesitate to negotiate with them and make deals that suited our purposes. While denouncing every agreement with the manufacturers concluded without our participation as a sell-out, the same sort of agreement concluded under our sponsorship was hailed as a brilliant victory for militant trade unionism. We savagely attacked the entrenched trade-union officials for resorting to the services of professional gangsters and drew the bitter moral that this was the morass into which reactionary leadership was leading the honest trade unionists, but when we hired gangsters and resorted to gangster methods, we pointed to the heroic achievements of the rank and file, glorifying in the revolutionary upsurge of the class-conscious masses. What venom we spilled on the heads of certain Socialist officials in the unions for alleged squandering of union funds on bribes to police officials, while at the same time some of our Communist officials far outstripped the Socialists in this branch of trade union technique! [18]

Meanwhile Foster reaffirmed the Party's role in labor affairs.

> The time is at hand when we must give much more attention than in the past to the organization of Party fractions [cells] in the trade unions. . . . At the recent sessions of the enlarged executive committee of the Comintern the question of building trade-union fractions was one of those stressed greatly. . . . Our Party must always act as a unit in the unions. This can only be accomplished through the fraction system. . . . The fractions are Party organs for working within the unions.[19]

The TUEL campaign, however, had only limited success; and in 1928 the RILU changed its American policy from boring from within to the establishment of rival unions. The Trade Union Unity League (TUUL), which took the place of the TUEL, set up separate unions in the mining and needle trades, and made plans for new organizations in other industries. Except for the Needle Workers Industrial Union, which had general jurisdiction in the garment trades and ultimately took over in the fur industry,[20] none of these adventures succeeded at the national level. They did, however, serve as a proving-ground for Communists interested in trade-union work. Their turn was to come.

Communist labor policy changed again during the New Deal. At first the Party was unsympathetic with the Roosevelt administration. The President was a "sly Fascist manipulator . . . [who] operates with all the arts of 'democratic' rule, with an emphasized liberal and social demagogic cover, quite in contrast with Hoover, who was outspokenly reactionary. Yet behind this smokescreen, Roosevelt is carrying out more thoroughly, more brutally than Hoover the capitalist attack against the living standards of the masses and the sharpest national chauvinism in foreign relations." [21] Even the effort to encourage the organization of trade unions through the National Industrial Recovery Act (NIRA) was "a movement toward the *militarization of labor*. This is the most direct and open part of the fascist features of the New Deal." [22]

But the NIRA and subsequent legislation facilitated the substantial increase in union membership, and a program was now announced for the creation of a revolutionary opposition within the AFL. The whole Party was to be mobilized, Communist-led unions were to affiliate as units wherever possible, and where this was impractical Communists were to join unions as individuals. Alex Bittelman gave recognition to the source of inspiration.

> In short, at every stage in the development of the revolutionary trade-union movement in the United States . . . it was with the help of the Comintern that the American revolutionary workers were able to find the correct way to correct their errors and, through manifold changes in tactics, to press on to the goal of building a revolutionary trade-union movement in the United States.[23]

A substantial mark was made on AFL unions in only two industries: the film industry and the culinary trades.

Active Communist Party interest in Hollywood evidently began about 1925. In that year Willi Münzenberg—a founder of the German Communist Party and head of International Workers Aid, one of the first international Communist fronts—declared that the American film industry presented "tremendous cultural possibilities in a revolutionary sense." [24] Thereafter the Party's cultural committee began to concern itself with Hollywood.

In 1935, according to a variety of witnesses, the Party dispatched an agent named Jeff Kibre to organize the infiltration of the talent and technical unions. Considerable Communist influence developed in one of the former, the Screen Writers Guild,[25] but the major success was among the technical workers. The International Association of Theatrical and Stage Employees (IATSE), the largest of the technical unions, was under the control of racketeers. George Browne had been elected president of the union in 1934 with underworld support. William Bioff, his chief assistant and the *de facto* leader of the union, had been a minor figure in the Capone organization in Chicago. Between them, Browne and Bioff extorted hundreds of thousands of dollars from the employers, but in return for limited collective bargaining demands received the support of their victims in organizing the industry.

Several opposition groups to the IATSE developed, influenced in varying degree by Communists or Communist sympathizers. In 1941 the rebel elements joined to form the Conference of Studio Unions (CSU), which for some years adhered to Party policy on most issues. The leader of the CSU, Herbert Sorrell of the Painters, always denied he was a Communist and in fact openly disagreed with the Party on a number of issues, but generally enjoyed its support. The tensions of the postwar years hardened the lines between the Communists and anti-Communists. The IATSE and the CSU fought each other in bitter strikes during 1945 and 1946. In 1949—now with considerable community as well as labor support—the IATSE defeated the CSU in an industrywide election conducted by the National Labor Relations Board. This election, together with a series of hearings on the industry conducted by the House Un-American Activities Committee,[26] put an end to effective Communist infiltration of Hollywood unions.

The only other AFL union seriously affected by the Communist drive of the 1930's was the Hotel and Restaurant Employees (HRE). The Communist-led Food Workers Industrial Union (FWIU) was founded in the early part of the decade to fight racketeers in the New York area. With the decline of corrupt practices in the HRE itself, the FWIU was absorbed by the larger union in 1936. Objections in the HRE to the admission of a Communist-led group were passed over in the interest of a stronger organization and the need for combined efforts to eliminate the racketeers altogether.

Discontent with the alliance, however, remained and grew. The 1940 convention of the HRE took note of the dissemination of Communist propaganda in certain sections of the union, and ordered the expulsion of any member found to be fostering the Communist cause. Because of the war, the next convention of the HRE was not held until 1947, by which time the anti-Communist sentiment in the union had crystallized. The HRE General Executive Board, declaring that substantial Communist influence existed among its New York affiliates, had previously ordered the local unions involved to clean house. No local action had been taken. The convention then passed a constitutional amendment barring Communists, fascists, and other extremists from elective or appointive office, and put the HRE Joint Executive Board in New York City into trusteeship. The trusteeship was challenged in the courts, which ruled in favor of the international union. Pro-Communist elements succeeded through a series of internecine battles in maintaining a foothold until 1951, when their last adherents were voted out of office. A few lodgements in other parts of the country were eliminated by 1953.

These were the only instances of important Communist influence among unions which remained with the AFL.[27] It was a different matter with its rival federation.

III

John L. Lewis founded the Committee on Industrial Organization—which later became the Congress of Industrial Organizations (CIO)—in 1935. Its purpose was to organize mass-production workers by industry rather than by craft. This policy, however, ran counter to the dominant traditions of the AFL and clashed with the jurisdictional interests of a large number of craft unions. The Committee was told to disband, and when it ignored the order was expelled from the parent federation.

The CIO then launched a major campaign in the automobile, steel, rubber, textile, and other industries. The time was propitious and the drive phenomenally successful with no help from the Communists. In 1935 the Party, following the Comintern policy in favor of working-class solidarity against fascism, denounced dual unionism, dissolved the TUUL, and ordered a resumption of boring from within. For two years the Communists attacked the CIO; but the new federation succeeded, while the Communists failed against the AFL. In 1937 they turned again and moved into the CIO.

There was need for their services. The early campaigns of the

CIO were largely staffed and financed by the UMWA and a few other unions. But now the CIO claimed some three million members, with thousands evidently at the door. There was a great demand for men of experience. The Communists were available, and Lewis accepted their aid. "In a battle," he said, like Henry of Navarre, "I make arrows from any wood." [28] He believed he could control the Communists and discard them at will. It was a costly error.

Several Communists soon became senior staff officials in the national office of the CIO. They also moved into high elective or appointive posts in the United Electrical Workers (UE), the American Newspaper Guild, the National Maritime Union, the International Woodworkers of America, the International Longshoremen's and Warehousemen's Union (ILWU), the Cannery Workers, the United Office and Professional Workers (UOPWA), the United Public Workers (UPWA), the United Farm and Equipment Workers, and other unions. By 1938, according to one estimate, they had partial or complete control over 40 percent of all unions affiliated with the CIO. [29]

There was, for a time, little friction on policy. The New Deal, in Communist propaganda, had been transformed from a fascist conspiracy into a bulwark against monopoly capitalism, and the Communists supported the alliance between Roosevelt and the CIO. In foreign affairs there was general agreement on the menace of Nazi Germany but also on the generally isolationist position of both American labor and the community at large. Later, when the non-Communist CIO leadership supported intervention, Lewis remained an isolationist and received the support of the Communists. The Hitler-Stalin pact of 1939 cemented this friendship, while aggravating the estrangement between Lewis and the non-Communists in the CIO. Roosevelt now became an agent for Wall Street and an advocate of imperialist war. There was a Communist rhyme of the time:

> Old Franklin Roosevelt
> Told the people how he felt
> We damn near believed what he said.
> He said, "I hate war
> And so does Eleanor,
> But we won't be safe till everybody's dead. [30]

The 1940 CIO convention was the first test of strength. Lewis had endorsed Wendell Willkie for the presidency and promised to resign as CIO president if Roosevelt was reelected. In a skillful intervention Sidney Hillman, president of the Amalgamated Clothing Workers and a Roosevelt supporter, anticipated Lewis's resignation and urged the convention to elect Philip Murray of the Steelworkers as the new CIO president. The Communists counterattacked with a move to draft Lewis, but failed. Lewis left, and Murray took his place.

The Communists dropped isolation and substituted intervention when the Germans invaded the Soviet Union.[31] The imperialist war became a struggle for democracy, and the isolationist allies of yesterday became appeasers, fifth-columnists, or enemy agents. Communist support for the war effort, however, did not entirely heal the breach within the CIO. When Soviet police arrested and eventually shot two prominent Polish socialists, Victor Alter and Henryk Ehrlich, the national CIO joined with many prominent Americans in condemning the Soviet Union; the Communists termed the campaign a deliberate move to create dissension among the Allies and to weaken the war effort. There was disagreement on conscription and permanent selective service; the non-Communists opposed both measures, the Communists supported them. The Communists also wanted to extend the wartime no-strike pledge into peacetime; the non-Communists did not.

The issues were joined after the war. The earlier policy differences, the fact that the Communist-controlled unions still represented some 15 percent of the total CIO membership, and the waning emotions of the Grand Alliance, moved the non-Communists in the CIO to more drastic action. Murray was at first hesitant to risk a further schism in the labor movement, but he presented to the 1946 convention a strong statement criticizing Communist activities in the CIO and allied himself unequivocally with the anti-Communists. The convention also acted to limit the political influence of the CIO's state and local councils, many of which were Communist-controlled. Anti-Communist revolts then broke in many councils with considerable success. A number of CIO international union presidents—Joseph Curran of the National Maritime Union, Michael Quill of the Transport Workers, Morris Muster of the Furniture Workers, and Frank McGrath of the Shoe Workers—broke publicly with their former Communist allies. Muster and McGrath resigned from office, but Curran and Quill retained their posts while driving Communist officials from their unions. CIO secretary-treasurer James B. Carey, ousted from the presidency of the UE by the Communists in 1941, organized in 1947 the "UE Members for Democratic Action," a dissident group which rapidly gained support and formed the nucleus of a new union. In 1948, after Murray and president Harry Bridges of the ILWU disagreed violently over the Marshall Plan, Bridges was discharged as West Coast regional director of the CIO. In the same year Murray dismissed CIO counsel Lee Pressman as a Communist, and ordered the Communist-dominated Farm and Equipment Workers to merge with the United Automobile Workers (UAW). Meanwhile the million-member UAW, under the presidency of Walter Reuther, was becoming one of the strongest advocates of disciplinary action against the Communists in the CIO.

The campaign of Henry Wallace on the Progressive Party ticket was a major catalyst in the final break. In 1947, a group of liberals formed Americans for Democratic Action, declared Communists ineligible for membership, and attracted the support of a number of CIO leaders. In the same year several Communist fronts united into the Progressive Citizens of America, promoted the presidential candidacy of Wallace, and enlisted the aid of the Communist leaders in the CIO. The division deepened, and the bitterness of the Wallace campaign brought new strength to the non-Communists.

Michael Quill, who had long worked with the Communists in his own union, later testified before the CIO investigating committee on his experiences. In October 1947, he said, he was invited to meet in New York City with Eugene Dennis, the general secretary of the Communist Party; John Williamson, the labor secretary of the Party; Harry Bridges of the ILWU; James Matles and Julius Emspak of the UE; and other CIO leaders. Eugene Dennis informed the meeting that "the national leaders . . . of the Communist Party have decided to form a third party led by Henry Wallace . . . [and that] the Communist Party was asking all the Left-wing-controlled unions to start to petition and campaign now, to start the publicity, to line up support for Wallace as soon as he announced himself on the radio." [32]

Quill later went to see William Z. Foster, then the national chairman of the Party. "I expressed to him," Quill said, "fear that this move will split the unions, and weaken our position locally and

nationally against the employers. He said the Communist Party
. . . decided that all the unions it can influence within CIO are
to go down the line behind Wallace if it splits the last trade union
down the middle. He said, 'We have also decided to form a Third
Federation of Labor in the United States carved out of the A.F.
of L. and the CIO in order to implement the Henry Wallace movement.' " [33]

Wallace's defeat was a victory for the anti-Communists in the
CIO. The 1949 convention was decisive. The CIO expelled the UE
and issued a new charter to Carey and his associates for the International Union of Electrical Workers (IUE). It also passed a constitutional amendment authorizing a two-thirds majority of the CIO
executive board to expel any union that followed the policies of an
authoritarian political party. Committees were then named to hear
charges against ten CIO unions. After hearings, a number of these
were expelled: the UOPWA, and UPWA, the Food and Tobacco
Workers, and the Mine, Mill and Smelter Workers; and somewhat
later the American Communications Association, the Fishermen,
the ILWU, the Fur Workers, and the National Union of Marine
Cooks and Stewards. A change in leadership averted the expulsion
of the Shoe Workers.

That was the end of any important Communist influence in the
CIO. There were further reprisals. The IUE raided the UE and
now represents most of the latter's former membership. The Steelworkers have made major inroads into the membership of the Mine,
Mill and Smelter Workers. Most of the other expelled unions either
have been absorbed by other unions or eke out a marginal existence
with little influence on industrial relations in the United States.
Only the ILWU retains its former strength, due partly to the ability
of its leadership and partly to the fact that it is an emotionally
close-knit union with a limited jurisdiction and strong geographical
concentration in membership. According to recent charges, Communist influences linger on in one or two former CIO unions, but
if they exist they are not serious enough to prompt disciplinary
action by the parent federation.

IV

The success of American Communists as union leaders, such as
it was, derived from several factors. The Communist theory of trade

unionism was specific, authoritative, and evangelic. It was implemented usually by men of considerable ability, courage, and energy, who believed deeply in their cause, knew what they wanted, and were less restrained by consistency and candor than were their competitors. Further, the superior discipline of the Communists and their willingness to outsit and outtalk the opposition helped them to gain power over organizations whose membership in general had not the slightest sympathy with Communist aims. Their bargaining achievements were often impressive; and even when higher loyalties prompted them to engage in political strikes and other activities not in the interest of their constituents, their superior organization and warmer faith generally enabled them to hold their own.

There were other reasons. In the AFL, Communist strength grew largely from the existence of racketeering elements in various unions. In the CIO, the enormous and unanticipated victories of the new organization created a demand for specialized services the Communists were uniquely prepared to provide. The great prestige and authority of Lewis, once he had decided to use the Communists, sufficed to silence or nullify the misgivings of others. The miseries of the depression, the social criticism of the period, the popularity of antifascism, and the missionary quality of the CIO gave the Communists a natural setting for their rhetoric and a certain immunity against democratic opposition. The Nazi-Soviet pact was a setback, but the Communists gained a reprieve from the war, when the immediacies of battle were the *bona fides* of allies.

But in the end they failed.[34] They failed in the AFL largely because that organization, committed to business unionism and private enterprise, was a natural enemy; it had no taste for crusades, no large ambitions for obscure ends, and—because of its more stable membership—no need for armies of questionable friends. With the postwar disillusionments, the deep reservoir of American criticism for the radical, and the deadly investigations of Congress, the Communist embrace of the CIO might have become a mortal one. The Communists failed in the CIO because of public opinion, but also because of the private conviction of growing numbers of union leaders that, no matter how effective Communists might be as short-run allies, their true loyalties were to a system in which free trade unionism has no place.

Fraternity had become a luxury, but it was not simply a matter of safety at home. The lines of the cold war had been drawn, and

the leaders of American labor believed that democratic trade unionism had a major responsibility for the shaping of free societies.
Victorious at home, they also looked abroad, where encouragement
was harder to find.

V

The Russian revolution had a direct impact on the international
labor movement. Prior to 1917 there had been a general unity in
international trade unionism, residing mainly in the International
Federation of Trade Unions (IFTU) and a number of trade secretariats for unions in particular industries. The RILU, as soon as it
was formed, attempted to capture the leadership of existing labor
organizations all over the world and gained ground in some parts
of Western Europe, Latin America, and the Far East.

But neither the RILU nor the IFTU wielded great influence
during the interwar years, particularly after the onset of the depression, the growth of military dictatorships, and the heightening of
international political tensions. By the outbreak of World War II,
both organizations had practically ceased to exist.

International trade unionism revived with the war. Formal and
continuing relationships established between the labor movements
of the Allied powers prepared the ground for a new international
labor movement in peacetime. In 1945 the British, French, and
Russian labor movements combined with the CIO to form the
World Federation of Trade Unions (WFTU), based on a comprehensive program of postwar reconstruction, social reform, national
political independence, and international cooperation. The idea
was popular, and within two years the WFTU claimed a membership of 67 million workers. The AFL, which had left the IFTU after
World War I because of the latter's socialist orientation, refused
to join the WFTU because of its Communist affiliates.

The WFTU was an understandable outgrowth of the military
alliances of World War II and the desire for international peacetime cooperation, but it did not long survive the cold war and the
fundamental conflict between Western and Soviet concepts of trade
unionism. The break came in 1949, after several attempts at conciliation by the British and other West European labor movements
had failed. The Western affiliates left the WFTU on three specific
grounds: the conviction of the job-oriented trade secretariats that

the dominant Communist element in the WFTU was using the federation for political purposes; the anger of the Western labor movements at the violent opposition of the Soviet Union to the Marshall Plan; and the continuous opposition of the AFL to participation in an organization dominated by Communists. Negotiations were opened with the AFL; and in December 1949, the AFL, the CIO, the British and almost all other free labor movements joined to form the International Confederation of Free Trade Unions (ICFTU), which now claims a membership of some 65 million in over 100 countries.[35]

The primary emphasis of the ICFTU is on free trade unionism and democratic government. Its rules permit the admission only of those unions or federations which are voluntary in character, democratic in management, and not sponsored or controlled by political parties or governments; they specifically forbid the affiliation of labor organizations in Communist or fascist countries. Its general purpose is to encourage the development of free collective bargaining, the equitable distribution of wealth by democratic means, and the cooperation of free governments in world affairs. Programmatically it concentrates in five areas: resisting totalitarian ideas and organizations in the trade-union field; encouraging the growth of free trade unionism in the developing countries; rendering similar but naturally less-concentrated assistance to affiliated organizations in the more advanced industrial countries; supporting the United Nations as the most hopeful agency for collective security and world peace; and attempting to obtain effective labor representation in the various agencies of the UN and other international bodies.

For these purposes it engages in publicity and propaganda work throughout the world, gives financial and administrative aid to labor movements beset by Communist attempts at infiltration, maintains an International Solidarity Fund to help union officials harassed by their governments, and conducts training schools in Africa, Asia, and Latin America to train the future officialdom of the labor movements in those areas. It attempts to influence the UN General Assembly on such questions as self-government for colonial countries, racial segregation in South Africa, and the international control of nuclear weapons. Through the Economic and Social Council of the UN, it works for the elimination of forced labor and for full employment, higher labor standards, increased technical assistance, the international financing of economic development, and the representation of labor on missions sent to underdeveloped countries. In UNESCO it is particularly concerned with both general and workers' education. It works in the International Labor Organization on such issues as the forty-hour week, higher productivity and wages, vocational training, and aid to migrants and refugees. It also maintains liaison with or is represented on various commissions of NATO, OEEC, the Council of Europe, and the European Coal and Steel Community. Regional organizations in Europe, Africa, Latin America, and Asia, operating under the general direction of the ICFTU headquarters in Brussels, engage in specialized activities in their own territories.

The WFTU has not been idle, and enjoys a number of advantages. Since the affiliation of the mainland Chinese, it now claims a membership of some 95 million, and is probably much richer than the ICFTU.[36] Programmatically, it offers to uncommitted labor movements the prospect of a speed in economic and technological progress which, it avers, is impossible in non-Communist societies—an argument of some force for those who compare the ostensible progress of Red China with that of democratic India. It has exploited racial discrimination in the American and other Western labor movements, and has gained strength from the reluctance of various Western powers to surrender their colonial possessions.

It has also been more flexible than the ICFTU. The latter generally demands that uncommitted labor organizations make a clear choice between the two federations. The WFTU does not compromise where it is strong; but where its position is uncertain, especially in Africa, it demands no more than nonaffiliation with the ICFTU and the pursuit of a neutralist policy. Once disaffection with the ICFTU has been achieved, the WFTU has disbanded its own affiliates and merged them with indigenous and uncommitted organizations. Such self-effacement has been profitable. An increasing number of nonaligned labor movements and even ICFTU affiliates have been attending WFTU conferences; visiting the Soviet Union, Red China, and other Communist countries; accepting WFTU financial aid and policy guidance; and sending students to Communist labor colleges in various parts of the world.

The WFTU, of course, has its own problems. With the consolidation of non-Russian Communist regimes, particularly Red China, the demand has grown within the WFTU for a greater degree of national or regional independence from the Soviet Union. The problem is serious enough already, and will certainly grow with any further estrangement between Red China and the Soviet Union.[37]

But there is division within the ICFTU as well. The prevailing American view, as expressed by the merged AFL-CIO, is that the European labor movements—not to speak of the African, Asian, and Latin American—do not understand the need for an absolute choice between free and Soviet-style trade unionism. On the other hand, the Europeans and others—including many Americans—generally believe that the official policy of the American labor movement is too rigid in its anti-Communism and insufficiently sensitive to the variety of social reform and trade union structures needed to satisfy the needs of the emerging countries. The division is a serious matter. Whether conceived as a question of trade union organization alone, or of the contribution of free trade unionism to democratic political institutions, or of the protection of vital sources of raw materials, the odds are high.

The choice is real. If free trade unionism can embrace a variety of forms and policies, it is nevertheless committed to the principle of free association, to a system of decisive collective bargaining, to the right to strike, and to the self-conceived contribution of an independent labor movement to the welfare of a free society. The Communists have a different view. "In the Bolshevik system," Prime Minister Janos Kádár of Hungary has stated, "trade unions have become transmission belts: their role is restricted to the intensification of production, the organization and popularization of work competition, the affirmation of the leadership of the Party." [38] According to *Trud,* the official organ of Bulgarian labor, "It is politically incorrect to speak today in our country of defending the interests of the workers and employees as it was done in the past, and trade unions do not and cannot have such a task." [39]

Ernest Thornton, former federal secretary of the Australian Ironworkers' Association, informed the 15th National Congress of the Australian Communist Party, "The policy of the Ironworkers' Union is decided in consultation with the leaders of the Communist Party. The great achievements of our union in the last few years should be credited to the Communist Party. But they are not so credited. Because the Party does not appear as the Communist Party to the members of the union, the achievements of our leaders are credited to individuals and not to the Party." [40] The advice of Lenin prevails: control, but hide the instruments of control.

The choice, once made, has political implications of the highest order. "The outlook for nonpolitical unionism in the newly developing countries," according to Walter Galenson, "is not bright." [41] In most such countries the indigenous labor movements have little economic power. Weak unions turn to politics, and can help to determine by their philosophical choices the political systems under which their organizations will live. The WFTU, by appealing to national unity and independence, to nonalignment in international affairs, and to the need for draconian reforms, has gained strong allies. "Political developments in Africa and Latin America," George Lichtblau has written, "now enable the labor organizations of the Soviet-bloc countries to contribute tactical and technical guidance, training of cadres, and financial assistance to a growing number of labor movements, helping them thereby to transform their societies into socio-economic structures resembling those of the 'People's Democracies.'" [42]

The Communist effort is formidable. The Soviet Union, according to one estimate, has trained a reserve of ten thousand experts on development available for service overseas. [43] There is already, in countries such as Indonesia and Japan, a substantial body of support for Communist causes. In Costa Rica, Brazil, Chile, and Peru, the WFTU has an estimated 447 full-time organizers, compared with the ICFTU's seven. [44] In Africa, the WFTU has helped to set up the new, nonaligned All-Africa Trade Union Federation, which has made inroads into ICFTU strength in many parts of the continent. The Confederation of Arab Trade Unions, partly due to WFTU efforts, vacillates between nonalignment and anti-Westernism. [45] In India, the mantle of respectability assumed by the Communist-controlled All-India Trade Union Congress has raised the prospect of alliance and merger with the ICFTU-affiliated Indian National Trade Union Congress. [46] Inroads are being made, exchanges are multiplied, and the lines are blurred. There is a final, ominous note. Red China, according to West African testimony, is now training foreign trade unionists in the arts of sabotage and guerrilla warfare. [47]

The obvious response is to expand free trade-union activities through greatly increased investments in men and money; but skill is demanded no less than scale. A commitment to free trade unionism does not preclude flexibility in application. Native soils produce different needs, and the price of cooperation should not be identity in institutions.

The final decisions, in any event, are not in our hands. They will be made by complex men who—exalted by independence, driven by nationalism, sensitive to discrimination, courted by giants, and pressed by their followers—are eager for achievement. In every case the choice between impatience and tolerance, between authority and consent, will be a crucial one. In almost every case the absence of a native democratic tradition, the hunger for status, and the absence of a native democratic tradition, will counsel discipline rather than dissent, the authoritarian rather than the democratic measure, the unitary rather than the pluralist state. The degree of transitional concession to the free society will depend in good measure on the quality of understanding which is given. There is, and can be, no assurance that the outcome will be in our favor.

FOOTNOTES

[1] V.I. Lenin, "What Is To Be Done?" in Lenin, *Collected Works: The Iskra Period* (New York: International Publishers, 1929), p. 189. In general see Thomas Taylor Hammond, *Lenin on Trade Unions and Revolution* (New York: Columbia University Press, 1957).

[2] "What Is To Be Done?" p. 189.

[3] *Ibid.*

[4] Lenin, "Novoe poboishsche," in *Sochineniia,* 4:115, June 1901.

[5] "What Is To Be Done?" p. 191.

[6] *Ibid.,* pp. 143, 172.

[7] *Ibid.,* p. 123.

[8] *Ibid.,* pp. 194, 196.

[9] Quoted in Hammond, *op. cit.,* p. 73n.

[10] Lenin, *Left-Wing Communism: An Infantile Disorder* (Moscow: Foreign Languages Publishing House, 1952), pp. 58-59. Italics in the original.

[11] "Pismo 'Severnomu Soiuzu'," in *Sochineniia,* 5:129 (April 1902).

[12] *Left-Wing Communism,* p. 57.

[13] *Ibid.,* pp. 61, 64.

[14] Isaac Deutscher, *Soviet Trade Unions* (London: Royal Institute of International Affairs, 1950), pp. 135-136.

[15] *Left-Wing Communism,* pp. 52-53. Italics in the original.

[16] *Theses and Statutes of the Third (Communist) International* (Moscow: 1922), p. 35.

[17] *Resolutions and Decisions Adopted by the First International Congress of Revolutionary Trade and Industrial Unions* (Moscow: 1921), pp. 19, 31, cited in the testimony of Philip Taft, "Communist Domination of Unions and National Security," *Hearings,* Senate Committee on Labor and Public Welfare, 82d Cong., 2d sess. (Washington, D.C.: U.S. Government Printing Office, 1952).

[18] Benjamin Gitlow, *I Confess* (New York: Dutton, 1939), p. 339.

[19] William Z. Foster, "Party Trade-Union Factions," *Workers Monthly,* July 1925, p. 414.

[20] The Needle Trades Workers Industrial Union, the Communist-led group, broke away from the AFL International Fur Workers Union (IFWU) in 1928. By 1932 it dominated the New York City fur market, the center of the industry. Following another change in Party policy, it reaffiliated with the IFWU in 1934 and brought that union under Communist control. The IFWU later joined the Congress of Industrial Organizations, was expelled in 1949, and after removing Communists from office was absorbed by the Meat Cutters in 1955.

[21] Earl Browder, "Why an Open Letter to Our Party Membership?" *The Communist,* August 1933, pp. 711-712.

[21] *Ibid.,* p. 715. Italics in the original.

[23] Alex Bittelman, "Milestones of Comintern Leadership," *The Communist,* March, 1934, p. 240.

[24] Cited in David J. Saposs, *Communism in American Unions* (New York: McGraw-Hill, 1959), p. 19.

[25] However, according to one observer, no Communist propaganda ever reached the screen except in "possibly rare instances." See Dorothy B. Jones, "Communism and the Movies: A Study of Film Content," in John Cogley, ed., *Report on Blacklisting* (Fund for the Republic, 1956), p. 197.

[26] See House Committee on Un-American Activities, *Hearings* (on the motion picture industry), 80th Cong., 1st sess., 1947.

[27] It is worth repeating that in both cases the Communists gained a foothold by opposing racketeering elements, thus winning the support of a substantial minority of non-Communists.

[28] Max H. Kampelman, *The Communist Party vs. the CIO* (New York: Praeger, 1957), p. 16.

[29] Herbert Harris, *Labor's Civil War* (New York: Knopf, 1940), pp. 129-133. Most of these were small unions. The Party-controlled unions never represented more than 20 percent of the CIO's individual membership.

[30] Kampelman, *op. cit.*, p. 22.

[31] See Joel Seidman, "Labor Policy of the Communist Party during World War II," *Industrial and Labor Relations Review*, October 1950.

[32] Kampelman, *op. cit.*, p. 144.

[33] *Ibid.*, p. 145.

[34] On legislative measures taken to control Communism in American unions, see Benjamin Aaron, "Statutory Regulation of Internal Union Affairs: The Control of Communism," *Proceedings of New York University Fifth Annual Conference on Labor* (Albany: Matthew Bender, 1952).

[35] Arne Geijer, "The Tasks Ahead," *Free Labour World*, August-September 1962.

[36] Otto Pick and Andrew Wiseman, "Moscow and the WFTU," *Problems of Communism*, May-June 1959.

[37] See G. E. Lynd, "Workers Disunite," *Problems of Communism*, March-April 1962.

[38] Robert Gabor, *Trade Unions: Transmission Belts of the Party* (New York: Free Hungarian Trade Unions in Exile, n.d.).

[39] *Trud*, February 22, 1952.

[40] Herbert E. Weiner, "The Reduction of Communist Power in the Australian Trade Unions," *Political Science Quarterly*, September 1954, p. 398.

[41] Walter Galenson, *Labor in Developing Economies* (Berkeley: University of California Press, 1962), p. 8.

[42] George Lichtblau, "The Communist Labor Offensive in

Former Colonial Countries," *Industrial and Labor Relations Review,* April 1962, p. 401. Among West European unions substantial Communist strength is confined to France and Italy.

[43] "The Soviet Bloc and the Developing Countries," *Forschungsstelle der Friedrich-Ebert-Stiftung* (Bonn: 1962), p. 37.

[44] A. Sanchez Madariaga, "The Communist Drive against Latin American Unions," *Free Labour World,* June 1961. For a historical review see Ben G. Burnett, "Communist Strategy in the Latin American Labor Movement," *Social Science,* April 1960. See also Robert J. Alexander, "Labor and Inter-American Relations," *Annals of the American Academy of Political and Social Science,* March 1961.

[45] Lichtblau, *op. cit.*

[46] Brij Moohan Toofan, "The Communists and Indian Labor," *Problems of Communism,* March-April 1959.

[47] *Sunday Telegraph* (London), July 23, 1961. According to various reports, Cuba is similarly engaged.

The Jacobin Left and the Future of the Communists in Latin America

Robert J. Alexander

The advent of the Castro government to power in Cuba opened a new chapter in the history of the Communist movement in Latin America. Not only did it result in the establishment of the first self-proclaimed Communist regime in the hemisphere, but it also allowed the Communist Parties to break out of a position of political isolation in which they had been for a decade.

However, although Castro's immediate effect was favorable to Latin American Communists, his long-range impact may be considerably less so. For there is good reason to believe that Communists will be faced with an important challenge from the Left, from groups temperamentally and politically a good deal more extremist than the Communist Parties themselves. Fidel Castro and the group most closely associated with him in Cuba have helped crystallize a current of Latin American political opinion which we shall call the Jacobin Left, or simply Jacobins, still somewhat amorphous and disorganized, but a potential extremist challenge to the Communists.

Of course, the Jacobin parties and groups are not the first competitors of the Communists for leadership of the revolutionary movement in Latin America. From their very inception, various of the Communist Parties have had to battle socialist parties for the loyalty of the workers, the middle classes, and the peasants. In several countries traditional liberal parties have also been formidable rivals. And during the last three decades the Communists have been confronted with an even greater competition in the national revolutionary parties, which in country after country reduced the Communists to little more than a nuisance.

However, in their competition with the socialists, liberals, and national revolutionaries, the Communists were generally the more extremist. They were the ones who urged the most drastic methods of revolutionary change, they were the most extreme advocates of jingoistic nationalism, they possessed the internally consistent doctrine that seemed to answer all questions. In contrast, the competing groups urged more pacific means of achieving power, sought to carry out social change through democratic processes, and sometimes seemed to reflect doctrinal confusion or controversy within their ranks. Democratic advocates of social and economic change faced an increasingly difficult dilemma. In the many countries where they came to power or to the verge of power, they encountered grave difficulties in carrying out their program. Elsewhere it seemed that nonviolent methods of gaining power and beginning the social changes advocated by the democratic Left would never succeed. This crisis of the democratic Left, which was highlighted by Castro's advent to power in Cuba, may have helped the Communists, at least in some countries. Certainly, the possible failure of the democratic Left in Venezuela, Peru, Colombia, and other countries would be a potential gain to extremists, which until 1959 meant principally the Communists.

It was at this point that the Jacobins began to contest for power in Latin America. This was not the first time the Communists had to face a competitor on their Left, but the two previous challenges of this type had been relatively insignificant. Anarcho-syndicalists, who had had considerable influence in the labor movements of several Latin American countries, were already on the decline by the time the Communists appeared on the scene, and changing conditions made their appeal less and less popular. By the end of the 1920's, the anarcho-syndicalists had ceased to be significant in most Latin American countries.

In the late 1920's and early 1930's, factions developed in several of the Latin American Communist Parties, reflecting the worldwide Stalin-Trotsky feud. In the Chilean Party, the larger of the two groups was the Trotskyite faction, which for several years competed successfully with the Stalinist Communists for influence in the labor movement and intellectual circles. In Cuba, a Trotskyite faction led by Sandalio Junco had a considerable influence in the labor movement. Later, the Trotskyites joined the Leftist democratic Auténtico Party of Dr. Ramón Grau San Martín, which for two decades constituted the Communists' principal opposition in the trade-union movement.

Subsequently, the Trotskyites in Bolivia attained briefly a greater significance in national politics than the Stalinists had. They had developed a close relation with Juan Lechin, the principal trade-union leader of the Movimiento Nacionalista Revolucionario (MNR), which in 1952 seized control of the government and began one of this century's most profound revolutions in Latin America. However, Lechin turned against his Trotskyite supporters at the end of 1952; and they lost most of their remaining importance in 1954, when most of their trade-union followers opposed their extreme sectarianism and joined the MNR. Since that time, the orthodox Communists have constituted the MNR's principal Left opposition.

Several other countries have had small Trotskyite parties, notably Peru, Argentina, Uruguay, Brazil, and Mexico. However, in no case could they long challenge the Communists as the principal Left element in national politics. Only with the rise of Jacobins since 1959 have the Communists had to confront such a challenge on a hemispheric scale.

II

The Communist movement in Latin America began in the aftermath of the First World War. The Left wings of the socialist parties of several countries were very much attracted to the Bolshevik revolution. In Uruguay, Mexico, and Chile the socialist parties themselves joined the Comintern, while in Argentina a dissident socialist group that had split off in 1918 became the Communist Party. Other Communist Parties were established partly by Comintern agents, who became active in the area very early. In Cuba, Costa Rica, Brazil, Peru, Paraguay, Ecuador, and Colombia, Parties were organized in the middle or late 1920's. Communist Parties were established in Venezuela and Panama during the 1930's; in most of Central America, Haiti, and the Dominican Republic during the 1940's; and in Honduras and Bolivia during the 1950's.

At the present time, therefore, a Communist party exists in every Latin American country. All of those in existence before the Comintern was officially disbanded belonged to it. All Latin American Parties have participated in recent international Communist gatherings, such as the meetings held in Moscow in 1960 and 1961. In short, the Latin American Parties have been loyal and orthodox members of the international Communist movement. To believe that the various Communist Parties of the area are "more Latin American than Communist," or that they are "merely agrarian reformers," is to suffer from a delusion.

Over the decades Latin American Communists have faithfully followed the various twists and turns of the international Communist line. In the 1920's they shared in the "bolshevization" that Communist Parties all over the world were undergoing. In the so-called Third Period of 1929-35, when the Comintern imposed an extreme sectarianism, every Latin American Party then in existence followed suit and established a dual trade union movement under its control. In Mexico, and in Cuba in 1933, the Communists violently opposed social and nationalist revolutions. Subsequently, the Latin American Communists conformed to the Popular Front, abolishing their dual labor movements and seeking to collaborate in national Popular Fronts in their respective countries. During the period of the Stalin-Nazi Pact, they conformed again, reverting to the extreme sectarianism of the Third Period and maintaining so great an "objectivity" toward World War II that in some instances they actually collaborated with local pro-Axis elements. After the Nazi armies invaded the Soviet Union, the Latin American Communists, like their confreres elsewhere, were superpatriotic, seemingly more pro-Allied than the Allies themselves. When the cold war began, they turned from eulogizing the United States to violent attacks against the "Colossus of the North."

Like Communists everywhere, the Latin American Parties throughout most of their history have shared the basic aims of the international movement—the "defense of the Soviet Union" and the attainment of dictatorial power in their respective nations. When the two aims conflicted, however, the Latin-American Communists sacrificed themselves to serve the interests of the Soviet Union. This loyalty to Russia has not been accidental. Most of the Parties' founders felt inspired by the Soviet experiment, and many top and junior leaders from all over Latin America were taken to the Soviet Union for intensive training. As long as the Comintern existed, it had leading Latin American Communists in its apparatus, and since its dismemberment a fair number have served on the staffs of the Cominform and of such peripheral organizations as the World Federation of Trade Unions, the International Union of Democratic Youth, and the World Peace Council.

Like all Communist Parties, those of Latin America have devoted much time and energy to the labor movements of their respective countries—participating in them and trying to gain control of them. Their effectiveness in the labor movement has varied a good deal from time to time and from country to country. The high point of influence was in the middle 1940's, when Communists had a major or dominant influence in most labor movements of Latin America and controlled the only hemispheric labor organization, the Confederación de Trabajadores de América Latina (CTAL). The Cali Congress of the CTAL in December 1944 elected an executive committee of eleven men, of whom seven were avowed Communists, three were fellow-travelers, and only one was openly anti-Communist.

III

In general, Communist influence in the labor movement has been associated with their broader importance in the politics of the particular countries. The Castro regime constitutes the fifth instance of important Communist influence on the governments of Latin America. The earlier cases were in Cuba under Batista in the early 1940's, in Ecuador in 1944, in Chile under González Videla in 1946-47, and in Guatemala under Arbenz in 1952-54. These are discussed briefly in turn.

Fulgencio Batista and the Cuban Communists formed an alliance at the end of 1937. Batista was promised Communist support for his ambition to become president, and in return he agreed to allow the Communists to function legally and assured them control of the labor movement. During his first term as president, 1940-44, Batista brought two Communists into his cabinet as ministers without portfolio, junior partners in the administration—Juan Marinello, who under Castro would become president of the University of Havana, and Carlos Rafael Rodríguez, who under Castro would be head of the National Institute of Agrarian Reform. This Batista-Communist alliance lasted for two decades.

In 1944 the Communist Party of Ecuador participated in organizing the successful insurrection against President Carlos Arroyo del Rio. Communists were officially represented in the provisional regime set up thereafter, but their period in the government was too short for them to establish any significant power over the administrative apparatus, though they made important gains in the labor movement.

In 1946, the Chilean Communist Party was one of the two principal partners, along with the Radical Party, in the coalition that elected the radical leader Gabriel González Videla as president. During the first five months of his administration, when Communists had three members in the cabinet, their influence within the regime was greater than this proportion of the top posts would suggest. However, in April 1947, following nationwide municipal elections which ran against the Communists' governmental partners, the Radicals and Liberals, the Communists were dropped from the cabinet, having refused to resign voluntarily. Shortly afterwards they turned violently against González Videla, who induced Congress to pass the so-called Law for the Defense of Democracy, which outlawed the Communist Party.

Finally, in Guatemala between 1952 and 1954, the Communists had more influence than in any Latin American government up to that time. President Jacobo Arbenz relied very heavily on their support, in return for which he assured them complete control of the labor movement and turned over to them such key parts of the administration as the National Agrarian Reform Institute, the Social Security Board, and the government propaganda office. They had no official representation in the government but held key posts in Arbenz' "shadow cabinet," composed of the heads of the four pro-government parties (including the Communist Party, or Partido Guatemalteco del Trabajo—PGT) and the peasant and labor confederations. Probably the president's closest political adviser was José Manuel Fortuny, secretary-general of the PGT. In all probability, if President Arbenz had remained in office until the end of 1954, the Communists would have attained as much control as their brother parties in Eastern Europe had shortly after World War II. He was overthrown in June of that year.

In addition to these experiences in various national governments, Communists have frequently had members in national and provincial legislatures, city councils, and other elective bodies. At the end of 1962, for instance, there were Communist deputies in the national congresses of Chile, Uruguay, Brazil, Venezuela, and Ecuador.

In summary, in virtually every country of the hemisphere, the Communists have won for themselves a recognized position in the national political spectrum. Although in more or less bitter opposition to all governments except Castro's, they have something significant to lose if a violent attempt on their part to seize power were to fail. After four decades or more of struggle, when Castro came to power the Communist movement in Latin America was at a low ebb. Their obvious allegiance to the Soviet Union, often aggravated by local factors, had brought them into greater isolation than for almost two decades. However, even in their isolation the Communists had a philosophy, a political direction, and enough investment in the *status quo* to make them hesitate before engaging in any insurrection.

IV

In Cuba, when Fidel Castro first opposed the Batista government, the Communists of the so-called Partido Socialista Popular (PSP) condemned him as a "putschist." It was not until shortly before his triumph that they decided to give at least some support to his efforts; they still maintained more or less cordial relations with Batista until as late as August 1958, only five months before Castro rode triumphantly into Havana. The Cuban Communists were suspicious of the romanticism, the personalism, the apparent irresponsibilty of Fidel Castro and his followers; and they joined with him only after it seemed profitable to do so. This ambivalence marks the relation between the Communists and the Jacobins in most other Latin American countries.

The Jacobin Left is still a somewhat amorphous and dispersed stream of public opinion which had been forming for more than a decade. The Jacobins recognized in the Cuban leader a symbol around which to organize, and since Castro's ascension to power in 1959, they have become a significant force in several countries.

Like the Jacobins of the French revolution, those of Latin America are nationalistic to the point of xenophobia. Like their French predecessors, they favor cataclysmic social change at virtually any cost. At best, they disparage the "formalities" of political democracy; at worst, they consider them to be a cloak to protect the interests of the ruling class.

Fundamentally, the Jacobins constitute the political expression of the frustration, even desperation, apparent in Latin America throughout the postwar period, the consequence of an economic development too slow to keep up with the masses' rising expectations and the explosive increase in population. Many have come to doubt whether the long-overdue social reforms could be achieved by the democratic process. Such attitudes were aggravated, moreover, by the spectacle of the United States, the self-proclaimed leader of world democracy and the symbol of material progress, whose policies often favored military dictatorship in Latin America and contributed but little to the region's economic progress.

Castro had at least two important Jacobin predecessors. Getulio Vargas, the dictator of Brazil in 1937-45, pushed forward rapid industrialization and enacted many reforms, which gave the urban poor at least the illusion that they were finally playing a part in their country's civic affairs. He had no pretensions to hemispheric leadership, but this was not true of Juan Perón of Argentina. While carrying out drastic labor and social reforms, favoring industrialization, and laying the basis for a totalitarian regime at home, Perón sought also to become the leader, the symbol, of an international political movement. In his aspirations at least, he was an important precursor of Fidel Castro.

Castro, the triumphant leader of a seemingly impossible revolution, was a catalyst to the dispersed Jacobin sentiment growing during the 1950's. He brought to the extreme Left enthusiasm and militancy, qualities that the Communists had long lacked. To many, Castro appealed as a native American revolutionist. He came to power with no extracontinental help, and if later he turned to a foreign country for support, he seemed to do so only to protect the revolution of which he was the author and leader. His romanticism, which may appear ridiculous to sober spirits, is attractive to many, particularly among the young. They could not doubt the profundity of the social changes he was bringing about, or his strident proclamations that he would industrialize his island. And his violent diatribes against the Yankees won him support even from those otherwise inclined to oppose his regime.

Of the various parties and groups in Latin American countries that are coalescing behind Fidel Castro, probably the most vociferous are those of Venezuela. The Jacobin tendency is represented there by the Movimiento de Izquierda Revolucionaria (MIR), and by part of the Union Republicana Democrática (URD). The for-

mer was established in 1960 by a group of young people who broke
away from the Acción Democrática, the Left democratic party of
which President Romulo Betancourt is the principal figure. They
proclaim themselves as "Marxist-Leninists," and some of their more
enthusiastic spokesmen have gone so far as to label Domingo Al-
berto Rangel, their principal spokesman, "the Venezuelan Lenin."

The URD is a more complex institution. Organized in 1946, it
had no well-defined ideology. Its spokesmen frequently referred to
it as a "liberal" party, and until 1959 frequently attacked the Acción
Democrática as "too socialist." However, after Castro came to power,
many of the younger people in the URD were attracted to his support and began to attack Betancourt's administration even while
the URD was still in the government. The party withdrew from
the government in November 1960, and since then the Communists, the MIR, and the URD have generally cooperated in Congress, in the labor movement, and among the students. As a party,
the URD has not taken a position on the Castro regime, although
it tends to favor it. However, early in 1962, when one of its principal
younger leaders, Fabricio Ojeda, attempted to organize a Fidel-like
guerrilla campaign against the Betancourt government, the party
expelled him. There is little doubt that the MIR, on the other
hand, together with some elements of the Communist Party, attempted to organize an insurrection against Betancourt, following
the example of Castro in Cuba. They have also sought to subvert
the country's armed forces, and have terrorized the principal cities.

In Peru, also, there are several different Jacobin groups. The
Apra Rebelde, a dissident faction that broke away from the Left
democratic Aprista party in the late 1950's, in 1962 changed its
name to the Movimiento de Izquierda Revolucionaria. The Partido Social Progresista is another such group, formed in the late
1950's. The Trotskyite party, the Partido Obrero Revolucionario,
is small but active. The old Partido Socialista has also tended to
side with the Jacobins. These various Jacobin parties in Peru have
tried to incite Indian peasants to appropriate private land, to develop several strikes into violent clashes, and in isolated areas to
organize small guerrilla bands.

Peru's 1962 election campaign had at least two Jacobin candidates, one named by the Partido Social Progresista and the other
by the Partido Socialista, as well as a Communist nominee. When
the election resulted in a virtual deadlock, the Jacobins supported

a coup by the military, who seized power in July 1962. Later, however, the military regime accused the Jacobin groups of having organized a nationwide conspiracy to seize power through insurrection and guerrilla attacks.

In Colombia, likewise, various elements can be identified with Jacobin tendency. Onetime supporters of the Leftist liberal leader Jorge Eliecer Gaitan (who was assassinated in 1948), now led by his daughter and her husband, follow this line. The Movimiento Liberal Revolucionario, organized in the late 1950's by dissident members of the Liberal Party, more or less repudiated Fidel Castro in 1962 through its principal leader, Alfonso Lopez Michelson, but its Left wing still ardently support Castro. The Colombian Jacobins have actively sought to stir up guerrilla conflict, for which that country presented fertile ground because of the violent Liberal-Conservative conflict intermittent since 1948.

In Costa Rica the principal Jacobin group is small. It was formed in 1961 by dissidents from the Leftist democratic party of José Figueres, Liberación Nacional, including one or two of this party's deputies. But it made an exceedingly poor showing in the 1962 general election, and up to the beginning of 1963 it had not seriously attempted to launch a guerrilla conflict.

In 1961, a heterogeneous group of Mexican intellectuals and lower-echelon trade-union leaders established a Jacobin group, the Movimiento de Liberación Nacional, under the titular leadership of ex-President Lázaro Cárdenas. It has devoted its energies mainly to stimulating discontent among peasants, whose demand for land had not been satisfied under the government's agrarian reform program. As of the beginning of 1963, it had not organized any serious guerrilla efforts.

In several countries, elements of formerly democratic socialist parties constitute the Jacobin force. This is the case in Argentina, where several factions of the much-divided Socialist Party support the Cuban chieftain, together with dissident elements of the Unión Civica Radical Intransigente, the party of ex-President Arturo Frondizi. The socialists of Uruguay have also pledged their support to Castro. Those of Ecuador were badly split on the subject. In Brazil, Francisco Julião, socialist leader in the northeastern state of Pernambuco and an important organizer of peasant leagues in that area, made a particular point of his admiration for the Cuban leader.

V

The distinction between the Jacobins and the orthodox Communists is relevant even in Castro's Cuba, in spite of the fact that the two groups have now joined in a single party. This formal unity has by no means ended all differences between the two groups.

The original 26th of July Movement of Fidel Castro included within its ranks large numbers who wanted the Cuban revolution to be achieved democratically, as well as many who preferred totalitarian solutions to the country's problems. At the end of 1959 Castro threw in his lot with the latter group, and the democratic elements were purged from the movement. Subsequently the remnants of the 26th of July Movement and the orthodox Communists (the Partido Socialista Popular—PSP) moved closed together, while PSP leaders were being given increasingly important posts in the regime. On July 26, 1961, Castro announced the merger of the 26th of July Movement, the PSP, and another small Fidelista group, the Directorio Revolucionario, into a new organization to be called the Organizaciones Revolucionarias Integradas (ORI). The consolidation was managed by Aníbal Escalante, a leading PSP figure, and he made certain that the new group was controlled by orthodox Communists. At the same time, Fidelistas holding key posts in the administration were ousted. In November 1962, Communists took over the national labor movement, and Lázaro Peña, onetime Communist deputy who had headed the Confederación de Trabajadores de Cuba under Batista, returned as its secretary-general. Shortly afterwards, Juan Marinello was chosen as head of the University of Havana, and Carlos Rafael Rodríguez was put in charge of the country's national economic planning and succeeded Fidel Castro himself as President of the National Institute of Agrarian Reform.

This Communist drive to take over full control of the Castro regime, however, came to a sudden halt. Starting on March 18, 1962, Fidel Castro began a series of violent attacks on the leadership of the former PSP, accusing it—accurately—of trying to seize control of the government. Aníbal Escalante was designated the chief scapegoat, but Castro's oratory was certainly directed at the whole Communist leadership. This conflict between the Fidelistas and the orthodox Communists was covered over after the Communist Party of the Soviet Union endorsed Castro, but the bitterness between the two groups undoubtedly continued, and was even aggravated in October 1962 by the matter of the Soviet missile bases in Cuba. At a time when Castro was fulminating against Khrushchev's decision to withdraw the missiles, prominent Communists were enthusiastically endorsing it. The important distinctions between the Jacobin Fidelistas and the orthodox Communists of the PSP remain relevant in Cuba, and may become more so in the years to come.

VI

As in Cuba, so also in Latin America generally, the rise of the Jacobins at first meant considerable gains for the Communists. Since Jacobin parties and groups were willing and even anxious to work with them, the Communists could escape from the almost complete isolation of the recent period. When Cuba became an avowedly Communist state, Latin American Communists no longer were restricted to countries outside of the Western Hemisphere for examples of the Communist revolution. Enthusiastic young Party members and gullible fellow-travelers could be sent to the Caribbean island "to see for themselves"; there a Communist revolution was being carried out in an economic, social, and cultural milieu highly reminiscent of their own country. Communist Cuba, finally, facilitated the preparation and shipment of propaganda to the rest of Latin America. Party functionaries could be trained there, and the Cuban diplomatic missions could distribute propaganda, money, and personnel for the Communist movement throughout the hemisphere.

However, in the long run these immediate gains for the Communists may be counterbalanced by conflicts between them and the Jacobins. As we have noted, some such dissension was evident by the end of 1962, and it seems likely to grow. The parties are largely based in different social classes, the orthodox Communists in the working class, and the Jacobins in the middle and upper classes.

The latent disagreements will probably become acute as the split between the Soviet and Chinese factions of the international Communist movement comes completely out into the open. When the various Communist Parties all over the world have to choose sides, in Latin America this is likely to result in a major crisis in Jacobin-Communist relations. If such a worldwide split in the Communist movement developed to the full, in all likelihood most of the parties of Latin America would align themselves with the Soviet Union, and the Chinese would be supported by at least some of the Jacobin groups. The loyalty of the orthodox Communist Parties to the Soviet Union is deeply ingrained. As we have noted, many leaders of these organizations were trained there for longer or shorter periods, and they have spent most of their adult lives extolling Soviet virtues, in which the vast majority of them undoubtedly honestly believe. In any case, the Soviet line of "coexistence," with a primary reliance on legal methods to seize power, appeals more to the leaders of the Communist Parties. These Parties have something to lose, and their leaders are not likely to be anxious to risk what they have for an attempted coup. This caution is reinforced by the fact that most of the Latin American Communist leaders are either middle-aged or old. In some cases, the founders of the Parties are still heading them; this is the case, for instance, with Victorio Codovilla in Argentina. Such men are not likely to break with their lifelong loyalties, or to take to the hills to organize a guerrilla war.

A few of the orthodox Communist parties may nevertheless not adopt a pro-Soviet position. In 1961, Brazil's Communist Party split into two factions, with the one headed by the Party's principal leader, Luis Carlos Prestes, loyal to the Soviet Union, and the rival group backing the Chinese. In Venezuela, too, there have been evidences of such a division of opinion. Some Communist leaders there are certainly opposed to the insurrectionist and terrorist tactics the Party has tended to follow since the end of 1960. However, during and after the Pérez Jiménez dictatorship (1948-58), the Party recruited many younger people, especially university students, who are more favorable to the Fidelista mode of seizing power than to the more cautious approach traditional to the Latin American Parties. If such differences of opinion were to lead to a Party split, one faction might well align itself with the Chinese and the other with the USSR. Similar differences of opinion undoubtedly exist in other Latin American Communist Parties. It seems highly likely that as the Soviet-Chinese split develops, the orthodox Communist Parties will lose a sizable proportion of their younger members.

For their part, the Jacobins have no lifetime investment in adulation of the Soviet Union. There were two major Communist powers when most of them came to political maturity, and they will perceive no treason in supporting one of these against the other. Because they are new in politics, the Jacobins have no assured position in their respective countries. They have few elected officials, little or no influence in the labor movement, little to lose by an attempted guerrilla uprising. The tendency to rashness is reinforced by their youth: Jacobins are mainly in their twenties or early thirties, university students or young professionals. For all of these reasons, the violent, insurrectionary line favored by the Chinese Communists is more likely to appeal to the Jacobins than the more moderate advance advocated by the Soviet Communists, as was the case in several countries on the issue of the Cuban missile bases.

In summary, the rise of Jacobins as a coherent element in Latin American politics has had an important impact on the hemisphere's Communist movement, and it is likely to have an even greater one in the future. During the first years after the Castro revolution, the Jacobins helped the Communists to break out of the isolation in which they had festered for two decades, and probably brought them many new recruits. But in the proximate future this cooperation is likely to present the Communists with very serious problems. The Jacobins threaten to become the most serious opponent that the Communists have ever had on their Left. As the worldwide dispute develops within the international Communist movement, the Soviet Union will probably have the virtually solid backing of the orthodox Communists, while the Jacobins will become the "Chinese" Communists of Latin America.

World Communism: A Reading List for Nonspecialists*

William Petersen and Paul E. Zinner

In the 1930's intellectuals aspired to know all the important books about Communism; today scholars find it difficult to keep up with their own specialized areas. More than ever, the general reader needs a guide through the growing literature. There are two excellent bibliographies, but neither quite satisfies his needs. Philip Grierson, *Books on Soviet Russia, 1917-1942: A Bibliography and Guide to Reading* (London: Methuen, 1943), is limited to Russia and to a period that ended more than two decades ago. R. N. Carew Hunt, *Books on Communism* (Essential Books, 1959), covers both scholarly and popular works on Communism anywhere in the world up to mid-1958. Our list was prepared independently and then checked against Professor Carew Hunt's recommendations. There is a surprisingly small overlap, in part because of the large number of works published in the interim, in part because each bibliography reflects to some degree the backgrounds, preferences, and prejudices of the compilers. Robert Finley Delaney, *The Literature of Communism in America: A Selected Reference Guide* (Catholic University Press, 1962), is largely an uncritical compilation of congressional hearings and reports.

Our reading list is not "objective" in the sense of balancing each criticism of totalitarianism with an apology for it; in this sense, we are no more "objective" about Communism than we were about Nazism. The works have been chosen and described from the point of view of a Western democrat, but also from the point of view of a Western scholar: the two criteria do not clash. The first and most important standard by which the books have been chosen is that in

---

* This list is based in part on the recommended readings suggested by some of the other contributors. We are especially grateful to Gregory Grossman and Nancy Heer, who reviewed a draft of this paper. But the opinions expressed and the responsibility for them are ours.

our opinion reading them would contribute significantly to a general reader's understanding of Communism. Some of the works are more important than others; the best, in our opinion, are marked with an asterisk. We prefer good writing to bad; all of the books are in English, and many of them in well-written English. Except for a few items of special interest, all are currently available in bookstores, many in paperback editions. While the most recent trends are given their due, the philosophical and historical background is not skimped.

The Ideological Background

The writings of Marxism-Leninism are not intrinsically interesting or stylistically engaging. How much of the original texts the general reader should absorb is somewhat a matter of taste, but he would do well to become acquainted with at least the most important figures and their major works.

The best biography of Marx is Isaiah Berlin, *Karl Marx: His Life and Environment* (Oxford paperback). The most useful compilation of the founders' writings is Lewis S. Feuer, ed., *Marx and Engels: Basic Writings on Politics and Philosophy* (Doubleday-Anchor paperback). Of the large library of interpretations, perhaps the best short work for the general reader is Alfred G. Meyer, *Marxism: The Unity of Theory and Practice* (Harvard, 1954). Henry B. Mayo, *Introduction to Marxist Theory* (Oxford paperback), is a more frankly hostile interpretation. Several more recent works also stand out: George Lichtheim, *Marxism: An Historical and Critical Study* (Praeger, 1961); R. C. Tucker, *Philosophy and Myth in Karl Marx* (Cambridge paperback).

By a considerable margin the best sympathetic interpretation of Marxian economics is Paul M. Sweezy, *The Theory of Capitalist Development: Principles of Marxian Political Economy* (Oxford, 1942); this is not an easy book, but its difficulty derives from the subject matter rather than, as often in Marx, from the convoluted language. A more elementary presentation, mainly through passages from Marx's various works, is Robert Freedman, ed., *Marx on Economics* (Harvest paperback).

Lenin is considerably more important for our subject; he is the Father of Bolshevism, and his repetitious and bludgeoning language shaped the whole movement. An antidote to the worshipful commentary of all schools of Communists is a muckraking biography from the Menshevik point of view—David Shub, *Lenin* (Mentor paperback). Much more significant both as biography and as interpretation of the Russian revolution is Bertram D. Wolfe, *Three Who Made a Revolution* (Beacon paperback). Among Lenin's own writings, three pamphlets are especially important—*What Is to Be Done?*, *State and Revolution*, and *Imperialism, The Highest Stage of Capitalism;* they are available most cheaply in the "Little Lenin Library," International Publishers, New York. An important Marxian commentary is in Rosa Luxemburg, *The Russian Revolution* and *Leninism or Marxism?* (Ann Arbor paperback). Most works on Communism and especially those on Communist theory discuss Lenin's ideas and acts at length; they are listed below under other headings.

It is commonplace these days to denigrate Stalin as a theorist, and no one with any pretensions to objectivity ever acclaimed him as a stylist. Yet one can hardly appreciate Soviet civilization, or the credulity of its Western admirers, unless one reads some of the speeches that Stalin was making in the very years that he was being acclaimed as a Friend of All Mankind. They are collected in *Foundations of Leninism, Problems of Leninism,* and *Leninism: Selected Writings,* all available in various editions. A convenient selection of Stalin's writings is M. R. Werner, *Stalin's Kampf* (Howell, Soskin, 1940). By far the best biography-interpretation is Boris Souvarine, *Stalin—A Critical Survey of Bolshevism* (Alliance, 1939); this American translation unfortunately omitted the footnote references, which in the original French take up about thirty pages of small type. Leon Trotsky, *Stalin: An Appraisal of the Man and His Influence* (Harper, 1946), is as hostile as one would expect (a Soviet agent murdered Trotsky while he was working on the book, which was finished from his notes by Charles Malamuth); but the documentation is thorough. Isaac Deutscher, *Stalin: A Political Biography* (Oxford, 1949), is also thoroughly readable.

Alone among the great figures of Bolshevism, Leon Trotsky was a first-rate writer, and if only for that reason his appeal to intellectuals has been great. His *History of the Russian Revolution,* recently published by the University of Michigan Press both in its entirety and as an abridged paperback, is not reliable as history, but as an interpretation of the revolutionary movement that he helped lead, it is a work of art. His most important literary products were those of his exile, when he was denouncing Stalinist "aberrations" from the true Leninist course; see in particular *The Revolution Betrayed* (Doubleday, 1937), and also the parallel, better-organized volume of Victor Serge, *Russia Twenty Years After* (Pioneer, 1937). If anyone confuses Trotsky's anti-Stalinism with a defense of liberal principles, however, he should read *Terrorism and Communism* (Ann Arbor paperback), in which Bolshevik ideas are promulgated with an almost super-Leninist brutality. A sympathetic and well-written interpretation of Trotsky's role is given in Isaac Deutscher, *The Prophet Armed* and *The Prophet Unarmed* (Oxford, 1954, 1959).

By far the most important work of Khrushchev is his "secret" speech denouncing Stalin at the 20th Party Congress, available in a number of editions. The most thoroughly annotated is Bertram D. Wolfe, *Khrushchev and Stalin's Ghost* (Praeger, 1957). Myron Rush, *The Rise of Khrushchev* (Public Affairs Press, 1958), and Lazar Pistrak, *The Grand Tactician* (Praeger, 1961), analyze Khrushchev's successful struggle against the other would-be successors to Stalin.

The ideas of Marxism-Leninism and the ways that these have influenced behavior are implicit to any extended discussion of Communism, and only those works specifically on Bolshevik ideology are noted in this place. There are two excellent elementary presentations, soundly based and well written—R. N. Carew Hunt, *The Theory and Practice of Communism* (Macmillan, 1961); and Alfred G. Meyer, *Communism* (Random House, 1960). A more demanding work, and more interesting for a reader with some background, is Leopold Labedz, ed., *Revisionism: Essays in the History of Marxist Ideas* (Praeger, 1962). An important if difficult work is Philip Selznick, *The Organizational Weapon: A Study of Bolshevik Strategy and Tactics* (McGraw-Hill, 1952).

Czeslaw Milosz, *The Captive Mind* (Vintage paperback), analyzes the moral bondage of the Polish intellectuals, and by implication of all those in Communist countries. A parallel description of Communist sympathizers in the West is Raymond Aron, *The Opium of the Intellectuals* (Norton paperback), which of course is not religion but Communism. The intellectual links between tsarist and Soviet Russia are fascinatingly analyzed in "The Russian Intelligentsia," *Daedalus*, Summer 1960. One of the contributors to this symposium is Gustav A. Wetter, a Jesuit priest whose principal work is acknowledged even by hostile critics to be an outstanding contribution—*Dialectical Materialism: A History and Systematic Survey of Philosophy in the Soviet Union* (Praeger, 1959). A stimulating series of essays arguing the importance of ideas in Soviet practice is Zbigniew K. Brzezinski, *Ideology and Power in Soviet Politics* (Praeger paperback). David Mitrany, *Marx Against the Peasant* (Collier paperback), is a profound analysis of the hostility of Marxism-Leninism to the social class that has suffered most from Communism. Two works in the history of ideas place Marxism, broadly interpreted, in its relation to the development of Western thought—Karl R. Popper, *The Open Society and Its Enemies* (Princeton, 1950), and J. L. Talmon, *The Rise of Totalitarian Democracy* (Beacon, 1952); both argue that in some important senses the totalitarian nature of Communist society derives from Marx.

The Soviet Union

The best general history of Russia, tsarist and Soviet to 1960, is George Vernadsky, *A History of Russia* (Yale paperback). For various purposes, this can be usefully supplemented by Michael T. Florinsky, *Russia: A History and Interpretation* (2 vol.; Macmillan, 1953), which is much more detailed for the period it covers; and Sir John Maynard, *Russia in Flux* (Macmillan, 1948), which analyzes the situation especially of the Russian peasant before and after the revolution.

The classic Bolshevik interpretation of the Russian revolution, at least for Americans, is John Reed, *Ten Days That Shook the World* (Vintage paperback). The two best-known, fuller accounts are by Trotsky, already mentioned, and by William H. Chamberlin, *The Russian Revolution, 1917-1921* (2 vol.; Macmillan, 1952), which is objective and well written. Georg von Rauch, *A History of Soviet Russia* (Praeger paperback), is a scholarly work somewhat inelegantly translated from the German. The most ambitious recent analysis is in the six volumes of E. H. Carr, *A History of Soviet Russia* (Macmillan, 1950-59), which learnedly propounds his particular point of view. Raphael R. Abramovich, *The Soviet Revolution, 1917-1939* (International Universities Press, 1962); and N. N. Sukhanov, *The Russian Revolution, 1917* (2 vol.; Harper paperback) are informed and eloquent analyses by two of the last survivors of the Menshevik group. Robert V. Daniels, *A Documentary History of Communism* (2 vol.; Vintage paperback), covers the history of doctrine and the international expansion of Communism as well as Soviet history itself. Portions of several of the classic analyses are intelligently contrasted in Arthur E. Adams, ed., *The Russian Revolution and Bolshevik Victory: Why and How?* (Heath paperback).

Among the histories of the Party, Leonard Schapiro, *The Communist Party of the Soviet Union* (Random House, 1959), is outstanding. John A. Armstrong, *The Politics of Totalitarianism: The Communist Party of the Soviet Union from 1934 to the Present* (Random House, 1961), and John S. Reshetar, Jr., *A Concise History of the Communist Party of the Soviet Union* (Praeger paperback), are also good. A convenient edition of the important 1961 Party program is Herbert Ritvo, ed., *The New Soviet Society* (New Leader paperback), where the full text is thoroughly annotated. Thomas P. Whitney, ed., *The Communist Blueprint for the Future* (Dutton paperback), includes this and also the original *Communist Manifesto* of 1848 and several programatic statements of the intervening century. Leonard Schapiro, *The Origin of the Communist Autocracy: Political Opposition in the Soviet State* (Harvard, 1956), is a detailed discussion of how the Leninist wing of the Communist Party ousted all other factions. For an account of the struggle between the Communist and other Left parties, several early anarchist chronicles are still exciting reading; see especially Emma Goldman, *My Disillusionment* and *My Further Disillusionment in Russia* (Doubleday, 1923, 1924). For the post-Stalin intraparty disputes, see the books by Rush and Pistrak, cited above.

There are several general surveys of Soviet society, which overlap only in part. In David J. Dallin, *The Changing World of Soviet Russia* (Yale, 1956), the author gives in a relatively short book the fruits of a lifetime of analysis of Communism and Soviet institutions. Merle Fainsod, *How Russia Is Ruled* (Harvard, 1953), though it ranges over the whole of Soviet life, is best for its analysis of how the Party controls other institutions. This is also the principal emphasis of Wladyslaw W. Kulski, *The Soviet Regime: Communism in Practice* (Syracuse, 1954), and of Julian Towster, *Political Power in the USSR: 1917-1947* (Oxford, 1948), which is excellent for the period it covers. Herbert McClosky and John E. Turner, *The Soviet Dictatorship* (McGraw-Hill, 1960), has a wider coverage and is especially to be recommended for its carfeul documentation from translated sources. A frequently cited if somewhat dated survey is Raymond A. Bauer *et al., How the Soviet System Works* (Vintage paperback), which describes from interviews with Soviet refugees certain features of the Stalinist period. A more intensive analysis, based on documents captured by the Nazi army and then by the Americans, is Merle Fainsod, *Smolensk Under Soviet Rule* (Harvard, 1958). For someone with as much background as one of the general surveys could furnish, this may be the best single book on daily life in prewar Soviet Russia.

The several collections of articles on the Soviet Union vary greatly in quality. The best is still one of the earliest, a remarkable review of the first thirty years of Soviet rule—Julien Steinberg, ed., *Verdict of Three Decades* (Duell, Sloan and Pearce, 1950). Also excellent is Abraham Brumberg, ed., *Russia under Khrushchev: An Anthology from* Problems of Communism (Praeger, 1962). More academic but still useful is Alex Inkeles and Kent Geiger, eds., *Soviet Society: A Book of Readings* (Houghton Mifflin, 1961). Philip E. Mosely, ed., "Russia Since Stalin: Old Trends and New Problems," *Annals of the American Academy of Political and Social Science,* January 1956, is an interesting survey only three years after the death of Stalin. Bertram D. Wolfe, *Six Keys to the Soviet System* (Beacon, 1956), brings together a number of this first-rate analyst's articles.

As one would expect, the literature on the Soviet economy is enormous and, in large part, too specialized or too difficult for the general reader. The best general books on this subject are Alec Nove, *The Soviet Economy: An Introduction* (Praeger paperback), and Robert Campbell, *Soviet Economic Power: Its Organization, Growth, and Challenge* (Houghton Mifflin paperback), both of which are solidly based on scholarly research, relatively short, and generally nontechnical. Also good is Harry Schwartz, *Russia's Soviet Economy* (2d ed.; Prentice-Hall, 1954). The best pro-Soviet account is Maurice H. Dobb, *Soviet Economic Development Since 1917* (London: Routledge & Kegan Paul, 1948).

One of the main problems in discussing the achievements of the Soviet economy is how to evaluate Soviet economic statistics; but on this matter the best analyses are excessively technical for this list. There is a good elementary discussion in Campbell, cited above; and the interested reader might want to supplement this with Naum

Jasny, *The Soviet 1956 Statistical Handbook: A Commentary* (Michigan State University, 1958), which illustrates with a hundred examples how tricky the problem is. An excellent summary article is Gregory Grossman, "Thirty Years of Soviet Industrialization," *Soviet Survey,* October-December 1958. Those with some background in economics will benefit from Abram Bergson, *The Real National Income of Soviet Russia Since 1928* (Harvard, 1961), a definitive statement by a recognized authority. The most complete comparison with the American economy is Joint Economic Committee, Congress of the United States, *Comparisons of the United States and Soviet Economies,* 3 vol.; and *Dimensions of Soviet Economic Power.* The contributions to these works are generally excellent, up-to-date reviews of particular fields by recognized authorities. A good short comparison is given in Marshall Goldman, "The Soviet Standard of Living, and Ours," *Foreign Affairs,* July 1960.

The standard work on labor is *Labor in the Soviet Union* by Solomon M. Schwarz (Praeger, 1951). Isaac Deutscher, *Soviet Trade Unions: Their Place in Soviet Labour Policy* (London: Royal Institute of International Affairs, 1950), is the only work on its subject. David Granick has written two works on the Soviet industrial elite— *Management of the Industrial Firm in the USSR: A Study in Soviet Economic Planning* (Columbia, 1954), and the more popular but still solidly based *The Red Executive: A Study of the Organization Man in Russian Industry* (Doubleday, 1960). A parallel study by Joseph S. Berliner, *Factory and Manager in the USSR* (Harvard, 1957), derives primarily from interviews with Russian émigrés and reports in the Soviet press.

Forced Labor in Soviet Russia, by David J. Dallin and Boris I. Nicolaevsky (Yale, 1947), a vast compilation from hundreds of sources in various languages, is still the most complete account of its subject. Indispensable for an understanding of the Stalinist period, it can be usefully supplemented with personal accounts by former Soviet forced laborers or guards, and of such books there are dozens in various languages. Among the best are Jerzy Gliksman, *Tell the West* (Gresham, 1948), a personal chronicle by a Polish socialist who is also an acute social analyst; Margarete Buber-Neumann, *Under Two Dictators* (London: Gollancz, 1949), a comparison between Soviet and Nazi camps, by a woman who was in both; Joseph Scholmer, *Vorkuta* (Holt, 1955), an exciting account of the slave revolt by a German physician; and Gustav Herling, *A World Apart*

(Roy, 1951), by a Pole who was arrested when the Russians occupied his country during World War II.

Simon Wolin and Robert M. Slusser, eds., *The Soviet Secret Police* (Praeger, 1957), is the standard work on the structure and functioning of the Stalinist terror apparatus. A somewhat broader, more theoretical work, is Zbigniew K. Brzezinski, *The Permanent Purge: Politics in Soviet Totalitarianism* (Harvard, 1956). A very good article on the post-Stalin relaxation is Paul Barton, "An End to Concentration Camps?" *Problems of Communism*, March-April 1962.

There is no wholly satisfactory analysis of Soviet law, which poses difficult problems for Western legal experts. The best known work on legal institutions under Stalin is that edited by the chief prosecutor in the notorious show-trials of the 1930's—A. Y. Vyshinsky, *The Law of the Soviet State* (Macmillan, 1948). Vladimir Gsovski, *Soviet Civil Law* (2 vol.; Michigan, 1948, 1949) is a mammoth work beyond the level of the usual nonspecialist. George C. Guins, *Soviet Law and Soviet Society* (The Hague: Nijhoff, 1954); John N. Hazard, *Law and Social Change in the USSR* (London: Stevens, 1953); and Harold J. Berman, *Justice in Russia* (Harvard, 1950), represent efforts to analyze the function and operation of law in a totalitarian social order.

The standard work on *The Population of the Soviet Union* is the book of that title by Frank Lorimer (Princeton, 1946). A very good supplement, emphasizing migratory trends, is Eugene M. Kulischer, *Europe on the Move: War and Population Changes, 1917-47* (Columbia, 1948). The best analyses of postwar population trends are the articles by John F. Kantner and Warren W. Eason in *Comparisons of United States and Soviet Economics,* cited above; and by James W. Brackett in *Dimensions of Economic Power,* cited above. For a shorter account see William Petersen, *Population* (Macmillan, 1961), chap. 15.

There is an extensive literature on the Soviet Union's policy toward its ethnic minorities, a question of considerable importance in this multinational country. For the theoretical background, see Alfred Low, *Lenin on the Question of Nationality* (Bookman, 1958). The best-known work of Richard Pipes, a recognized authority, is *The Formation of the Soviet Union: Communism and Nationalism, 1917-1923* (Harvard, 1954). Of the books on the Stalin and post-

Stalin periods, the best are Walter Kolarz, *Russia and Her Colonies* (Praeger, 1955); Frederick C. Barghoorn, *Soviet Russian Nationalism* (Oxford, 1956); and Robert Conquest, *The Soviet Deportation of Nationalities* (St. Martin's, 1960). An outstanding work on a subject of special importance is Solomon M. Schwarz, *The Jews in the Soviet Union* (Syracuse, 1951), which is brought up to date in an informative article, Erich Goldhagen, "Communism and Anti-Semitism," *Problems of Communism*, May-June 1960. See also Peter Meyer *et al., The Jews in the Soviet Satellites* (Syracuse, 1953). *Religion in the Soviet Union*, by Walter Kolarz (St. Martin's, 1961), is the definitive survey; John Shelton Curtiss, *The Russian Church and the Soviet State, 1917-1950* (Little, Brown, 1953), also provides an authoritative account.

In general, analyses of the Soviet social structure are less satisfactory than those of its political system or its economy. Totalitarian institutions are interesting mainly because of the contrast with their Western counterparts, and political scientists have analyzed the Party, or economists the planned economy, from this point of view. Very often sociologists, on the contrary, have sought some sort of all-inclusive generalization, measuring the implicit worth of all societies by whether they "function"—or, in effect, persist—and depreciating the idea that they can persist for a long period on the basis of terror.

Jules Monnerot, *Sociology and Psychology of Communism* (Beacon paperback), an insightful interpretation in vigorous prose, is not less good because it does not really fall into what we ordinarily understand by "sociology." A somewhat similar range is covered in Klaus Mehnert, *Soviet Man and His World* (Praeger, 1961). The most important book on the Soviet class structure, *The New Class: An Analysis of the Communist System*, by Milovan Djilas (Praeger paperback), is of great interest in part because of the background of the author—a close associate of Tito and former vice president of Yugoslavia.

The Spring 1960 issue of *Social Problems* contains a "Symposium on Social Problems in the Soviet Union," including articles on mental illness, alcoholism, etc. There is no adequate analysis of the family; Rudolf Schlesinger, ed., *Changing Attitudes in Soviet Russia: The Family in the USSR* (London: Routledge and Kegan Paul, 1949), is a useful compendium of translated documents. Mark

G. Field, *Doctor and Patient in Soviet Russia* (Harvard, 1957), is the best work on its subject, as is also Alex Inkeles, *Public Opinion in Soviet Russia: A Study in Mass Persuasion* (Harvard, 1950).

A comprehensive survey of Soviet education is given in George Z. F. Bereday *et al., The Changing Soviet School* (Houghton Mifflin, 1960). George S. Counts and Nucia P. Lodge, *The Challenge of Soviet Education* (McGraw-Hill, 1957), and Nicholas DeWitt, *Education and Professional Employment in the USSR* (National Science Foundation, 1961), assess various educational practices especially as they affect Russia's competitive position vis-a-vis the United States. *The Big Red Schoolhouse* (Doubleday, 1959), by Fred M. Hechinger, the education editor of the *New York Times,* is journalistic but well based.

The most succinct statement of the Bolshevik position on the arts is Trotsky's *Literature and Revolution* (Ann Arbor paperback), which was written, paradoxically, as a protest against the regimentation of literature. The best overall critique, in spite of its date, is Max Eastman, *Artists in Uniform* (Knopf, 1934). George C. Counts and Nucia P. Lodge, **The Country of the Blind: The Soviet System of Mind Control* (Houghton Mifflin, 1949), is an incisive account of how conformity was achieved under Stalin. Abram Tertz, *On Socialist Realism* (Pantheon, 1960), is an attack on Soviet literary policy by a pseudonymous Russian writer. On this subject, see also Harold Swayze, *Political Control of Literature in the USSR, 1946-1959* (Harvard, 1962), and Robert Conquest, *The Pasternak Affair: Courage of Genius* (Lippincott, 1962), which analyzes cultural controls in the case of one of Soviet Russia's major poets. Gleb Struve, *Twenty-five Years of Soviet Literature, 1918-1943* (London: Routledge, 1944), is the standard work.

Eric Ashby, **Scientist in Russia* (Penguin paperback), is an excellent, sympathetic postwar survey. See also the more specialized study, Alexander S. Vucinich, *The Soviet Academy of Sciences* (Stanford, 1956). A difficult work for a nonspecialist, but important enough to be worth the effort, is Cyril E. Black, *Rewriting Russian History* (Vintage paperback).

World Communism

Soviet foreign policy, the activities of the Comintern and its successors, the expansion of Communism to states outside the Soviet

Union and to institutions of still other countries, are interrelated processes. One fault of many books in this area, whatever their virtues, is that they view separately the parts of this single dynamic complex.

Max Beloff, *The Foreign Policy of Soviet Russia, 1929-41* (2 vol.; Oxford, 1947, 1949), and Louis Fischer, *The Soviets in World Affairs: A History of the Relations between the Soviet Union and the Rest of the World, 1917-1929* (2 vol.; Princeton, 1951), are standard works. George F. Kennan, *Soviet Foreign Policy, 1917-1941* (Anvil paperback), is a shorter, generally more sympathetic interpretation, written by a former U.S. ambassador to the Soviet Union, who is also author of *Russia and the West under Lenin and Stalin* (Little, Brown, 1961). Philip F. Mosely, *The Kremlin and World Politics* (Vintage paperback), is a collection of articles by a leading authority, mostly from the postwar period and with an emphasis on post-Stalin strategies. David J. Dallin's *The New Soviet Empire* (Yale, 1951), is a detailed account of Soviet imperialism, and his *Soviet Foreign Policy after Stalin* (Lippincott, 1961) brings the story up to 1960. Ivo J. Lederer, ed., *Russian Foreign Policy: Essays in Historical Perspective* (Yale, 1962), is an excellent compendium of articles with greater depth than the general works cited. See also Alexander Dallin, ed., *Soviet Conduct in World Affairs* (Columbia, 1960).

Two of the most important books analyzing the underside of Soviet foreign policy are David J. Dallin, **Soviet Espionage* (Yale, 1955), a fascinating work; and Franz Borkenau, **European Communism* (Harper, 1953), an analysis of how Communist Parties were used to further Soviet foreign policy in various countries. **World Communism* (Ann Arbor paperback), also by Borkenau, is the standard work on the operations of the Comintern up to the middle 1930's. Hugh Seton-Watson, *From Lenin to Khrushchev* (Praeger, 1960), is a sweeping survey of Communist activities outside Russia. Gabriel A. Almond, *The Appeals of Communism* (Princeton, 1954), is based on case studies of former Party members in several Western countries. A more pertinent book today is **The Unfinished Revolution,* by Adam B. Ulam (Random House, 1960), which argues that Communism has a special appeal to underdeveloped nations.

The establishment of Communism in countries outside Russia has meant not only the extension of the system but its partial differentiation and the emergence of potential or actual conflicts among Communist states. The growing literature on this range of problems includes a number of very interesting works, some of which are listed below with the references on China. See in particular Zbigniew K. Brzezinski, *The Soviet Bloc: Unity and Conflict* (Praeger paperback; rev. ed., 1961), which places the current intra-Communist disputes against their prewar background; and Hugh Seton-Watson, *The East European Revolution* (Praeger paperback), a standard work. A livelier discussion is that in "Polycentrism," a special issue of *Survey*, June 1962. See also John H. Hallowell, ed., "The Soviet Satellite Nations: A Study of the New Imperialism," *Journal of Politics*, February 1958; and Henry L. Roberts, ed., "The Satellites in Eastern Europe," *Annals of the American Academy of Political and Social Science*, May 1958. Some of the vast literature on Communism in Eastern Europe is compiled in an excellent reference work, Robert F. Byrnes, ed., *Bibliography of American Publications on East Central Europe* (Indiana, 1958).

Detailed analyses of each country in Eastern Europe are given in the volumes that Praeger has published in its series on "East Central Europe under the Communists," namely: Stavro Skendi, ed., *Albania* (1956); L. A. D. Dellin, ed., *Bulgaria* (1957); Vratislav Busek and Nicolas Spulber, eds., *Czechoslovakia* (1957); Ernst C. Helmreich, ed., *Hungary* (1957); Oscar Halecki, ed., *Poland* (1957); and Stephen Fischer-Galati, ed., *Rumania* (1956). The way in which Soviet power was established in one country is eloquently described in *Allied Wartime Diplomacy: A Pattern in Poland* (Wiley, 1957), by Edward J. Rozek, who had access to the private files of Stanislaw Mikolajczyk, the premier of the London Polish government. After the Stalin-Tito break in 1948, Yugoslavia became the first Communist country opposed to the Soviet Union, a special circumstance that warrants particular attention. On the break itself, see the book of Djilas, cited above; and Robert H. Bass and Elizabeth Marbury, eds., *The Soviet-Yugoslav Controversy, 1948-1958: A Documented Record* (Prospect Books, 1959). On the country, two of the best analyses are Adam B. Ulam, *Titoism and the Cominform* (Harvard, 1952), and Charles P. McVicker, *Titoism: Pattern for International Communism* (St. Martin's, 1957).

The revolts in Soviet satellites following the death of Stalin, and particularly the Hungarian revolution, are of fundamental importance; and they have been analyzed in several of the books already cited. Paul E. Zinner, ed., *National Communism and Popular Revolt in Eastern Europe* (Columbia, 1956), gives a documentary account of the reverberations of de-Stalinization, particularly in Poland and Hungary. Rainer Hildebrandt, *The Explosion: The Uprising behind the Iron Curtain* (Duell, Sloan and Pearce, 1955), is a journalistic account of the uprising in East Germany. Flora Lewis, *A Case History of Hope* (Doubleday, 1958), and Konrad Syrop, *Spring in October* (Praeger, 1957), best portray the Polish events of 1956. Of the eye-witness accounts of the Hungarian revolution, one of the most interesting is Peter Fryer, *Hungarian Tragedy* (London: Dennis Dobson, 1956); its author was a Communist, who resigned from his job as correspondent of the *London Daily Worker* when it refused to print his dispatches. A very good compilation of such chronicles, together with documents and photographs, is Melvin J. Lasky, ed., *The Hungarian Revolution* (Praeger, 1957). Of the analyses in greater depth, two are eminently worth reading—Paul Kecskemeti, *The Unexpected Revolution: Social Forces in the Hungarian Uprising* (Stanford, 1961); and Paul E. Zinner, *Revolution in Hungary* (Columbia, 1962).

Of the many books on Cuba, whether pro-Castro or anti-, only one is both scholarly and well written—Theodore Draper, *Castro's Revolution: Myths and Realities* (Praeger paperback).

Communist China is as important to the United States as the Soviet Union—or considering China's population, potential power, and present aggressive proclivity, even more so. Perhaps the best analysis of the Communist regime's first period is Richard L. Walker, *China under Communism: The First Five Years* (Yale, 1955). This is brought up to date in Peter S. H. Tang, *Communist China Today* (rev. ed.; Research Institute on the Sino-Soviet Bloc, 1961); see also the second volume of this work, subtitled *Chronological and Documentary Supplement* (1962). Documentation is also given in Robert R. Bowie and John K. Fairbank, eds., *Communist China, 1955-1959: Policy Documents with Analysis* (Harvard, 1962). Interpretations more sympathetic to the regime than Walker's or Tang's are given in Guy Wint, *Common Sense about China* (Macmillan, 1960); and Edgar Snow, *The Other Side of the River: Red China Today* (Random House, 1962), which is the only work of this scope written by an American eye-witness. A work by an Indian scholar is of special interest: Sripati Chandra-Sekhar, *Red China: An Asian View* (Praeger paperback), which emphasizes social as well as political changes. Two collections of articles can be recommended: Howard L. Boorman, ed., "Contemporary China and the

Chinese," *Annals of the American Academy of Political and Social Science,* January 1959; and "The First Decade," *China Quarterly,* January-March 1960.

Of the various works of Mao Tse-tung available in English, two are of general interest: Samuel B. Griffith, ed., *Mao Tse-tung on Guerrilla Warfare* (Praeger, 1961); and "Let a Hundred Flowers Bloom," usefully edited by G. F. Hudson in the *New Leader,* September 9, 1957. On the latter work, see also Roderick MacFarquhar, *The Hundred Flowers Campaign and the Chinese Intellectuals* (Praeger, 1960). The Party's position on various matters is presented regularly in *Peking Review,* the official English-language weekly, and *Translations of the Mainland Press,* issued by the U.S. Consulate in Hong Kong. There are several solid works on the rise of the Party in China; in particular: Harold R. Isaacs, *The Tragedy of the Chinese Revolution* (Stanford, 1951), a Trotskyist interpretation of the early period; and Benjamin I. Schwartz, *Chinese Communism and the Rise of Mao* (Harvard, 1951), a standard work. A provocative work, especially relevant to Communist China but actually an attempt to analyze totalitarianism generally, is Karl A. Wittfogel, *Oriental Despotism: A Comparative Study of Total Power* (Yale, 1957).

The Sino-Soviet dispute, its range and meaning, are subjects to which all analysts rightly give much attention today. The differences go back farther than many accounts would suggest; see Howard L. Boorman *et al., Moscow-Peking Axis: Strengths and Strains* (Harper, 1957). Among the most interesting and important works analyzing recent trends, see Donald Zagoria, *The Sino-Soviet Conflict, 1956-1961* (Princeton, 1962), the standard work on the subject; G. F. Hudson, Richard Lowenthal, and Roderick MacFarquhar, eds., *The Sino-Soviet Dispute (China Quarterly,* 1961; reprinted as a Praeger paperback), which includes extensive excerpts from original documents; and Robert A. Scalapino, "Moscow, Peking and the Communist Parties of Asia," *Foreign Affairs,* January 1963.

China's general foreign policy is analyzed at length in A. Doak Barnett, *Communist China and Asia: Challenge to American Policy* (Council on Foreign Relations; Harper, 1960). Herbert Feis, *The China Tangle* (Princeton, 1953), includes a discussion of Chinese-American relations. Frank Moraes, *The Revolt in Tibet* (Macmillan, 1960), provides some background to the Sino-Indian conflict, as seen by a distinguished Indian journalist.

Communist activities in non-Communist countries, and especially the Communist infiltration of democratic institutions, have been analyzed in an enormous number of books, which vary greatly in reliability and interest. The best general works are by Borkenau and Seton-Watson, cited above. For particular countries of Western Europe, these can be usefully supplemented by the following: Ruth Fischer, *Stalin and German Communism: A Study of the Origins of the State Party* (Harvard, 1948), a partisan interpretation by a former leader of the German Party; Angelo Rossi, *A Communist Party in Action* (Yale, 1949), an analysis of the French Party by a former high-ranking Italian Communist; Mario Einaudi *et al.*, *Communism in Western Europe* (Cornell, 1951), especially good on Italy; Hugh Thomas, *The Spanish Civil War* (Harper, 1961), which manages to be both objective and stirring; and Neal Wood, *Communism and British Intellectuals* (Columbia, 1959).

The two best books on Communism in the United States are by Theodore Draper, *The Roots of American Communism* (Viking, 1957), and *American Communism and the Soviet Union* (Viking, 1960), which carry the history of the Party only up to the 1930's. A more superficial survey, restricted to the Party's legal activities, is given in Irving Howe and Lewis Coser, *The American Communist Party* (Beacon, 1958). Eugene Lyons, *The Red Decade* (Bobbs Merrill, 1941), is a journalistic account of the Communist-front activities in the 1930's; especially for one too young to remember the period, it is worth reading still. Perhaps the best one-volume interpretation is Clinton Rossiter, *Marxism: The View from America* (Harcourt, Brace, 1960), which consistently emphasizes the contrast between Communist and democratic practices. This contrast is pointed up even more sharply in Sidney Hook, *Heresy, Yes—Conspiracy, No!* (John Day, 1953), and in a group of essays by the same author, *Political Power and Personal Freedom: Critical Studies in Democracy, Communism, and Civil Rights* (Collier paperback), which continue his cogent argument for differentiating Communism from "the Left." Among the more specialized studies, those worthy of attention by the general reader include David J. Saposs, *Communism in American Unions* (McGraw-Hill, 1959); John P. Windmuller, *American Labor and the International Labor Movement, 1940-1953* (Cornell, 1954); Wilson Record, *The Negroes and the Communist Party* (North Carolina, 1951); and Dwight Macdonald, *Henry Wallace: The Man and the Myth* (Vanguard, 1947), a marvelous combination of wit and scholarship. For a truly excellent symposium on * "The Western Image of the Soviet Union, 1917-1962," see *Survey*, April 1962.

Communist activities in underdeveloped countries have been analyzed in fewer works, of which several deserve attention. Walter Z. Laqueur, *Communism and Nationalism in the Middle East* (Praeger, 1956), is based on an intimate knowledge of sources in, among other languages, Russian and Arabic. John H. Kautsky, *Moscow and the Communist Party of India* (Wiley, 1956), is the best book on its subject. J. H. Brimmel, *Communism in Southeast Asia* (Oxford, 1959), authoritatively covers a lot of territory. The rise of the Hukbalahap movement and its decline, one of the very few cases of a wholly successful effort to combat Communism in a poor country, is analyzed in Alvin H. Scaff, *The Philippine Answer to Communism* (Stanford, 1955). The best work on the Party's activities in Japan is Rodger Swearingen and Paul Langer, *Red Flag in Japan: International Communism in Action, 1919 to 1951* (Harvard, 1952). The best work on Latin America is Robert J. Alexander, *Communism in Latin America* (Rutgers, 1957); it can be brought up to date with an excellent symposium on this subject in *Problems of Communism*, January-February 1961. For a hostile but well-documented account of Communism in Negro Africa, see Pieter Lessing, *Africa's Red Harvest* (John Day, 1962).

General

Two elementary presentations, both especially suitable for beginning classes or discussion groups, are Sidney Hook, *Marx and the Marxists: An Ambiguous Legacy* (Anvil paperback), and Moshe Decter, ed., *The Profile of Communism* (New York: Anti-Defamation League of B'nai B'rith, 1961). While these are less difficult than most of the works in this list, they lack the faults typical of popularizations.

Michael T. Florinsky, ed., *Encyclopedia of Russia and the Soviet Union* (McGraw-Hill, 1961), though its subject and price ($23.50) put it beyond the usual range of this bibliography, is so interesting for browsing and so useful for reference that some nonspecialists may be tempted to own it.

Rodger Swearingen, *What's So Funny, Comrade?* (Praeger paperback), reproduces some of the self-critical cartoons from the Soviet periodical *Krokodil.*

Relevant periodicals can be divided into three classes:

(a) Those especially recommended for the general reader. *Problems of Communism,* published six times a year by the U.S. Information Agency (subscription $1.50 per year from the Superintendent of Documents, U.S. Government Printing Office, Washington 25, D.C.). This covers the whole range of Communism, with emphasis on recent developments; articles are written by specialists, who typically base their findings on original sources, but the intended audience includes the layman. *Survey: A Journal of Soviet and East European Studies* and *China Quarterly;* subscriptions to either $3 (or $2 to students) to Ilford House, 133 Oxford Street, London W.1 (or the American agent: Eastern News Distributors, 255 Seventh Avenue, New York 1, N.Y.). These are remarkable quarterlies which combine the best qualities of journalism and scholarship in an eminently readable amalgam.

(b) Professional journals too specialized to interest the usual general reader. The most important is *The Current Digest of the Soviet Press,* a weekly in which the most significant articles in *Pravda, Izvestia,* and other Soviet publications are translated or abridged. Nothing else will give the person who reads no Russian so rich an idea of what is going on in the USSR. Other relevant periodicals include: *Russian Review, Slavic Review,* and *Soviet Studies* (Glasgow).

(c) General magazines with occasional good articles on Communism. Here the list could be very long, but the most important are *New Leader,* which varies greatly in quality but has published, particularly in its occasional supplements, excellent commentaries; *Foreign Affairs,* which publishes articles by first-rate journalists, diplomats, and scholars; and *Encounter* (London), the English-language publication of the Congress for Cultural Freedom.

Fiction can often give one valid impressions of totalitarianism or of Communist countries. The best novel about life in the Communist movement is Victor Serge, *The Case of Comrade Tulayev* (Doubleday, 1950). Also excellent, and of course much better known, is Arthur Koestler, *Darkness at Noon* (Signet paperback), a psychological analysis of the reasons for the confessions in the Moscow show-trials. Godfrey Blunden, *A Room on the Route* (Lippincott,

1947), is even more successful in conveying the fear that pervaded Stalinist Russia. Two novels by George Orwell are relevant—*Animal Farm* (Signet paperback), a wry fable on the degeneration of Soviet society; and *1984* (Signet paperback), a terrifying picture of the totalitarian future. Less well known but more believable is a novel of the future Communist domination of Britain—Constantine Fitz-Gibbon, *When the Kissing Had to Stop* (Bantam paperback). Eric Ambler, who writes excellent, more or less credible adventure stories, surpassed himself in *Judgment on Deltchev* (Black, 1951), which apparently was modeled on the Kostov trial.

Soviet literature in translation now includes many titles, only a few of which are noted here. Bernard G. Guernay, ed., *An Anthology of Russian Literature in the Soviet Period, from Gorki to Pasternak* (Modern Library paperback), is an excellent collection. In Ernest J. Simmons, ed., *Through the Looking Glass of Soviet Literature: Views of Russian Society* (Columbia, 1953), the several authors use themes from Soviet literature to analyze the way the society is structured. See also the anthology of fiction in Hugh McLean and Walter N. Vickery, eds., *The Year of Protest, 1956* (Vintage paperback), which includes a very good introduction. Social protest is also the main theme of two novels by Vladimir Dudintsev, *Not by Bread Alone* (Dutton, 1957), and *A New Year's Tale* (Dutton paperback). Boris Pasternak, *Doctor Zhivago,* which became the subject of an international scandal (see the book by Conquest, cited above), is available in a number of editions, including a Signet paperback. The most startling evidence of the literary thaw to date is the semi-fictional account of forced labor by a former camp inmate—Alexander Solzhenitsyn, *One Day in the Life of Ivan Denisovich* (Praeger, 1963). See also the more or less fictional account by a former NKVD official, now living in exile—Vladimir Andreyev, *Gamailis, and Other Tales from Stalin's Russia* (Regnery, 1963).

NOTES ON THE CONTRIBUTORS

Robert J. Alexander is professor of economics at Rutgers, The State University. Ph.D., Columbia University. Associated for short periods with the Board of Economic Warfare, Office of Inter-American Affairs, and Economic Cooperation Administration. Publications include: *The Peron Era* (1951), *Communism in Latin America* (1957), *The Bolivian National Revolution* (1958), *The Struggle for Democracy in Latin America* (with Charles O. Porter, 1961), *Prophets of the Revolution* (1962), and *Labor Relations in Argentina, Brazil and Chile* (1962).

Gregory Grossman is professor of economics at the University of California, Berkeley. Ph.D., Harvard University. Research fellow, Russian Research Center, Harvard University; member of the team of American economists visiting the USSR, 1960. Author of *Soviet Statistics of Physical Output* (1960), editor of *Value and Plan* (1960), and author of numerous articles in professional journals on the Soviet economy.

John E. Hutchinson is coordinator of labor programs and research political scientist, Institute of Industrial Relations, University of California, Berkeley. Ph.D., London University. Author of articles and monographs on the labor movement and politics; *Labor and Corruption in America* (in process).

Paul Kecskemeti is senior research analyst with The RAND Corporation and was visiting professor (1962-63) at the Russian Institute, Columbia University. Ph.D., Budapest University. Author of *Meaning, Communication, and Value* (1952), *Strategic Surrender* (1958), *The Unexpected Revolution* (1961), and articles in professional journals on totalitarian governments.

William Petersen is professor of sociology at the University of California, Berkeley. Ph.D., Columbia University. Hendrik Willem van Loon fellow; senior research fellow, National Science Foundation. Author of *Planned Migration* (1955), *University Adult Education* (with Renee Petersen, 1960), *Population* (1961), and articles on Marxism and Soviet society; editor of *American Social Patterns* (1956) and *Social Controversy* (with David Matza, 1963).

Robert A. Scalapino is professor of political science, University of California, Berkeley. Ph.D., Harvard University. Author of *Democracy and the Party Movement in Pre-War Japan* (1953), *The*

Chinese Anarchist Movement (with George T. Yu, 1961), *Parties and Politics in Contemporary Japan* (with Junnosuke Masumi, 1962), and numerous articles on Communist China's foreign policy, Japanese socialism, the Japanese intellectual, and related topics.

Bertram D. Wolfe is a free-lance writer and historian; he was visiting professor of history (1961-62) at the University of California, Davis. Senior fellow, Slavic Studies, Hoover Library; senior fellow, Russian Institute, Columbia University. Publications include: *Diego Rivera* (1939), *Three Who Made a Revolution* (1948), *Six Keys to the Soviet System* (1956), *Khrushchev and Stalin's Ghost* (1957), and many articles on Communism, Russian history, and Hispanic culture.

Paul E. Zinner is associate professor of political science at the University of California, Davis. Ph.D., Harvard University. Editor of five yearly volumes of *Documents on Foreign Relations,* Council on Foreign Relations; and of *National Communism and Popular Revolt in Eastern Europe* (1956). Author of *Revolution in Hungary* (1962) and of articles on Soviet and East European politics.